'Admirably candid' *The Times*

'Daffy charm . . . the reconstruction of confused emotions rings true' *Independent on Sunday*

'Very honest . . . very open' *Manchester Evening News*

'Naïve charm . . . a child's eye view of childhood . . . she reminisces without any gloss of self-justification' *Sunday Times*

'Gripping autobiography' *London Evening Standard*

Sarah Miles married the writer Robert Bolt (twice).
They have a son, Tom, and live in the country.

A Right Royal Bastard

SARAH MILES

PAN BOOKS
LONDON, SYDNEY AND AUCKLAND

FOR MY TWO HUSBANDS
ROBERT BOLT

First published 1993 by Macmillan London Limited

This edition published 1994 by Pan Books
a division of Macmillan General Books
Cavaye Place London SW10 9PG
and Basingstoke

Associated companies throughout the world

ISBN 0 330 33142 6

1 3 5 7 9 8 6 4 2

A CIP catalogue for this book is available from
the British Library

Printed and bound in Great Britain by
Cox & Wyman Ltd, Reading, Berkshire

CHAPTER ONE

ONE OF Father's passions was tennis, so he made Mother promise to deliver him a tennis four, and ideally at least one left-handed player. She complied with his wishes, and gave birth to a mixed doubles match all in a row. Daddy came from a family of nicknames and so that's how it was. Jukes was the eldest (Christopher). Then there was Chuzzlewit (Martin) after Martin Chuzzlewit – or just Chuzzer. I arrived third, with a year and a half separating each of us. The fourth was miscarried so Pooker, (Vanessa) my little sister, wasn't around for another five years.

I was the only one born at home, arriving some time around midnight, gate-crashing a New Year's Eve party they were giving. My father and Dr Mary Adams, family friend-cum-gynaecologist-cum-midwife, who brought all four of us into the world, were present. They all had conflicting evidence as to the exact time. My birth certificate states before midnight, but my mother said they just took a guess.

Perhaps it's a blessing that I've never been able to get an astrology chart done. I remember once ringing Mummy, and asking her for the exact time, for that very purpose. 'I don't know, darling,' she said vaguely, 'I wasn't wearing a watch.' All that's definite is that I was born, and it was at the Mill House, Fryerning, near Ingatestone, Essex. I was named

Sarah Elizabeth (though everyone called me Pusscat), Sarah after Sarah Bernhardt, and Elizabeth after the Queen. Poor Mummy – such high expectations.

Looking the way I did those expectations were bound to be lowered. Quaint would be a fair description, thanks to my strangely resilient, almost pubic hair sprouting upon my head, framing an equally resilient pair of transparent, shapeless radar scanners. These ears upset Mummy so much that she put an ear-flattening bonnet, tight as a strait-jacket, on me at night, which did nothing to bend or flatten them, but sent *me* totally round the bend and almost into the real thing. After two years of failure with the monstrous bonnet, I got stuck with sticky tape as a bed-fellow, but again it had no effect whatsoever.

For those first years my ears didn't worry me too much, nor did they worry my father. In fact Daddy quite liked them. 'If the worst comes to the worst, Pusscat, you can always join the circus,' he said with a glint in his wicked green eyes. He had a quite terrible stammer, which he inherited from his father, and which, apart from lucky old Pooker, the three of us had the rotten luck to inherit as well.

Owly was my first memory, a big china owl guarding me night and day. He was bound to be the first, with his powerful presence peering down at me, judging all things with a gentle uncluttered knowingness from high on his perch, the walnut tallboy beside my cot. He's still peering down at me, in the conservatory as I write, smashed up many times, but still here, if not in one piece, then in a million lovingly glued together pieces, still able to vouch for me – or not, as the case may be. Silly, perhaps, to find such comfort in the continuity of old Owly.

But I know, and he knows that I couldn't tell the tale without him, because Owly saw it all. When I look into his dark eyes, he jogs my memory by nudging echoes into recollections then out into the light.

Pip, too, was pretty big, he was very nearly my size when I was six months old. Pip was a black and white squishy penguin, knitted for me by Granny. What I loved most about Pip was his thick sausage beak, which hung like a long nose right down between his legs. This floppy beak was knitted in an orangy-yellow, a colour I still tend to associate with happiness.

The next three memories to step into my consciousness were barriers – prison bars preventing me from shooting back to the place where I knew home to be, far up above the sky. These three shapes were the bars of my cot, the criss-cross weave of the cat net over my pram in the garden and the diamond shapes of the lattice windows in my nursery.

I know I'm risking disbelief right here up front, nevertheless I can only give you the truth as I remember it. The desire to return whence I had come was such an aching need that I almost felt I was being magnetically pulled. I felt so alien, as if being here on Earth was a terrible mistake, and that someone would soon come to rescue me if I was unable to escape for myself.

'DOODLEBUGS COMING OVER!' shouted Jukes and Chuzzlewit. I believed that those lethal flying bombs were sent to rescue me, they were the chosen ones, sent to whisk me away, back home at last. Whenever I heard the wail of the warning siren my hopes soared because I knew my saviours had arrived. Mother would glide into the nursery in her silk dressing gown and swoosh me up under her right arm. I'd scream, not because I was frightened but because she squeezed me so tight that I couldn't breathe. Why wouldn't she let me take Pip with me?

'Pusscat, stop screaming!' Beastly having to leave Pip alone in my cot, sweet, loving Pip with the tiny soft hole under his floppy beak, a hole that went up somewhere . . . somewhere inside him. I couldn't quite push my finger up Pip's soft hole . . . yet . . . 'Shush, Pusscat – come here, you two boys!' And we'd be marched off down the cobwebby stone steps to the dank cellar below.

Why was she hiding me from the doodlebugs, didn't she know why they had come? I could hear them screaming outside, desperately trying to crash through the walls and carry me up, up and away.

'Doodlebugs gone!' shouted the boys. Once again those selfish doodlebugs had run away without saving me.

Mother tossed me into the bottom bunk, next to the smelly floor.

'Oh, no, they haven't,' warned Daddy.

'Say a prayer,' said Mummy.

The whole cellar shook and rumbled. I was delighted because I thought the bang was the doodlebug returning with a last cracking effort to get me home.

'Get the gas masks, Wren [Mother's nickname],' ordered Daddy, who didn't seem very jolly. 'I'll go and investigate the damage.'

When a doodlebug finally came into the cellar, I screamed with fright, for it had an unexpectedly evil face, yet I think its voice was Mother's. 'There are only four gas masks, John.' This 'Mother Thing' came rushing over, and quickly put the same frog-like heads on my brothers. 'We must get one more gas mask for Pusscat,' it said.

Now they all looked like evil frogs, except Daddy who said, 'In that case, Wren, she must wear mine.' Mummy put something dark and smelly over my face. Oh, no! I wasn't going to wear one of those – and I bellowed from the bottom of my lungs. 'Take if off her, Wren, I can't stand the noise.'

Next day Mummy took me by the hand, or rather hauled me from the arm socket because I couldn't walk yet, and opened the door into our drawing room. The prettiest half of it, which was up two steps where three beautiful lattice windows overlooked the garden, had been shattered by the doodlebug.

How hard he had tried to save me, poor doodlebug, how very close he'd come to succeeding. It must have been the wicked frog-like faces that had finally scared him away once and for all. To be so near and yet so far from my real home, way up there beyond the sky. What a shame! Never mind, those back home'll just have to be patient, that's all there is to it.

'We must thank our lucky stars, it could have been the whole house, not just the drawing room. Don't cry, Pusscat, Jesus saved us once again, we must say a prayer.'

What was she on about? I wasn't crying for the drawing room – stupid woman!

Later 'doodlebug' was the first word I ever uttered out loud, which shows what an effect they must have had on me, apart from my wanting to impress Jukes and Chuzzer with a real tongue twister like 'doodlebug'. Father always insisted that 'pickled onion' was my first word. Of course it was, in front of him, because I had a pickled onion passion and Daddy was always eating them.

Like a lot of babies I had a terror of the dark. It became so unbearably noisy that a night-light was installed, the flickering kind. When Mummy and Daddy put out the lights and kissed me goodnight, leaving me all alone, strange imaginings took place . . . or were they?

As the night-light comforted me with its stealthy patterns caressing the nursery walls, quite suddenly these feathery creatures plopped in to sit beside Owly on the tallboy. I didn't know if they were friends of Owly's or where they came from, for they were curious, these beings. Perhaps they were hairy, not feathery, I can't fully recall, but they were furtive and shadowy, as they alighted on the rim of my cot, without even a 'May I?' Some were very fierce, wicked even, others merry and full of goodliness. They settled themselves in hooded rows, crowding and jostling together, a feathery, hairy shroud of silent nosy parkers.

Later I called the benevolent ones 'Drumwins' and the fierce ones 'Drummoids'. Not only did they seem to know everything about me, but they could see right through me too. I didn't like the Drummoids and I asked them, most politely, to leave, but they had no intention of doing so. I think I called them Drumwins and Drummoids because my heart would always beat like a drum whenever they fluttered down.

I wish I knew at the time how lucky I was to be able really to see. I didn't think it anything special, then. The same went for the bright colours I often saw around Mummy and Daddy. Sometimes their heads were framed in amazingly vivid shades, Jukes' and Chuzzer's heads too, but less so. I saw paler shimmerings around animals, even the trees had an outer coating at their tops, but I thought nothing of it, for I suppose I thought everyone saw the same as I – they probably did but, like me, have sadly lost the knack.

One early spring day I was playing as usual with my ducks, hens, cocks and bantams down in the stable yard.

I was just walking, with huge nappies between my legs. Suddenly I heard a cry. 'Pusscat! Come quickly, *HELP!*'

Where was it coming from? 'Pusscat! Come quickly! There's a toad drowning in the loo!' It was Chuzzlewit, calling me from the garden lav, I'd know Chuzzer's stammer anywhere. He was asking me to save a toad! I'd never been called upon to *save* anything before.

That was my first real journey with a purpose to it. I was being asked to fulfil a mission. I knew what a toad was, because Daddy had pointed one out to us in the long grass beside the mill pond. Getting from the stable yard to the garden loo was fraught with many pitfalls, for there were no smooth level surfaces anywhere in the vicinity. With the heavy nappies hanging round my knees and a safety pin always unlocking and digging into my bottom, it seemed to take for ever. (I returned to the Mill House quite recently, and the distance from the stable yard to where the outside loo used to be is a matter of a mere twelve yards.)

Climbing the stone steps to the loo for the first time was,

for me at the age of two, as exhilarating as the top of Everest must have been for Hillary.

There stood Chuzzlewit, leaning over the loo hole, stuttering with despair. 'Hurry, Pusscat, I think you're too late.'

I peered into the loo hole, and there, looking at me from the murky depths of the filthy water, was this gigantic forlorn-looking toad. I was sure he wasn't dead yet and the need to save him was overwhelming. I quickly plunged in my hand and pulled him out. I felt such a sense of accomplishment at that moment, like a grown-up for the first time. Then, as I proudly stroked my prize, bringing him back to life with my finger, I began to have strange doubts . . .

I remained stock still as, slowly, the horror began to dawn on me. Every ounce of compassion that had previously welled up in abundance quickly dissolved, through the humiliation of being duped, into an overwhelming revulsion, and what was worse, a profound loathing for my brother. Toady wasn't a toad, after all, but my brother's very own newly created masterpiece.

I suppose it was no more than a childish game, a bit of lavatorial tomfoolery, because Chuzzer was never cruel – not on purpose. But for whatever reason this prank backfired, leaving a trail of hurt dignity and the need for revenge.

And I got it. One afternoon I spied Chuzzer from my favourite nook inside my old oak tree. This oak had giant's fingers, which spread over the ground before disappearing into the earth. At one place they were shaped like a boat. I felt so safe and snug because I could fit inside perfectly, as if the old oak had spread his fingers just wide enough for me. (Though not, alas, wide enough for my gigantic bow, for Mother insisted that all my dresses had a great bow. This had to be tied completely even and puffed up to look as chunky as possible. The damn thing began its bossy day on my waist, but within seconds of playing in the stables would gravitate to my bum, to which it clung ruthlessly till bedtime. Perhaps Mother thought that if she gave me a gigantic flamboyant bow it would detract attention from my bat ears. No, I think she just had a thing about bows.)

So there we were, my bow and I, snug inside my oak tree's boat fingers. It was a sticky afternoon, the far-off thunder rumbled, heralding a summer storm. I spied my brother Chuzzlewit crouching beside the mill pond, sailing boats made of tiny box leaves. It was quite comforting to see him looking so thin and frail, as he crouched all hunched up with his asthmatic wheeze, because I hadn't forgotten the toad episode, oh no.

I watched Chuzzer creep nearer to the edge, his concentration so focused on his box-leaf boats that he had failed to notice me in my scarlet frock, or the storm gathering in huge angry bundles behind the mill pond, turning it black as ink. My revenge welled up within me, tasting dark as the mill pond, rich and sweet as treacle. With a great deal of heave-ho-ing I managed to pick two fat juicy dock leaves. Waving them excitedly above my head, I skipped up to Chuzzer, with my huge scarlet bow tripping me up.

'Ch-Chuzzer, look,' I stammered, placing a dock leaf on

the water and watching it float majestically away, the *Queen Mary* surrounded by silly little box-leaf tugs.

'What a lovely big boat.' Chuzzer was impressed, and turned to see where it came from. I enticed him with the other dock leaf, which he tried to snatch from me. I did a snappy little spin and as usual trod on my beastly bow, ending up flat on my face.

Chuzzer grabbed the dropped dock leaf, and as I tried to retrieve it he pushed me away. I fell again, but scrambled up and stood behind him, fierce as a Drummoid. It was definitely a Drummoid wickedness that overcame me at that moment because, watching Chuzzlewit so bent over the liquid blackness, I knew what I was going to do. I felt the evil rise within me, that evil we all have hidden away, if we really care to look.

One – two – three – I pushed him in. SPLOSH!

Did I consider the consequences of my actions? Of course I did. I wanted Chuzzer to drown. I wanted him to – VANISH! To go away for ever. I didn't know what for ever meant, or indeed what death was, but I had to get Chuzzer out of my way – that's all I knew, but that I knew for sure.

'*DROWN!*' I kept screaming.

But Chuzzer didn't drown, he floated, so relaxed on the surface, all stretched out like Christ, as if he was lying on a cross in bed. As the thunder roared and the rains came down, the mill pond's velvet inkiness was transformed by a stampede of hefty speckles. But it didn't bother Chuzzer, he just kept floating and smiling at me, quietly victorious.

I couldn't understand why he didn't disappear. Then I saw a tangled mass of slimy green stuff beneath him, the only area of reeds on the whole mill pond, and it was a fair size mill pond at that. Just my luck to push him into the miracle of Moses in the bulrushes.

Brand the gardener appeared from nowhere carrying a pitch fork, and bloody well saved Chuzzer. Some people are born lucky, and there's an end to it.

When Mother returned from her weekly outing to London town, she heard the news as we all sat in the kitchen being rubbed down with a towel. Suddenly I was whisked upstairs, enclosed in the iron vice of Mummy's under-arm and tossed on to the bed. 'You are a very naughty – no, much worse – a wicked little girl!'

What a baptism of raging fire I received from that antique silver hair-brush of hers! The stinging went on well after she had stopped. Little did I know that day was just the beginning of many years of such rituals. Poor Mummy, it was the only way she could get a handle on my naughtiness. Talking of which, one day she hit me so hard that she bent the handle of her precious silver hair-brush and had to exchange it for a tougher wooden one.

About twenty years ago I had a spate of experiences that came to me out of the blue. As a result of one of these experiences, whole sections of my past came back at me with an overwhelming and violently uncomfortable clarity.

But so shocking was the net result of all these awesome experiences (and I wasn't on drugs) that I went into catharsis. Something was telling me to spend the next three years alone, to listen and lean on silence. I didn't question this, because

I'd been brought up to deal with things on my own. It was the way Daddy wished it to be. Deal with it, act upon it and shut up.

It was as if my life, up to that point, had been a garment chaotically, almost blindly, knitted, and that after the catharsis I had a great desire to gather together all the loose threads of newly acquired memories and knit a different garment with some kind of shape to it – perhaps even use. The result of this silent nonsense was to discover parts of me that had lain hidden for nigh on half a lifetime. It was a strange choice of mine to commit to this lonesome journey, especially at a time when I was at the top of my profession. Logic, however, had done a runner.

When it came to writing this book I was given a clear choice. I could either dwell on the memories that lurked in dingy pockets marked 'victim' or 'villain', or pick those that glimmered, for in many ways I'd had a privileged upbringing and a rare gift of freedom. The truth was to be found somewhere between these two extremes.

I recall a moment when Mother and I (both Capricorns with the ability to be down-to-earth and realistic) simultaneously observed the same sunbeam.

'Look at that sunbeam, Ma, like gold and silver rainbows swirling through the window.'

'Humm,' she said, in her usual business-like fashion, as she went off to get the duster. 'Aggravating the way they highlight every speck of dust.'

It was the same sunbeam, but at that moment we both chose to paint it differently. This gave me a new respect for truth. I never realized what an infinitely malleable substance it was, moulded from all angles of perception, awareness and, most of all, mood.

I mention all this only as a backdrop to being beaten on occasion with the hair-brush. What I tried to recall was beneath the pain, to what had caused the beating in the first place. What was it about me that forced Mother into such acts of fury? She didn't beat the boys, or my little sister when she came along, so what was it about me that she found so exasperating?

It has been fashionable over the past century to put nurture ahead of nature in character development. I believe that most of what we are is assimilated in that awesomely mysterious period before conception. Parents have some influence during that equally awesome period between conception and birth, and naturally more from birth on; but to dump all one's ugly traits, all one's might-have-beens on the poor parents is perhaps a bit unfair. Dumping one's own mess on others is so unBritish somehow, unbefitting our true nature.

I was born with something hugely unresolved, which is partly why I can remember so eagerly wanting to return to where I considered home to be. My missing parts, so to speak, gave my personality jagged edges upon which Mummy was always catching herself.

Ashamed, I have to admit that on most occasions I knew perfectly well the difference between right and wrong. I can even remember a strange sense of safety when being punished, for it allowed me a clearer recognition of the 'right and wrong' boundaries. (I'm not advocating the rod for others, it just worked for me.)

I have a feeling we are born sublimely selfish, ignorantly cunning – not innocent at all. Innocence, I maintain, is a state that lies beyond all other virtues. Once any one of us has attained a state of innocence in its true and purest form, we have finally reached a State of Grace.

CHAPTER TWO

M Y RESPECT AND love for animals was an integral part of my nature from the very beginning. I had no choice but to be drawn towards the stable yard, just as a bee has no choice but to home in on the honey.

As I grew, gradually I forgot my real home, the one out there somewhere. The stable yard became my kingdom and all the feathered creatures were my friends. What was it about that timelessness of the stable yard that kept me so implacably spellbound, giving me such a sense of well-being and peace? I felt such a oneness with nature in those early days, and because I was able to see further into that oneness – in fact much further than I have ever been able to see since – have I, unconsciously, spent the rest of my life attempting to recapture it?

Though we didn't have a dog at this time, we had Gerty the goat, who could sometimes be a bit of a devil, and charge at me for no reason that I could think of. Maybe he didn't like my scarlet frock, but only bulls charge at red, or so I was led to believe.

Daddy had a splendid hackney pony called Soldier, and sometimes Mummy would take us shopping in the trap to the local village of Ingatestone about two miles away. I found the rhythm so comforting compared with the sickly swoops of the motor-car.

One day I was playing with Berty my rainbow cock. 'Pusscat, can you please come and help me?' stammered Jukes politely.

Why not? Always happy to be in Jukes's good books. I waddled eagerly towards Jukes, who awaited my arrival patiently, holding three shoes in his hands. He couldn't carry the fourth so asked if I would be kind enough to carry it up the three steep steps to the playroom.

Naturally I complied. When I arrived at the top, I couldn't believe my eyes, because usually the whole playroom was covered in bits of Meccano, but today scattered all over the floor was a mass of shoes of all shapes and sizes, both Mummy's and Daddy's, with lots of toys strewn amongst them.

I didn't recognize Chuzzer as he entered the playroom, he was one great mound of shoes and toys.

'C'mon, Pusscat,' said Jukes firmly, 'hurry up and help.'

I wasn't sure what Jukes wanted me to help with, but it seemed very important. They both turned ominously silent as they stacked all the shoes and toys in a neat pile in the centre of the playroom. 'Right,' said Jukes, 'where are they?'

'I gave them to you,' stammered Chuzzer.

'Have you stolen them, Pusscat?' asked Jukes. I didn't know what I was supposed to have stolen, but thought it safest to start searching for the mysterious something.

'Here they are,' said Chuzzer, wheezing away with his asthma, as he produced a box of matches.

Jukes opened the box and struck a match to the shoe and toy bonfire. The flames failed to catch at first, but with a little help from some *Beano*s, the fire began to flare up, sparkle and spit. Spiffing it was, so warm, bright and cosy!

What a feeling of accomplishment we all shared in the playroom that afternoon. It was a profoundly satisfying sight, those growing flames, and just the three of us sitting there mesmerized. Jukes must have got this spiffing idea from our bedside story where Harriette burnt the house down.

Enter Mother. I can't remember how large the flames were

17

by then, but there was great urgency in her voice as she called Brand to help, covering up the blaze with water and blankets.

'On Miss Cripps's day off too [our governess]. How *could* you all?' She stood there stamping her feet, banging towels, and chucking water at the flames. Then she began climbing up the Polly Tree.

The expression 'climbing up the Polly Tree' came to me one day when my parents took me to the pet department in Harrods. High above me was a livid parrot on a long broomstick of a pole. 'Pretty Polly,' he squawked through exceedingly colourful, yet sparse plumage. For a balding bundle of feathers waddling to and fro on a tiny perch, he was possessed of a mighty power, spitting down on the whole of humanity with a raw and heartrending pent-up fury. 'Pretty Polly! Pretty Polly! Pretty Polly!' Just like Mother when she got going.

'Who is responsible for this?' she shouted, almost at the top of her tree. Jukes looked politely across the room at me, then Chuzzer too, while his wheezing multiplied. I just sat there, not knowing if I was being accused – nor what I was guilty of.

On this one occasion, it was the hair-brush all round.

That blasted drowning episode branded me for life. I was never really successful in shaking it off. Whatever happened – whoever did it – it was always, 'Pusscat!'

CHAPTER THREE

BEING IN AWE of my mother in those early years was easy, loving her wasn't. I felt I was always looking at her, talking to her, through a long telescope, for she kept herself at a busy distance. She was certainly the most beautiful creature I had ever seen, yet there was something else that she had, or was it just that she was my mother? I don't think so, because everyone who met her reacted in the same way. You could hear men sighing as they brushed her legs with a glance; legs which stretched way up to Kingdom Come.

She carried her seductive mixture of contradiction like the Queen of the realm that she was. She had all the natural grace of Kelly mixed in with the vixen heat of Leigh. Her hair was silky as the moon and her skin, as if somehow peached with the early morning dew, was never caught lacking its lustre. How she flummoxed all comers, children and adults alike. She would prowl around, mysteriously soft and panther-like, and then quite suddenly start to bustle like that demented Harrods parrot.

No one, except Daddy maybe, got close enough to crack the outer shell of her charisma – or was it just a pose? I don't think so, because she was too busy to create an image for herself, too busy even to be vain.

She was a threat to those who liked everything neatly pigeon-holed into a category or typecast into some cliché. The only part of her that lacked contradiction was her whole-hearted respect and devotion for my father. They were truly in love. She was his little wren-bird. Actually, she didn't resemble a wren at all, but hated her real name, Clarice, and Wren came from her surname Remnant.

When out shopping, Mummy's sexy elegance had some of the men gawping like goldfish as they bumped into each other. I remember on one occasion some fellow giving her such a lingering 'come hither' that he was blissfully unaware of an approaching lamp-post. As he received a mighty crack, Mummy gave me a wee conspiratorial wink, as if the punishment fitted the crime. Fortunately all the attention that was showered upon her helped to brighten those boring outings quite considerably.

The reason Mummy looked like a queen was because she was related to one. She was the eldest child of Francis (Frank) Remnant, bastard son of Prince Francis of Teck, Queen Mary's brother. Sexy old Frank, as he was known, came over when Mary married Prince George, who became George V, and had a cuddle with the seamstress in the White Lodge at Richmond. Bingo – and the seamstress ended up with one of the White Lodge grooms as a surrogate Dad for Grandpa.

My maternal grandmother was a Baskerville and we found this sufficiently intriguing for Jukes to go and check out our family tree at Somerset House. A Baskerville indeed she was, from Clovelly, but what he found out quite by chance was that the record of my grandfather's birth wasn't entered anywhere. Poor old Francis Remnant had no proof of his existence. So how could Mummy exist – or any of us lot come to that? Carelessness on behalf of the chambermaid (a second time) – or merely the power of royalty? Acknowledged bastards are given a 'Fitz' in front of their names as in 'FitzWilliam' – or so I'm told – with the honour of your birth being recorded at Somerset House. But if you're an unacknowledged bastard, your birth isn't recorded at Somerset House, and you're sometimes given, so Mother said, the name of Remnant, an unwanted piece of old cloth. If that be so, then Mother was quite some bargain piece of unwanted cloth.

CHAPTER FOUR

MAUZIE WAS the little girl who lived up the lane. I thought the sun shone out of Mauzie's silky plaits. She was three years older than me, and as 'pretty as a postcard', so Mummy kept telling me. Her house was very grand, and she seemed to have the best that money could buy. She had two fat uncles, Uncle John and Uncle Willy. As if Mauzie being pretty as a postcard wasn't enough, she was blessed with an even prettier Shetland pony called Kitty.

It was easy, I suppose, for someone like me to fall in love with someone like Kitty because, like me, she was left pretty much to her own devices, what with Mauzie's gang leading such a busy social life, always partying and shooting off to London.

I remember taking up my position, squatting hidden in the front hedge – I was roughly three and a half at this time – waiting patiently for Mauzie and her family to leave. They'd drive off, full of importance in their posh silver motor car, Uncle John at the wheel, Mauzie sitting on Uncle Willy's lap in the front, and Mauzie's mother always in the wrong hat, usually a conglomeration of bows and feathers, relentlessly at odds with her grim down-to-earth rather podgy features. There was something sad about her too, always alone in the back, with no Daddy as far as I could make out. Where were they off to on these outings, all dressed up like the dog's dinner? Blurred memories of a grand yet cloudy Irish mystery.

But I wasn't hiding in the front hedge merely to spy on this somewhat flamboyant exodus. Now that the coast was clear I could safely steal Kitty. I'd waddle through the stable yard and across the field through Mauzie's hedge and into her stable yard.

Kitty always gave me such a rowdy welcome. I knew it wasn't only greed for the pony-nuts I took for her, because when I had none she still whinnied, which I took to mean that Kitty loved me as well.

Opening the stable door was tricky. Having dragged a bucket across the yard to stand on to reach the bolt, I couldn't open the door because the bucket and I were in the way. Sometimes the bucket's clatter would frighten Kitty: she'd flatten her ears back and disappear into the far darkness of her stall. With Kitty trapped in the far corner, I could grab hold of a clump of mane and heave myself on to her back. Often I fell off before the final haul because the stupid bucket would tip over before I was quite up.

I was lucky on three counts: (1) Kitty had such a very long mane to hold on to; (2) her back was so safe and flat you could eat a picnic off it; (3) Kitty was without a doubt the laziest pony in the world, for I could never get her to venture further than the feed store, which was a great pity for me.

There was one occasion when I was clinging on to Kitty's mane for grim death, as usual, when she decided she wanted to go a little further than the boundary of the yard, and I had absolutely no say in the matter whatsoever. She made a beeline for the vegetable garden. It was the height of summer, so everything was ripe for picking – or squashing, as was the case that afternoon. With great precision she demolished the lot. Like a bulldozer she went through it, flattening the gooseberries and the redcurrants, scratching her back on the sweet-pea poles, snapping a pole in half, pawing the ground ferociously to expose a carrot or two. She knew what she was doing, no doubt about it. If I was frightened I can't recall it. Probably because in early childhood it was natural to remain firmly skewered to the moment, never looking back with regret or forward to the consequences – something I'm trying to achieve once again, but it's hard.

While Kitty ran amok in the vegetable garden, I can only remember how blissful it was. Thoughtfully she gave the rhubarb a great fresh dump of dung before finally flattening the asparagus. A butterfly landed to bask on my naked, sun-warmed knee. It tickled unbearably so I really had to concentrate on keeping still.

'Little devil!' It was Uncle John shouting as he stomped up from behind, rudely plucking me off Kitty. That I could swallow, but when he began rough-handling her, even hitting her, I began to cry. After all, it wasn't *her* fault.

Enter Mauzie's mother, Mrs Malone. 'Shoosh now, you scallywag, I've rung up Wren, she'll be here shortly.' The whole family just stood in a row wagging their fingers at me. How silly they all looked, like bad-tempered Drummoids on the bars of my cot.

While we all waited for Mummy to arrive, my eyes drifted to the orange stick Mauzie was nibbling with ravenous glee. I thought at first it was a carrot, but then she pulled some orange paper further down the stick, and stuck her tongue deep down into something gooey and chocolaty. Watching her dribbling got me going too. I asked her what it was.

'Crunchie bar,' said Mauzie, tossing back her golden locks.

'Want some.'

'Certainly not!' glared Mrs Malone. 'You need a spanking, not a Crunchie bar.'

Finally Mummy hurried up the drive and it all got ten times worse, the Polly Tree shuddered with the weight of them all 'Pretty Pollying' at me. My eyes strayed sideways again, squinting towards Mauzie's Crunchie bar – I'd never seen anything like it before.

Did I know I had done wrong? Did I know I had stolen Kitty and destroyed their vegetable garden? Of course I did – just as Mother knew I never listened to a single word she said. As soon as I drifted off to better places, she would hold my face between her hands in her familiar iron vice, trying to force me to concentrate. But I'd plug out the sound and simply watch her mouth moving. I still do this, especially with politicians. Body language tells the truest tales, and that day Mother's body language, together with her ruffled feathers stiff as a ramrod signalled one thing only – HAIR-BRUSH.

So, I thought to myself, there's no harm in finding out about Mauzie's orange stick. 'Mummy, can we have Crunchie bars, like Mauzie?'

'How dare you talk of Crunchie bars at a time like this!'

'After the hair-brush, can I?'

'No,' she said, squeezing my knuckles even harder. 'There aren't any to be found – anywhere.'

'Why not? Mauzie finds them.'

She gave me a quick, vixen look. 'They're only available on the Black Market.'

I was determined to find out where this Black Market was.

CHAPTER FIVE

MY FATHER WAS twenty-four years older than my mother. He couldn't get a divorce from Pat, his first wife, so Jukes, Chuzzlewit and I were born out of wedlock, although we never knew it.

Mother was working as a temporary secretary and was called in to work for my Father while his faithful Ruby Droop was away over the Christmas holiday. Mother went into his office one day to put some papers on his desk, in he came and that was that.

She didn't take my father away from his first wife. Pat had previously gone off with some Indian doctor; she was a left-wing intellectual and being feminist, a vanguard for women's rights, wasn't interested in having babies. It gradually dawned on Daddy that he wasn't going to get his mixed doubles match from those academic hips.

My father was mostly Welsh. His father, Thomas Miles, was a steel magnate, building a great many of those massive steel works (carbuncles, I'm ashamed to say) all over the place. Sheffield, the Holwell Foundry, Stanton Iron and Steel Works and Newton Chambers.

However, I'm delighted to add that the first railway ever built from Stockton to Darlington wasn't a carbuncle and Daddy's great-grandfather, also Thomas Miles, and his brother Richard were two of the four responsible.

Father was the second brother, which was usually seen as

rotten luck. However, he proved himself to be an extremely successful construction engineer, designing steel works all over the world (more carbuncles). Nevertheless he gave the best value for money, usually pipping the rest of world-wide competition to the post. His company was John Miles & Partners, with offices in a lovely old building in Cannon Street. (I'm boasting a little on his behalf because he never did so himself.)

Father was cuddly and accessible, yet all-knowing; a cross between Owly and a perfectly proportioned and co-ordinated minute Tarzan. Perfect in every way, but then all heroes are perfect, are they not?

Everything he did he did beautifully, or so it seemed to me. Whether it was an oil painting of Mummy in the bath, a bust of Jukes in bronze, a landscape in water colours, or a hand-carved wooden stool for me; whether he was playing the piano, darts, ping-pong, tennis, badminton, croquet or simply digging the asparagus bed, it all delighted him and he put his whole heart into it.

He was brought up to be a winner, so naturally he never questioned the pressures he put on all of us to be high achievers too. Is this wrong, I wonder. (Because I felt a definite pressure on me to succeed I, in turn, let my own son hang loose and not worry about winning or losing. This turned out to be just as wrong. Oh, for some wise instruction, or for that happy balance between the two! In fact, anything rather than to keep stunting human growth by blundering for ever onward into the generation chain reaction.)

Once home in the evening, Father would put the city behind him, and dedicate what remained of the day to us and his hobbies. We were easily spellbound, as he sat at his treasured Bechstein grand for hours playing Beethoven, Mozart, and other classical composers, forties favourites such as Cole Porter, Gershwin, Noël Coward, songs such as 'Uncle Tom Cobleigh', 'Danny Boy', 'John Peel', and most of the Negro spirituals as well. He had a mellow, honey-coated voice, and a natural style and sense of rhythm, always emphasizing the off-beat, so very rarely seen in the West, especially in the 1940s. When black people dance, they seem to flow like water through the ground, whereas we whites have a tendency to peck away on top – like one of my chickens. But Daddy never pecked away on top: his movements were laid back, real easy. As he shuffled along with all that frizzy hair on his head and that mysterious, endless repertoire of Negro spirituals I often wondered . . . I would have been greatly chuffed to have had some black blood tucked away somewhere in my veins.

We have photographs of Daddy looking so tiny, mounted on his great war-horse. He was a captain at the age of nineteen in the Royal Field Artillery in the First World War. (I still find it amazing to think that my father rode to war on horseback!) This horse, ironically called Kitty, had been with him for some years and a real bond had developed between them until on the battlefield one day she was shot dead from under him. I tried to get him to tell me more about Kitty, but he never would. He turned his face away once, ashamed of his welling tears.

His desk drawer was stuffed with medals including the Military Cross, but he never told me what he'd won it for. 'I was in the midst of a battle one dusk, sniffed the air, smelt the enemy approaching, and being the coward that I am, I panicked, gave the command to retreat and found myself charging into the enemy, who promptly turned tail and ran.' That was his story and he stuck to it. Whatever really happened, he preferred to shrug it off.

In truth, Father's sense of direction, like mine, was never his strong point.

After he received his Military Cross at Buckingham Palace, Daddy bowed graciously to King George V, and made for the exit, relieved to have got the whole occasion behind him. In the corridor he put up his hand to pat his medal proudly, only to discover that it wasn't there. He panicked and began to retrace his footsteps. He got down on his knees, hell bent on finding his Military Cross. What on earth was he going to say when he finally bumped into someone, and had to confess that he'd lost it within the space of two minutes?

As he was rehearsing the dreaded moment, he came across a pair of highly polished black boots. 'What are you doing here, crawling about in His Majesty's private quarters?' said a gruff military voice.

Poor Daddy was too embarrassed to look up, he had obviously taken the wrong turning. 'King George has just pinned on my medal, and it's gone – I've lost it!'

The voice replied, less gruff, more patronizing, 'Sir, the King hasn't time to fiddle with pins, he merely makes the gesture. Your medal is waiting for you at the exit.'

Daddy was a Communist in his early days. He used to hang around with the Bloomsbury Set in the twenties and thirties and bring them down to the Mill House for weekends with his first wife Pat. Apparently Mill House became a barmy Bohemian den of decadence every weekend, which of course Mummy promptly put a stop to when she became its mistress. The neighbours used to gossip of the risqué goings-on. One neighbour complained that they danced on the lawns naked at night, doing amazing Isadora Duncan swirls around the ancient sun-dial, erotically highlighted by the headlights of Daddy's car.

Daddy had a moving camera, even way back in those days, so we have some very rare footage of that gang in their era. What astonishes me is that, despite all their academic very left-wing Bohemian ways, they somehow still had the wherewithal to flaunt such a richness of style and flair with very little money – often no money at all. Where have we gone wrong? Why is it that they all seemed to possess a stronger sense of identity combined with such elegance and sparkling energy? Probably because there was no television to live their lives for them.

He also owned a small aircraft, a Hornet Moth, and sometimes he would fly over Mill House, tossing out far-things, and even halfpennies on to the lawn for us to collect. What fun it was, Daddy dropping down from the heavens, in his beautiful silver bird, scattering golden poo everywhere.

Jukes was allowed up to fly with him one day, so was Chuzzer. Daddy's best friend was called Hoppy, and he told us the tale of how he and Hoppy nearly took the top off one of the French Alps, because they over-estimated the little Hornet's climbing capacity. In fact, he and Hoppy went on some most illegal and dangerous journeys across Europe, sometimes frightening my mother half to death.

But Mummy had a lot to be thankful for. During the Second World War Daddy found himself in Lisbon on business where he met up with his friend the actor Leslie Howard. Leslie had finished his business earlier than he had antici-pated and wanted to return to England urgently, but his private plane wasn't due in till late the next day. Daddy's plane, however, left early the next morning so between them they decided to do a swap.

Leslie took Daddy's place on the flight home and got shot down. There were many rumours flying about at the time, one being that Churchill was supposed to have been on the flight. Mummy was at London Airport, expecting not only Daddy but also her first child to arrive. Booming over the Tannoy came the news that the plane had crashed. Daddy had been unable to inform her of his change of plan, so she assumed that he'd been shot down.

John Miles turned up the next day safe and sound in the comfort and splendour of Leslie's private plane. He remained shattered by the news for quite some time – not only a friend but a remarkable talent gone with the wind. Some of the papers had it that Daddy had been shot down because the ticket still remained in his name.

With all that shock and confusion, Jukes popped out prematurely. Usually babies born as small as Jukes didn't survive, and if it hadn't been for the expertise of Mother's doctor and friend Mary Adams feeding him with a fountain pen, Jukes wouldn't be with us today.

Daddy had many a narrow escape during both the First and Second World Wars. I wonder what God was saving him for? My tickles probably, because he would tickle my arms at night to send me to sleep. The electric combination of Daddy's soft yet firm tickling technique and my rather raw sensitive skin shot me straight up to Heaven's gates, never to return till morning. There's never been a tickler to match him and, believe me, I've searched. The only person to come within throwing distance of his brilliance is me, sadly. Brother Jukes appreciated Daddy's refined tickling skills too, and even to this day he'll unconsciously slip into a trance while stroking his hand just like Daddy used to do.

I longed for the evenings, when Daddy would come home and all would be well. Jukes, Chuzzer and I had a bath together twice a week because hot water was scarce in those days. I didn't mind bathing with the boys as long as Daddy was back from the City to watch over me.

Mummy is playing with the boy's dangly bits, polishing them with soapy water, and rubbing them up and down. Daddy says it's very important to loosen the skin, yet it seems to me their dangly bits are too loose already. If they get any looser, they'll look just like Pip's fat sausagey beak.

For our bedtime story Daddy's reading us *Struwwelpeter*, where this fierce fellow called the Scissor Man comes swooshing in, chopping off the thumbs of naughty children who suck them. I wish he'd swoosh into the bathroom and chop off the boys' dangly bits, then they'd be all neat and tidy like me.

Mummy snatches my battleship away. 'Stand up, Pusscat.' Hooray, now comes my favourite bit, being washed. But why is Mummy in such a hurry all the time? I love the slippery feeling as the soapy sponge slides over my tummy, legs and botty. But, like all good things, it comes to an end, much too fast.

Why isn't Daddy home yet? He washes me much slower, as long as Mummy has brought up his whisky first. Oh, dear

me, Mummy is leaving us to go and put the oven on. I don't like being left alone with the boys, not one little bit.

'Jukes – look what Pusscat has done with your battleship – she's filled it up with water, it won't float.' Horrid Chuzzer telling tales.

'Pusscat,' stammers Jukes, 'how many times have I told you not to play with my battleship?' They're going to push me under, I know it.

Where is Daddy? HELP! Under the water I go. I hate it under here . . . I try and grab something . . . it moves. I can't breathe I'm in a foggy forest infested with toenails, sunken battleships, spiky yachts and dangly bits . . . nothing seems to matter any more.

*

But all the near-drowning struggles gave me considerable lung capacity, which was to prove very useful as time went on.

Even more defined are the tickling nightmares. I don't mean Daddy's kind of tickling, I mean being tickled almost to death by the two of them. One would put his knees on my arms, the other on my legs, and with their four free hands tickle me down into that dark hopeless valley of the last death-breath. Sometimes in the midst of one of my very last death-breath experiences, I'd see from my angle along the lawn my father's sleek brown City shoes coming towards me – my knight in shining shoes! I know it was only fun; I know my brothers didn't really understand what I was going through beneath their gruff giggling and rough handling and I bear them not a whiff of a grudge.

I'd be loath to paint myself as a victim here, because I was as far away from a victim as it is possible to be. Perhaps on some occasions I was a scarlet victim because, although never cherishing any need to be a boy, I sometimes yearned to be part of their world so much that I made a right royal nuisance of myself. But finally, when push came to shove, there was no contest whatsoever between us – the boys simply had more muscles and there's an end to it.

I was allowed to join in one early game; it was called 'Ee-ees' – crabs playing 'He'. The three of us would scamper around on all fours with our tummies facing upwards and try and catch each other. When we were caught we'd cry, 'Ee-ees' like a crab squealing, then stick our knees in the air and wiggle our legs together, or up against each other, excitedly. In retrospect this early game seems slightly obscene, but at the time it was all quite innocent fun. Or was it? Later both the word and the wriggling action led us on towards wanking which we also called 'Ee-Ees'.

I remember longing to join in one day when the boys were being pushed by Daddy on the swing which hung from the gnarled apple tree beside the scullery door. Their voices sounded so full of excitement. 'I see him! I see him!' cried Jukes with glee.

On top of the ancient barn in the stable yard there stood a fine haughty weather-cock that snootily spun around when the mood took him. It was only possible to see part of him from one angle, down by the mill pond. I wanted to see all of him. Was he as magnificent as Berty, my real life rainbow cock, I wondered.

Now I heard Chuzzer yelping with joy. 'Higher! I can see him! I can see him!' I couldn't resist any more, and made my way from the stables, quite determined that I too should get a full view of the weather-cock.

There was Chuzzer, flying so high and fearless, bent up and hunched with his wheeze. 'My turn, my turn, my turn!' Daddy had no choice but to take notice of me.

I was wearing the only frock I didn't mind too much. It was pale blue with little pink elephants all over it. Joy of joys, it had a smallish bow, soft and limp compared to the rest, giving me some respite. It was a warm summer's evening and I had no shoes or panties on. 'All right, Pusscat, but very gently.'

On I climbed. 'Up we go!' said Daddy. His pushing was insultingly half-hearted. 'Higher, Daddy! HIGHER! Please!'

I looked up, I couldn't quite see all the weather-cock.

'Higher, Daddy – push harder! PUSH!'

'Well done, Pusscat – hold on tight – you're as high as the boys!'

At last I was able to see the weather-cock in all his glory. Bursting with victory, I had a slight accident, realized I wasn't wearing any panties, turned to see – Mummy at the scullery door, at the top of the Polly Tree! 'John, you'll kill her!' I lost all sense of balance.

I landed from a great height, head first on to the ancient flagstones. Apparently I was unconscious for so long that the doctor had to be called in. Mother always claimed my stammer got worse after that crash. It certainly left a severe dent in the back of my skull – very convenient for stuffing my own hair into whenever I have to wear a wig (most of the time!).

CHAPTER SIX

I DREADED GOING up to London more than anything in the whole wide world. The sad grey faces, the black smoke, even the noise and the smell gave out waves of greyish yellowness. Worse still was the sight of the few skinny horses scattered between traffic, ponies and sometimes even mules dotted about the East End. Sometimes I saw ponies being harshly whipped as they tried to pull their great piles, so cruelly overloaded.

Often our London trips included shopping, usually a new outfit for Mother. I'd spend hours with the two boys picking up pins from the carpets of Harrods or Debenhams. We must have picked up millions of pins during our childhood while Mummy tried on her clothes.

At lunch we'd watch Mother craning her head round the restaurant looking for one of her cronies. Reba Marsham, who lived up the lane, was a shrewd vibrant woman, much older than Mummy in years, but not in spirit, and she's still young at the ripe old age of ninety-four. She was the sister of Baron, the photographer, and she had two sons, Anthony and Peter Blond, who came down to Ingatestone sometimes. Peter nice, Anthony naughty. 'Nice' and 'Naughty', Mummy called them.

Reba and Mummy would gossip while we sat watching the mannequin parade up and down. Mummy's favourite table was at the corner of the cat walk, where the models

37

would do their elegant twizzle, point their high heels, flaunt their flamboyant hats this way and that, and then saunter off again.

This was great fun, because we'd mark the place where they'd float up to do their twizzle, put a pea, carrot or sprout down, and wait to see if they'd ignore it, step over it, or squash it into the carpet. One time the model had to remove her shoe, for part of the sprout had stuck limpet-like to her heel.

Those forties fashions were so elegant. The mannequins looked glorious swathed in the luxury of exciting new materials emerging after the relentlessly drab war years. Dashing hats, too, making Mummy's mouth water, so much so that she forgot about her food and reached for her pen, noting down the favourites in her diary.

There was one particularly memorable day. We had been to the dentist, which was beastly enough, followed by London Zoo, the most miserable place I knew, but all dressed up in the name of a treat. As soon as the car pulled up in Regent's Park a dread came over me as I heard the birds, monkeys and lions all wailing to be set free.

Still a toddler, I could happily have stayed near the penguins all day comparing notes with Pip. So I was rather annoyed when Daddy swept me up on to his shoulders. 'Come along, Pusscat, your favourite, the lions.' I don't think he liked trapped lions any more than I did. There we stood in the drizzling rain staring into private lives, private parts and private hells.

Mother was all dressed up in cream and beige under both umbrella and cloche hat, Father in his City best, Jukes and

Chuzzer all polished and swish. Daddy was escorting two VIPs from America, trying to clinch a business deal, so we were all on our best deal-clinching behaviour.

'Give Pip to me, he'll get soaked,' whispered Mummy sweetly, in case they overheard.

'No.'

The lions roared with such profound hatred through their bars – just like the bars of my cot. Prowling back and forth, up and down, round and round in angry circles, snarling their great yellow teeth with a hopeless fury, while we all stood in our posh London clothes, oohing and aahing at them – why?

One lion was so livid that Daddy put me down. 'Maybe he doesn't like you on my shoulders, Pusscat.' Right at that moment, perfectly on cue, the lion turned away from us in disgust, flaunting a backside closely resembling a rather messy traffic accident. Just as I was thinking that I'd never seen a bottom quite like it, unheralded, it opened up its swollen fleshy botty gates, and hey presto! Great splooshes of pee came shooting out with impressive force over everyone, but mostly over Mummy and the VIPs. Thank God I'd held on to Pip!

So cold the day, so warm the pee that it steamed its way out with dashing aplomb. Daddy who, like me, was clear of the main blast turned and gave me an Owly wink.

Mother was about to climb up the Polly Tree, but seeing all of us, including the VIPs, hooting with laughter, she closed her redundant brolly with a shrug and surrendered to her fate as best she could. 'Wretched lion's ruined my suit.'

Daddy turned to her. 'I think, darling, you'll find, from

the general direction of things, that it's probably a lioness, unless he's especially talented.'

One evening, driving home from another beastly London experience, I remember Mother was at the wheel. As usual I was either trying not to think about being sick or wondering where to put it when it arrived. 'I feel sick!'

'Just keep looking out of the window, Pusscat, count the Gee-Gees.'

Why did they always call them Gee-Gees, I wondered.

I knew we were half-way home because of the high oak trees of Epping Forest. Mother and Father were nattering away in the front as usual, and the boys were squashing me in the back, as usual, fighting over the monkey puzzle tree game. (Whoever saw a monkey puzzle tree first won a penny from Daddy.) Why bother searching for such an ugly prickly tree?

I was happy and contented whenever my finger was securely up into Pip's hole. It was my sleeping pill, and it worked every time. I was very proud of Pip's secret hole of late because, thanks to hard work, my finger could now makes its way far up into the cosy squashy softness.

When I awoke it was to find Jukes trying to interrupt the argument babbling forth in the front. Interrupting the parents was forbidden. Jukes knew this full well, yet, 'Excuse me, Daddy,' persisted Jukes politely. Daddy was in the middle of saying something very important to Mummy, who couldn't have been listening because she was shouting even louder than Daddy, but Jukes had the audacity to top them both.

'Be quiet, Jukes, just keep counting monkey puzzle trees.' The whole car was shaking with angry voices for quite some distance, but I didn't mind because it stopped me thinking about throwing up.

Jukes had finally had enough, so he politely shouted, 'Excuse me, but Chuzzer's not here.' That stopped everything right in its tracks.

'WHAT?' they said together, finally agreeing about something.

'How long ago did he fall out?' stammered Daddy.

'A long time ago, way back in Epping Forest when you wouldn't listen to me,' Jukes stuttered back, crying politely. Daddy drove a maroon Lee Frances in those days, with an upward locking device, so if you leant down on the handles, you could easily fly out.

Was I too young to realize how much I loved Chuzzer? How much I would miss him? Did I really know what was happening or was I merely echoing my parents' concern? I don't think so.

If it was an echo, it disturbed me quite a lot. I remember keeping my eyes glued to the road as Mummy had ordered, hoping I'd be the one to see him first. I expected to find Chuzzer all mashed up like lumpy tomato ketchup – SPLAT – in the middle of the road.

It turned into hell that night in Epping Forest, searching through the dark and gloom amidst panic and the haze of misty rain swirling in foggy headlights, casting devious shadows across the forest, which in turn dripped tears of consolation, for both Mummy and Daddy feared the worst.

It was well after midnight when yet another police station gave us the news that he had been taken to a nearby hospital, apparently none the worse for wear. Typical! It wouldn't surprise me if Chuzzlewit ends up the sole survivor of the nuclear holocaust. He just had the knack, still has it as a matter of fact. Had he drowned in the mill pond, like I wanted, all this would never have happened.

CHAPTER SEVEN

MOTHER'S BEST FRIEND was Lady Petre of Ingatestone Hall, a magnificent Tudor house of rosy brick, with my favourite diamond-shaped windowpanes. Peggy Petre, a showgirl turned London society beauty, was a stunner. It was quite common for a chorus girl to pluck up a lord or even a duke, but to do so you had to be really hot stuff and Peggy Petre certainly was that.

Ingatestone was full of classy families all of whom loved partying and we were off to Ingatestone Hall for another ghastly party. I had a problem as a small girl (still do, as a matter of fact) in my relationship with the upper classes. I have never been totally comfortable in their company, and in those early days the more Mummy pushed me to join the county band wagon the more I ran in the opposite direction. I know this is an inverted snobbery, but I am unable to make a point of true contact. I don't dislike them, in some ways I respect them, but I just feel very different, and did so, even then, at the age of four.

Perhaps I associate the upper classes with my hatred of parties, and perhaps that very same hatred stems from the fact that I gate-crashed one at my birth. On the other hand Mother liked parties a lot, and once she was there they liked her, but gearing herself up for the occasion was quite a process.

She'd park the three of us on chairs all in a row right

behind her, where she could keep her beady reflected eye on us through her three-way dressing-table mirror. If any one of us dared move a muscle, we'd get our wrists slapped. Then with a business-like economy and a deft precision lacking any trace of vanity, she'd transform into the belle of the ball before our very eyes. A magical mystery.

Jukes put up with the dressing-up bit, and under his stiff upper lip seemed quite at home at the party itself; whereas Chuzzlewit hated dressing up and loathed parties as much as I did. But what I found most infuriating was that Chuzzer was often let off the party hook at the last moment, because of his wheeze. Mind you, his nightly wheezing was horrid. It was hard trying to sleep with Chuzzer silently screaming. His breath would suck itself out of his throat and disappear, running away from him as fast as it could, leaving him rasping, gasping and begging it to return to him.

He never ever moaned about his wheeze (still doesn't, and it's been relentless all his life) but I always wondered why his breath went on these strange walkabouts, perhaps it didn't like him very much? There were times when I didn't blame it because whenever Chuzzer's dark, powerfully broody moods fell upon him, I welcomed the sound of his struggle, because there was a chance his breath might run away for ever – and on those occasions a good job too, I thought. But other times I would wake with a shudder as an eerie soulful whine culminating in a kind of death rattle would creak up the corridors, making me feel so sad for Chuzzer, so very sad.

On the day of the Ingatestone Hall party, Chuzzer started his wheezing, and got stroked, cuddled and caressed. 'Poor darling boy, you needn't go to the party if you don't want to.'

Down on my haunches I went, crouching like a frog, wheezing away very realistically, but all I got was my bottom smacked and promptly bundled into my beastly party frock – not a drop of hugging to be seen. I used to wonder, as I watched him strutting back to his boring Meccano set in the playroom, whether he would still be wheezing when he got there.

One time I followed him, crept into the playroom, and there was Chuzzer, happy as Larry, constructing a most gigantic crane, with not a whisper of a wheeze. Just as I suspected – the rat.

'Keep still, Pusscat, for the last time.' Poor old Mother – still thinking, the bigger the bow the less chance of the neighbourhood noticing the occupant. 'Oh, God! Look at your ears, they're filthy! They must be kept pristine clean, since they're on parade for the whole world to see.'

Mummy was wrong about that, because I remember thinking that at last my hair was finally growing over my ears.

Ripping hair as she tugged at my fuzzy tangles, 'Good God! This time the manure's completely stuck to your hair!' Mother and I in those early days were probably no more than chalk and cheese clashing – sometimes, as that day, into chaotic poison. 'You'll never see your twenty-first birthday, just mark my words!' She threw down the comb as if it were a deadly enemy and marched off, returning with a big pair of scissors, and just like the Scissor Man in *Struwwelpeter*, she chopped my hair off. I looked in the mirror and saw nothing but ears. I gave an inward sigh, because I knew she'd have to pay for this latest humiliation, and it was all so exhausting.

With staggering serenity, a veritable poem of pink and

pearls, with a cluster of daisies in her cloche hat, Mummy parked the car in the great driveway of Ingatestone Hall. Staggering, because it seemed only a few seconds before that she had been bellowing at me like a fish-wife. As we got out of the car, Mummy glanced at me. 'You look so grown-up with that tidy hair, Pusscat.' But her nostrils, shaped like willow leaves were puckering inwardly. They always quivered when she was fibbing.

So there we were, the three of us, entering the great Hall as if butter wouldn't melt in our mouths with Mummy as cool and calm as a pearly cucumber. (That's why I hate parties, it's the pretence, the delusion, the falsehood.) Everyone who was anyone in our parish was there, and many more who weren't. The girls were comparing frocks, hair, ribbons, buttons 'n' bows – there was no discussion as to whose was the biggest on the bow front, so why hang around? Pip and I were about to sneak off on our own. 'Where are you going?' asked Lady Petre, as she puffed on her black shiny cigarette holder. 'We're about to play "Grandmother's Footsteps" and you can be Grandmother. I'll hold your penguin for you.'

'No!' She turned away, laughing at me.

I tried to escape to find the staircase, so Pip and I could have a slide, but before I had time tea was announced. 'Lots of birthday cake, ice-cream and jelly,' said Lady Petre, clapping her hands royally.

I hated ice-cream, jelly and birthday cake, worst of all. Why can't they make a birthday cake out of pickled onions?

I found myself sitting next to Ros de Worms, who with her older sister Anne lived down the lane from us. A very serious couple they were, but jolly good bricks really. Ros was wearing a smart tartan frock, so carefully I dumped my red jelly into her lap, because I hate red jelly. She gave me one of her dark glares, and dumped a great clump of green jelly into mine, which was lucky, because I loved green jelly.

'Pusscat!' cried Mrs de Worms. 'That's Ros's brand new frock. Wren!'

Mummy came, took me outside, and removed Pip from me, whereupon I shook the very foundations of Ingatestone Hall, thanks to my terrific lung capacity helped by the boys' attempts to drown me. Pip was reluctantly returned, and he and I snuck off.

I was drawn to banisters as powerfully as I was drawn to the stable yard. I judged people by their banisters. Undeniably Lord and Lady Petre had the greatest banisters in the county (for a four-year-old, that is – when I grew more daring I'd find the stops and starts infuriating). At the top I managed to squeeze my way between two banisters, and sat down with Pip beside me, watching all the partying going on from high up in the gods.

I remember Mummy all busy and glittering through the great Hall. Was it because she was my mother that she always had a golden shimmer around her skin? 'Shoosh, everyone,' said Lady Petre. 'Let Wren announce the winner of the tray game.'

I knew Jukes would be the winner because he always won the tray game, so I thought I'd be off.

I wandered down a corridor and got lost. I was reminded of Daddy and Buckingham Palace – thank goodness I had Pip with me. Eventually we found ourselves in front of a beautifully carved door which led into the most spectacular room. There was a four-poster bed smothered in creamy lace, and a dressing table draped in more lace, silver brushes and boxes everywhere, coloured scent bottles with little golden bags hanging from them. Many more than Mummy had, and there I was thinking that Mummy's dressing table took the biscuit! I saw strings of pearls, beads and silk scarves dangling from the mirror, all glowing in the evening light. I'd never seen anything like it before, Lady Petre's Aladdin's cave, glistening with all the colours of the rainbow.

I was about to leave when I spied a tiny object dazzling away like billyo. I'm sure I heard it tinkling at me, daring me to come a little closer. It was a minute watch with Roman numerals, surrounded by baby pearls. I loved pearls more than anything in the whole wide world. I still do.

I picked it up and stuffed it into Pip's hole, which had matured beautifully. (I'm sure Freud would have had a field day with all this, as he sat snorting cocaine in his private chambers!)

I didn't take the pearly watch out of Pip's hole for three whole days. Then, late one evening, when they'd all said goodnight, I thought I'd take my first peek by candlelight. I put three fingers right up inside Pip's hole, and slowly, very very slowly I took it out. Oh! The wonder of it in candlelight, even better than I'd remembered! Drummoids plopped down on to the bars of my cot to see what I'd been up to. There was such a drumming going on, from them and my heart, drumming with guilt.

I put the watch around Pip's head like a crown. He looked spectacular, like King George would have looked if I'd ever seen him, that is. At that moment in came Mummy, frightening both me and the dear Drumwins to death. 'Pusscat! What on earth have you got there?' I tried to hide it away.

'Stealing is very naughty. Jesus won't love you if you steal.' Who was this Jesus, anyway?

Perhaps I wanted to be caught, for those three days of waiting were truly dark and awful, as if a great and sickly gloom held my tummy in its clammy grasp. So many alien feelings, too complicated for me to understand at the time. The Drumwins left the bars of my cot, they were not inclined to seek out the company of a thief, but the Drummoids sat there in great clusters, clinging and cloying to my sorrow, silently squawking their gloat of glee.

Mother made me give it back to Lady Petre myself. I was too ashamed to look her in the eyes, I just did a little curtsey. 'Sorry, Lady Petre.'

'Thank you, Pusscat, I wondered where it had got to.' She gave me a knowing look as she slipped it into her handbag. She didn't hug it or look at it even, merely snapped the clasp crisply shut again, as she majestically puffed away on her black cigarette holder.

On the way home I do remember feeling a heavy load being lifted off me, followed by a slowly rising carefreeness, and everything became bright once more.

The power of guilt. It tripped me up and pitched me into its darkness, before I was even aware what it was.

CHAPTER EIGHT

Towards the end of the war, I fell in love. I heard a voice on the wireless in Daddy's dressing room one day while he was trying in vain to flatten his frizzy hair in the mirror.

'That you, Daddy?'

He left his disobedient hair swiftly to knot his tie. 'That's not me, Pusscat, that's King George,' he stammered.

'Where does he live?'

'In Buckingham Palace. Your mother has his picture.'

The moment Daddy fished King George out of the back of Mummy's bureau, all sepia and perfect in every way, something happened. He looked so kind and gentle, sad in a way, but beautiful too, I thought.

King George made me feel safe. Instantly he became one of my gang, and I taught Owly and Pip to curtsey whenever he came into the nursery. He went everywhere with me, to the stables, the chickens, the goat, into Soldier's stable, my laurel bush hidey-hole and up all my favourite trees. I even took him out with me when I borrowed Kitty. King George said it couldn't be called stealing because I always brought her home again. He knew Kitty was lonely and needed company, because he understood everything. How could he not? Here was someone who stammered like the rest of us, except *he* was a king! I couldn't see him on television, since we didn't have one yet, but whenever he came on the wireless

Mother would call me indoors and we would sit in reverence. I think Mummy loved him a little bit too, but then, of course, they were cousins.

Sometimes Mummy would shout from the window, 'Puss-cat, come quickly, King George is on!' I'd run like a mad March Hare, only to find that Mummy had tricked me. 'Come on, darling, lunch, we've rung the gong three times already.'

The boys enjoyed Christmas much more than I did, because there was nothing I really wanted except a hundred Crunchie bars maybe, or a dog, or a pony of my very own, but Mummy said they were too difficult for Father Christmas to carry down the chimney. Funny that. Mauzie's chimneys were smaller than ours, I checked, and Mauzie had a pony, kitten and millions of Crunchie bars – that's the Black Market for you. (If I spied a black man in London, I'd run up and ask him for the nearest Black Market. For some strange reason this used to embarrass Mother. 'So very sorry,' she would say, leading me off with her vice-like grip, squashing my knuckles together.)

I remember the Christmas when I was about five, we were all in the drawing room when, completely out of the blue, Father Christmas appeared – just like that. He was quite a big fellow with a long white moustache and a beard that went on and on for ever. He was cold, so Daddy put him by the fire, and gave him a Christmas drink of punch and a mince-pie. Mummy asked if I wanted to sit on his lap. 'Don't be shy, Pusscat, sit on his lap, and see what he has got for you,' said Mummy.

I ran into Daddy's arms, but he pushed me towards Father Christmas saying, 'He won't bite, Pusscat.'

He gave me a new doll, a very stupid doll with long silky

hair. I was angry. I wriggled, trying to escape from his lap. Mummy never listened to me, not once, not ever. 'I only want Crunchie bars!'

Mummy glared. 'They're nowhere to be found, I promise.'

The more I struggled to get off Father Christmas's knee the tighter he held me. I'd had enough, so I pulled his beard as hard as I could. It came away in my hands, and who was underneath but Brand the gardener! Not the ideal way to find out about Father Christmas but, then, what is?

School was looming, I could feel it. It was only half a mile down the lane, but Mummy insisted I came with her when she picked up the boys in the car, a chore that bored me rigid. Aggravated with my fidgeting, she let me climb the tree that stood outside the school yard. It was a perfect tree, huge but with ideal low branches. I knew that when the day came, if I was unable to conquer school at least I had a secret goal: I'd climb to the very top of that maze of complicated branches winding their way right up to heaven.

When the momentous day arrived, after I was forced into my new school clothes, I went and hid in the hay-loft in the barn, for I had a hunch that day that the future was going to be black. I was captured by the devious Brand, and stuffed into the back of the car, all hunched up between the two boys, with their business-like satchels. I screamed and screamed when we got there, so Miss Ingrams (the head and only mistress) suggested that perhaps it would be wiser for me to wait an extra term. So I won the first round. Yet I knew I'd be unable to stop school for ever. I could hear it charging towards me, a monstrous grey unfeeling three-ton truck. I'd given all the signs, I'd put up my hands and screamed, 'Stop!' But it took no notice of something as ephemeral as intuition, and just kept on coming, flattening me and what might have been.

In those days no one really knew what dyslexia was, or if they did it was a well-kept secret. So I went through a whole decade of school with the knowledge that I was just plain stupid, and then another decade of the same, out in the big wide world, and then almost another one after that. Is it any wonder I rebelled?

Through anguish, tears and hard work, I have conquered talking, writing and reading (still with difficulty) but numbers, left and right, map-reading, anything spatial, forget it! Not being able to read or write numbers has been a complete joke when it came to making money, because I cannot read a bank statement. Those whose job it was to take care of my finances knew I couldn't read numbers, which also meant I couldn't check them either.

It's hard to explain what happens. My mind goes blind, which affects my vision which goes a vivid blinding silver with a slightly misty black margin around the outside. I suppose that's where the expression 'blind panic' comes from (in the beginning my family used to say, conveniently blind).

Whatever dyslexia is, I don't like it. I was so ashamed of this blindness that I put up a tremendous bluff, grew up and became an actor, like lots of dyslexics do, because we're no good at anything else. It wasn't until my son was fifteen, and he'd been expelled from or asked to leave God knows how many schools that the penny finally dropped. We got ourselves tested for dyslexia: he was 85 per cent dyslexic and I was 83 per cent. That means as much to me as it probably does to you, because we still don't know much about dyslexia, but today children aren't so readily mocked for being thick as a plank. They're given more time, more patience and understanding – or so I'm led to believe.

'Come here quickly, Wren! Pusscat, catch the ball.'

Daddy threw it and I caught the ball with one hand. I couldn't understand why he hugged Mummy with such delight.

'I've never noticed before,' said Mummy surprised. 'You've got your left-handed tennis player at last.'

At school Miss Ingrams would come down the aisle and catch me all bent up over a blank page. Her firm brown eyes would look at me full in the face, then glance at my hands and, with a shake of her head, she'd gently but firmly remove the pencil from my left hand and place it in my right. 'I think you may find it easier in that hand,' she said kindly. I would look at the pencil, now in my right hand, try to write, fail to come to grips with the correct position, switch it back to my left, then back to my right again, and so on, back and forth all lesson long.

I began to ponder this new conundrum stretching before me, trying to remember which hand made Daddy happy, and which hand pleased Miss Ingrams.

Miss Ingrams finally persuaded me to use my right hand at school, but I was never sure which one *right* was, and I was frightened to tell Daddy this news, especially as he thought *right* was wrong, and Miss Ingrams thought *left* wasn't *right* . . . and there again, Miss Ingrams might have been wrong about the *right* being right, and Daddy might have been *right* about the right being *wrong*.

Predictably I ended up in no man's land. I have a mole on my left wrist, but that doesn't help at all, it just gets me into even more of a muddle, especially nowadays as hundreds more have appeared to keep it company. Besides, what's the advantage of being a left-handed tennis player if it's not to muddle your opponent?

Father and Mother set great store by the stiff upper lip. They were both monumentally strong people. Father instilled in us his belief in the necessity of putting the best foot forward and focusing on the blessings rather than the set-backs. He never liked us to cry, often sending us to our rooms if we did. Mother's stiff upper lip never cracked over import-ant things, only little things, just the servants and me, not much else, really.

Their attitude rubbed off on me. However miserable, frightened and confused I felt about my word blindness and the left/right business, I made a pact with myself that no one would ever know about it. Pride forbade me.

Once a week, on Fridays, a little old lady would come to school and play the piano, while we all stood on the large stage and sang songs. We had to learn the songs off by heart before we were allowed to sing them on stage. This used to put me under enormous pressure because I couldn't read the words, but once I grasped them committing them to memory was no problem. Finally the class realized, after waiting longer than they could bear, that they'd have to get behind me to help if we were ever to sing together.

So, on Fridays, I experienced that rare feeling of having the girls and boys unanimously behind me, as they helped me to learn a song. As if that wasn't wonderful enough, once we were up and singing, my stammer completely vanished, turning my tummy into a great bubble of happiness and my knees a wobble of ecstasy. On top of it all, there was the weekend winking at me the whole day through, turning Friday into my red-letter day.

Alas, I don't think my singing was anyone else's red-letter day. When I opened my mouth, the others would look at me oddly, and then start ever so slightly to shift away, but I was too blissed out to care! Miss Ingrams did care though, and I was removed from the centre stage (where she'd put me, I may add). With her brown eyes full of regret she gently took my hand and placed me at the back in the far corner. This didn't bother me two hoots, because I wasn't interested in singing for anyone else, I was too deeply absorbed in the pure joy that it was giving me.

And this is when my singing dream began.

I started to sing wherever I went. I was so pleased with being able to perform a few songs by heart without a stammer, that I plucked up the courage to go into the playroom, and sing to the boys, up to their eyes in Meccano, constructing their latest mind boggler. 'Go away,' said Jukes, 'we're concentrating.'

I'd sing all over Daddy while he sang 'Danny Boy'. He'd smile stiffly at me from his Bechstein grand. 'Listen to the note, Pusscat, and don't shout.'

Mummy would come in. 'Stop that racket, Pusscat, we can hear you all over the house. Go down and help Brand feed the chickens.'

I loved feeding the chickens and ducks, and serenading them at their dinner time would be great fun, so off I went.

'Miss,' said Brand, 'I think it'd be best if you didn't sing at mealtimes, not while they're having their dinner.'

'Why not?'

'Because the hens aren't laying too well.'

That was rubbish, I could tell. 'Don't you like my singing, Brand?'

'It isn't me, miss, it's the hens,' said Brand turning the colour of Berty the reddest rooster.

Perhaps I was as stupid as they all thought I was at school, because as I started to serenade them, they'd pause in horror, and then, as if by silent command, all turn their backs on me, and strut off towards the furthest fence.

I'd follow on, still singing with all my might and main, but it's hard singing to a load of wobbly feathered botties. Sure as eggs are eggs (or aren't, according to Brand) once I'd got my captive audience trapped against the far fence, I'd give them my dulcet tones and off they'd flee back to square one, squawking and hooting, quacking, clucking so loudly that I couldn't hear myself sing. Funny manners they had, my feathered friends.

Sometimes I'd manage to pin Floss (the stupidest hen) to the corner, and try again. Stupid or not, she'd shoot past me before I could open my mouth.

Another evening of back and forth, back and forth. At the time it never occurred to me that it had anything to do with my singing.

Soldier would whinny as I passed by his stable, so I'd sing for him, but he'd back up to the far end to his hay-net. (At the time I thought it was hunger.)

Pip seemed to like my singing, Owly too. The Drummoids and Drumwins used to mass up, mesmerized next to Owly on the tallboy, because my new bed had no bars to it. They sat there not budging for hours. A captive audience at last.

57

But as the weeks went by the numbers of Drummoids and Drumwins dwindled . . . funny, that.

I refused to be daunted by the 'Shut ups' and door-slammings. I was never going to give up singing, never. Luckily I found a wonderfully receptive audience in the trees. When I'd sung well they would applaud. I could see them waving their arms around in appreciation. I'd show them mine, bowing and curtseying.

I had become quite an expert at bowing and curtseying, I could hardly fail, what with all the thousands of visits I'd been receiving from King George VI. The woodshed was my salon. An important knock on the door and there he'd be, his crown dazzling along with his eyes and his chest more full of medals than Daddy's drawer.

'Pusscat, you have been awarded this cup, by all the oak trees, elm trees, chestnut trees, copper beeches, weeping willows, walnuts, apples, silver birches – because they, the trees of England, have voted you best singer in the land.'

Often I'd get interrupted because everyone knew that if I wasn't in the stable yard then I'd be in the woodshed with King George.

My curtseying got better and better thanks to George and the dancing classes we went to. Though it ended up only Jukes and me, because of Chuzzer's wheeze. Our teacher was called Madame Vacani. She taught the Royal Family, and though it was all very posh I found myself loving it.

It was the only time my bows came in handy. They added something unique to every spin, and didn't look out of place with the kilts, the full petticoats, white socks and patent leather shoes.

When you're dancing, I find, you haven't got to talk to your partner at all. I loved it so I became quite good, getting my bronze medal in the end. I took after Daddy, I suppose, well co-ordinated in the body but not, in my case, in the brain.

Daddy showed me how to do a hand-stand. I made a pact with myself that I'd walk fifty steps on my hands before I was ten. Although I kept at it, doggedly, I wasn't strong enough till I was in my teens. Finally, when appearing on the *David Frost Show* in New York, twenty years later, I made my entrance on my hands. David Frost came for lunch the other day, and he said I was the only person ever to make an entrance on their hands. I replied, 'Who else would want to?'

I could also make amazingly realistic cock and hen noises – but, then, if *I* couldn't, who could?

'Come on now, Pusscat,' said Miss Ingrams, 'let the school hear your wonderful cockerel noise.'

My turn to be belle of the ball – crowing and clucking for the whole school! 'CLUCK! CLUCK! COCK-DOODLE-DOO!' Bow, curtsey!

It's fear that blocks us. Each and every one of us has the voice beneath the fear. Unfortunately there are many who are willing to vouch for my total lack of singing ability, being completely tone deaf with no pitch or rhythm. Yet I have a bet with my sister Pooker that I'll sing one day, before I'm locked into my Zimmer frame. We shall see.

CHAPTER NINE

M Y RIDING'S GOT so good, thanks to Mauzie never being there, that I've finally forsaken Kitty for a bigger version called Mischief who lives at the riding stables in Ingatestone. I still stop by to give Kitty treats though, before popping indoors to see if Mauzie's there.

Today is special because it's the first showing of *Muffin the Mule*. Very few people have television, so Mummy says, only the rich, or very, very special people indeed. But I'm getting quite bored with Annette Mills smiling away at us, she smiles all the time. I bet she stops as soon as she clicks that we've switched off, just like Mummy does when Daddy turns off his film camera at home.

'Keep still!' says Uncle John. I jump.

'Mauzie, could we go exploring?' Mauzie gives me a look, so does Uncle Willy.

'No!' so firmly, that he sees me jump. 'You've come over here to watch *Muffin the Mule*,' says Uncle John.

'Keep still there's a good girl,' says Uncle Willy.

Mauzie suddenly gets up in her brand new blue frock with white spots, and twirls her long pig-tails, with their neat blue bows bobbing behind her. Doing a little wiggle she goes and sits on Uncle Willy's lap.

Uncle Willy is chuffed up to high heaven with this, and they kiss and cuddle, like me and Daddy sometimes do. Sometimes I kneel down at the rim of Daddy's bath, I love to watch him soaking himself, half asleep, watching his winkie, which always seems to take on a life all of its own. Sometimes, he lets me wash his back for him which I love.

Still, I have Pip with me, oh, yes, I wouldn't go anywhere without my dearest Pip. Only problem is Mummy went and sewed up Pip's hole again, after all the hard work I'd put into making it so warm and cosy, but that's life I suppose.

'Pusscat, stop biting your nails, you're a big girl now,' says Uncle John, who's in a bad mood, because Mauzie went and sat on Uncle Willy's knee first. Mauzie always sits on Uncle Willy's knee first.

Uncle John does a quick check to see that nobody's looking, then picks his nose with one swift fat-fingered scoop. Bingo! He pops his dreadful findings into – you know where! That's very naughty indeed, because he should have wiped it under the table like Uncle Willy does.

Mauzie has wiggled her skirt right up to her chin. Uncle Willy is gently smacking her on her pink panties, which Mauzie finds very rewarding indeed, because she keeps whispering, or is she kissing Uncle Willy's ear?

On the telly Muffin is going a merry jig, I like him a lot. Uncle Willy gets hold of the end of Mauzie's plait and starts to tickle his face with it. Mauzie doesn't like this very much, she pulls her plait free, takes Uncle Willy's hand and glides it down to her panties again, lifting up her botty ever so slightly, just enough for Uncle Willy to put his hand inside her panties this time. Yes. Mauzie really starts swaying now, softly wiggling to and fro. I think she really likes Uncle Willy's hand patting her bottom inside her panties. His other hand is stroking Mauzie up and down her leg, up and down, as if he's waiting for something. Uncle John doesn't like all this, I do believe he's going for another quick pick, no, he's going for a great fat cigar instead, which he stuffs into his big mouth.

Uncle Willy's still waiting for something, he's quite upset, as if he might miss whatever it is he's waiting for. Mauzie in the meantime has got bored with his hand in her panties. She takes it out and flips her plait into Uncle Willy's acres of face.

Uncle John is happier now. He opens his arms wide for Mauzie to enter his great fat smoky lap. 'What about a hug for Uncle John?' Mauzie does as she is told. She doesn't seem so keen to sit on Uncle John's knee and quickly rises, skipping towards the door. She turns, checks that both uncles are glued to *Muffin the Mule* and beckons me to follow.

I'd do anything for Mauzie, any time, anywhere, because I may get a bite of Crunchie if I play my cards right. Silently, we creep up the stairs trying to avoid the creaky bits, as Mauzie's Mummy might hear.

'Do you have a bite of Crunchie, by any chance?'

Taking no notice she bossily pushes me into a small dark gap, behind a triangle of painted wood in the corner of the box room; it's frightening and quite smelly. I always have to go first, because Mauzie has a 'thing' about cobwebs and spiders. I'm not sure what this 'thing' about cobwebs and spiders is, but I'm happy to go first, because I'd rather meet cobwebs and spiders any day than have to deal with Mauzie's 'thing'.

Today it seems to be darker than ever. 'Mauzie, shine the torch!' Funny, I can't hear her. 'MAUZIE!' Silence. 'Ouch!' I've stubbed my toe on something very big and hard. I can just make it out it's a suitcase by the light shining through the crack under a door. The suitcase isn't locked. I open it very slowly, in case I make a noise.

Gordon Bennett! (Daddy's favourite expression, don't know who he is, though.) It's chock-a-block with MONEY! Millions and millions of pounds of lovely juicy money, the whole case stuffed to the brim! 'Mauz—!' Best not call her in case she doesn't know.

'Come out of there!' That's Mauzie's mother shouting – I must run. Shall I steal some? Dash it all, my stupid frock hasn't got any pockets. I'll just put one pound in my knickers – no, I'd better not in case they come and count it.

Mauzie is calmly sitting on the stairs when I hobble out. 'Mauzie, where did you get to?' She shrugs her shoulders, while tossing back her pig-tails. 'I didn't feel like it, I went down to finish watching *Muffin the Mule* instead.'

Suddenly, there before us glowers Mauzie's mother. 'Where have you been, the pair of you?' I just look at the floor, what else can I do? 'You know very well this part of the house is forbidden.'

'I keep telling Pusscat that, Mummy,' shrugs Mauzie with those doleful great brown eyes, 'but she just won't listen to me, so I left her to it.'

Mrs Malone looks at me. 'Pusscat, have you anything to say for yourself?'

I look at them both looking at me. I want to say, What's that great suitcase of lovely juicy money doing hidden in the attic? But something stops me. I feel a terrible darkness in my tummy, just like when I stole Lady Petre's watch. Why? I've stolen nothing.

'Did something frighten you in there, Pusscat, because I heard someone shout?'

I clear my throat, a little dust has got caught. 'No, nothing frightened me, except Mauzie went off with the torch' (I thought I'd tell on Mauzie's meanness) 'so I tripped over a suitcase.' That's foxed her! And I gather by her slippery look that not only does she know about the suitcase, but she knows that I know that she knows that I know what's in it.

'Pusscat,' she says in her quiet Irish way, 'come, why not? Follow me.'

I'm not sure I liked the sound of that, maybe I'm in for it. Off we go, back down the stairs. Mauzie's mother looks just like one of my ducks, placing her feet so neatly. I suppose she has to be careful and poke her head forwards like that otherwise she might miss the step and fall over her great bosoms! I wish this house hadn't got such slippery shiny banisters. One day I couldn't stop and after I shot off the end I crashed into the hat-rack. It fell on top of me and I bent one of its hooks, but no one noticed.

Mrs Malone opens the door to the large gloomy dining room. Is this where she keeps the hair-brush, or does she have a whip? It smells of cold fish 'n' chips and Uncle John's socks, everything stale and unwanted. She opens a cupboard beneath the sideboard, and brings out a large box. She removes the lid and lo and behold – great clusters of bright orange scrummy Crunchie bars!

'There you are, Pusscat, you can have two.'

I can't believe my eyes, ears or luck. I choose to accept them with one of my little bobs rather than my King George curtsey. 'If I find you up in my attics again, there will be no more Crunchie bars – do I make myself clear?'

She's bent so close to me now, I can see she has very yellow teeth compared to Mummy's pearly white ones, and they have great lumps of gold at the back. She must be so rich with all that gold as well.

'Are you listening to me, Pusscat?'

'Yes, I am.' Thank you, thank you. Another little bob, just to round things off nicely, then home to eat my Crunchie bars.

I don't want the boys to see my two Crunchie bars so I stuff them in my panties.

'Oh there you are, Pusscat,' says Mummy. 'You're filthy! What on earth do you and Mauzie get up to?'

'Mauzie's Mummy keeps a suitcase full of money in the attic.'

'Yes, darling,' says Mummy calmly.

'B-b-but, Mummy!'

Mummy holds her head high like Berty when he's had enough of Gus flaunting her yellow beak right in his face. She squeezes my hand grimly, which hurts more than the hair-brush, and she knows it.

'Stacks 'n' stacks of money, Mummy – it's true!'

'Yes, darling, I'm sure it's true, if you say so,' pushing me indoors, 'but I wouldn't tell the boys, they'll only give you a bad time.'

I don't know why Mummy didn't believe my story, because I'd never lied about big things. It was stealing that watch and trying to drown Chuzzer that did it. I lost all credibility in two fell swoops.

So keen was I to keep my Crunchie bars to myself that I completely forgot about them in my knickers. They melted into a terrible mess.

Strange, isn't it, how we long for something we don't have and waste so much energy believing everything'll be different when we finally get it? I longed to be out of my high-chair, sitting up at table with the grown-ups. But when the day dawned, I didn't like it at all. I didn't bargain for the loss of power, so easy to wield from my high-chair's great wooden drawbridge and high yellow walls. I was no longer the centre of all things, looking down on my minions while they fussed over me, making sure I ate everything. I was their 'twinkle twinkle little star'. Mummy was kinder, more patient. 'Open your mouth, Pusscat, there you are,' she'd say gently, opening her mouth for me. Why do grown-ups always do that, and then chew air?

However much I yearned to go backwards again, into that 'diamond in the sky', I had no choice but to move on, into an invisible shrunken nobody. I couldn't see anyone's faces, and if I tried to crane my head upwards, I got a stiff neck. No one to talk to, except the bread basket, salt and pepper, napkins and the rim of the table-cloth. But however hard we try, we can't reverse the forward motion of our frail mortality. Today when I look at that same merry high-chair, with its firm wooden drawbridge, I get a warm feeling, knowing with hindsight how essential firm boundaries are to rage against.

I was given the freedom of the whole dining room when left alone to finish my meals. This was the new rule. I'd sit every day facing a nasty plate heaped with food. Semolina pudding, rice pudding, custard, pastry, cakes, trifles, bread and butter pudding, fatty stews, dumplings, junket, cooked cabbage – it made no odds, it was all profoundly gross.

Staring at me every mealtime on the opposite side of the dining room, stood an antique oak show dresser, with lots and lots of drawers across the back of it. I call it a show dresser, because it was used only for show, kept nicely polished, of course.

My routine was all worked out to a fine art. I'd drink all the milk on my plate, then wait for the semolina to congeal. Waiting for semolina to congeal is not the most riveting of occupations, but it had to be pretty solid before I could carry out my manoeuvre. When finally the semolina was nicely congealed I'd take the plate over to the dresser. Standing on tiptoe I'd manage to place it safely on the top; then drag a chair over to the sideboard and scramble on to the dresser. Opening one of the drawers, I'd scoop the whole caboosh into the farthest end, squeezing it into a neat little ball and closing the drawer very quickly, before wiping my fingers clean on my frock. Mission accomplished, I'd walk into the kitchen with my clean plate, and hand it to Mother.

I'd go over to Mauzie's house regularly. Although I was uninvited, I made up for it by being ever so nice to Mauzie, her uncles, and especially nice to Mauzie's mother, who had no choice but to give me Crunchie bars, because she knew that I knew that she knew that I knew . . .

Sometimes, when Mauzie, Uncle John, and Uncle Willy were playing their little games in the drawing room, I'd creep out and go to Mrs Malone in the kitchen. She'd turn to me, dragging herself away from her dreams, offering me a worn-out little smile. 'Oh, hello, Pusscat, care for a cup of tea?' What I had to put up with for Crunchie bars. I hate tea.

Sometimes she'd sing to me, beautifully sad it was too. 'If

you ever go across the sea to Ireland.' She stared out of the window, as if she wanted the garden to turn into Galway Bay. One day – quite out of the blue – two great fat tears leaked out from the inner corner of her inky eyes (black eyes flummox me, because I can't seem to find a way in).

I got my first whiff of how hard I'd have to work in the future to get what I wanted. I thought if getting what one wants entails so much bobbing, bowing and scraping then I'd be better off not wanting anything in the first place.

As the weeks trickled by, the continual flow of Crunchie bar economics around my personage became so apparent that Father and Mother had no choice but to change their tune about my finding a suitcase full of money. 'I must say it's all rather fishy,' said Daddy, when we heard that Mauzie's gang had upped sticks and left – just like that. The whole neighbourhood thought it very suspicious. There endeth the Black Market and Blackmail Crunchie Bar Saga.

CHAPTER TEN

ONE MORNING Mother drew my curtains to let in the grey rain, and sat on my bed. I'd noticed that her tummy was rather like a balloon lately, but it wasn't my place to say anything, because Mummy always kept herself very much to herself, she was the most private person.

'Pusscat,' she said, stroking my hair, something she never did, 'would you like a baby brother or sister?'

'No,' I replied, because it was true.

'But you must have one or the other,' said Mummy, taking my hand, 'because it's going to happen whether you want it or not.'

'TOOT – TOOT – TOOT!' went Daddy's beastly motor-car.

'We'll be another ten minutes, John,' shouts Mummy from the window. We were off to Devon for a holiday, and I didn't want to go one little bit. 'Pusscat, feel my tummy,' she said.

She put my hand on her tummy, and something was squirming, something really terrible was happening in there. I snatched my hand away for it made me jump. 'It won't bite, it's only the baby doing its exercises.' I sat there watching Mummy's mouth move, which was much better than watching her tummy move. 'If it's a little girl, you can help me to dress her, and push her in her pram, and comb her hair, we'll have such fun.'

Well, if that really was a baby in her tummy, then there was nothing I could do about it, so I grabbed Pip and headed for my hidey-hole, the laurel bush that crawled all along the front of the house. No one could get in there but me. It had come in handy on many occasions and once I'd hidden in it all day. Mummy came back from the hairdresser with wet hair, because our governess, Miss Cripps, had rung urgently saying I'd disappeared. I'd stayed there till evening when Daddy came home. It wasn't so effective lately, because they all knew about it – pity, that.

With a bit of a struggle I was forced to surrender. We were back in the smelly old motor-car again, in the pouring rain, going down to a place called Thurlstone in Devon. I was sitting squashed up in my usual corner, right in the firing line of Daddy's and Mummy's cigarette smoke, as usual, Chuzzer was wheezing as usual, and Jukes was winning at the monkey puzzle tree game, everything was as usual. Thank goodness I had Pip with me, helping to take my mind off being sick.

Daddy had attached a great thick chain to the bottom of the car, to stop us from being sick; that day was our first journey with this amazing new contraption. Apparently, the chain was to keep us all grounded, earthed as it were, but it was making me feel sicker than ever. After a few hours of this completely horrid experience, without any warning of any kind, I felt a great unexpected wodge of sick coming up into my mouth, so big that I couldn't swallow it down again.

'Stop the car!' stammered Chuzzer. 'She's being sick all over me!'

Mummy wrenched me out of the car, beside a five-barred gate. 'Look at your new dress, Pusscat. What are we going to do with you?'

We were just about to move off when Mummy said, 'Pooh! Where's that smell coming from?'

'It's Pip,' said Chuzzer. 'He's all covered in sick.'

I'll never forget watching her turn Pip this way and that, waiting for her to pronounce sentence.

'It's no use, Pusscat, Pip's had his day.'

'Are you sure?' I heard Daddy stammer, amidst my screams. 'Surely, Wren, he can be salvaged?'

That was Mummy's Polly Tree cue. 'No, he can't, I'll get Granny to knit her a new one.' Daddy tried fighting my corner, but this sent Mummy right to the top of the Polly Tree, and she threw Pip over the five-barred gate and into the wet cornfield.

Something died within me that rainy summer day, for not only was my closest friend tossed away, like a piece of old remnant, but I was convinced that Pip, dying in a wet cornfield covered in my sick, would never ever forgive me.

'Pull yourself together, Pusscat. Just because you're not enjoying the holiday, that's no reason to spoil it for everyone else,' said Mummy, at supper the third night, probably over the rice pudding.

Sometimes whole areas go blank in my mind, and that holiday at Thurlstone is one of them. Perhaps I was too busy trying to submerge my mourning to see what was going on around me, although trying hard to hide my tears. I do remember Daddy gently holding my hand, as we walked together down Snail Lane, which was smothered in millions of snail trails. 'Look at them glistening, just like the tears on your cheeks.'

I wasn't in the mood to be cheered up. 'I wanna go home.'

He gave me one of his Owly looks. 'We, unlike snails, Pusscat, can't carry our homes on our back.' Wistfully, he wiped away my tears, but even that didn't help much.

CHAPTER ELEVEN

PACKING UP MY nursery and leaving Mill House, to travel two miles down the lane was so disorientating that I couldn't regain my balance for quite some time. Daddy, too – after all, it had been his home for forty years, and he thought we'd all made a terrible mistake. He loved Mill House as much as I did, but Mummy didn't. So there you have it.

Anyone would have thought I was a homeless refugee, which I very nearly became, I may add, as soon as Mummy dismantled the show dresser. What a to-do! But even hairbrushes lose their effect in the end. When my Father came home and saw the drawers clogged with dried-up memorabilia, he winked his secret wink. 'Most enterprising, Pusscat.'

Sleeping for the first time in Barn Mead was very frightening. Although Chuzzer had kindly let me have Ted, Daddy's very own childhood bear, Owly had been taken away from me because I might break him. 'Where's Owly?'

'Shoosh,' said Mummy rocking Pooker, my baby sister, in her arms, 'you'll wake her.' Pooker never cried, of course. 'Pooker, my litle miracle.' Mummy's eyes bulged with pride.

Pooker had golden fluffy bits of hair like one of my new-born baby chicks. In fact she reminded me very much of a baby chick. Her ears were perfect little pink sea-shells nestling softly against her sparkling golden head.

Our new home was not, I have to admit, as bad as I had anticipated. It wasn't terribly old, and was rather plain compared to Mill House, but it rambled in a friendly higgledy-piggledy kind of way. My room was quite large and airy, Owly was reinstated, back safe on my new chest of drawers, where he and Ted gradually became friends.

Opposite was Mummy and Daddy's room, which had lovely windows everywhere, facing the south side of the garden. Chuzzer's room was quite small, at the top of the stairs. I think he chose it because he was self-conscious about his wheeze. In that room, it would conveniently whistle and rattle its way down the stairs, and into the hall, and hopefully right through and out of the front door, rather than along the corridors waking us all up. Jukes's room was at the far eastern end, the best room, taking the whole width of the house.

The gardens of Barn Mead were really special to me, because there was such an abundance of variety. The main lawns, which covered a great expanse, were beautifully smooth and carpeted, making croquet a joy. These were divided by three enormous beech trees in a row, separating the two levels of lawn. The lower level went down to the summer house, tennis court (not built yet), orchards, and rose gardens.

Down the west side it was all wooded and wild and stretched right down to a perfect outside shed, tucked away, in a secret garden all of its own. The shed had indoor heating, and we played table-tennis fiendishly down there, until Jukes bagged it for his sound recording studio, which then became the film studio, equipped with screening room, all that his heart desired.

The other side of the house was just as wild and woolly. The woodshed sat amongst pampas grasses and bamboos. This side wasn't quite so secluded, because there was always the possibility of bumping into Lucia or Mummy putting out the washing on the line. Lucia, our first Italian maid, often reminded me of Berty my rainbow cock because she would constantly sing (sending Mummy up the Polly Tree) these Neapolitan love songs, which sounded rather quaint amidst relentless English rain. Just like Berty she was crowing for her mate, across the width and breadth of the Essex countryside.

Up above the pampas grasses was a large and comical grass dome, looking like a great green mole. Leaping up and down it was wizard fun. 'Pusscat! Come down off my plants!' Mother turned my mole into a rockery – wouldn't she just? Inside was a little hidey-hole because it was once an air-raid shelter.

Sandwiched between the green mole and the most majestic of ancient oak trees, with an old rope-ladder stretching right up to a tree-house, there stood a swing and trapeze. Father made me promise not to climb the rope-ladder until it was fixed, since it was all frayed. I promised, but I kept nagging for it to be fixed pretty quickly, otherwise he might have found my promise fraying a bit too. This giant oak marked the boundary between my two worlds, them and me. Beyond the oak tree was an enormous vegetable garden for all seasons, leading down to the playing fields of my feathered friends, duck pond, play pens, the lot. And last but not least, there was the stable yard.

The day finally arrived when Brand trusted me to feed the chickens on my own. This meant standing on a chair with a thick stick, stirring the rusty-coloured powder mixture into a smooth porridgy substance. It smelt perfectly delicious so one day I took a nibble. How deceiving smells can be. The mixture expanded in the cauldron, making it hard work for me to haul the three great bucket loads down to the hens, but it was so worth it to watch them all come waddling towards me with enthusiastic glee, reminding me of the bowler hat and umbrella brigade rushing along the platform at Ingatestone station after a hard day in the City.

Unfortunately I could just hear the dinner gong from the stables. Mother made sure Lucia brought it to the french windows where she struck it with such a Mafia brutality that I had no excuse.

On the way back I'd pass the raw crisp vegetables. I so much prefer crunching on a carrot, than eating lumpy stew – who in their right minds wouldn't? By the time I got to the house I usually had a full belly.

It was a formal dining room. Daddy sat at the head of the table, in front of the serving board, Mummy at the other end, in front of the fireplace, with Michelangelo's Adam touching God's hand above her head. My two brothers were opposite me, with the garden beyond, and on my right my fair little sister, in my high-chair, playing King of the Castle.

The three of us, and Daddy, had the habit of twiddling one ankle (wiggling one foot) under the table. This truly exasperated Mummy, because the vibration of energy gave the whole table and all the cutlery an eternal jiggle. Instilling in us, as Father did, an overall need to excel, I suppose this 'keenness of will' shot straight down to our ankles. The funny part is we're all still twirling our ankles around. (Not Pooker.) Daddy was doing it right up to his dying day, the will to be immortal being his problem.

Mealtimes were always the same, rather like watching Wimbledon. Father was the occasional Communist, Mummy very right-wing, Mummy Freudian, Daddy Jungian. These particular arguments were always fiery and interminable. With hindsight I find them strangely out of character. Surely it should have been the other way round? Surely Mummy should have been fighting Jung's corner, being more spiritually minded? Even in their other pet argument, religion versus science, Mummy was much keener on the Darwinian theory, Daddy had the reservations. Which adds to my own theory that Daddy, beneath his raging atheism, was the most spiritual of men. To be fair they argued rather than fought. Hugh Gaitskell was Daddy's friend and a neighbour. Mummy couldn't stand him. She was keen on Anthony Eden, he on Nye Bevan. Daddy wasn't enthralled with the royal family, for obvious reasons. Mummy was Church of England, and said her prayers; Daddy, being an atheist, mocked her belief.

And so the differences went on and on, both savouring the challenge of bringing the other into their court. If it wasn't neck-aches from too much Wimbledon, it was usually me alone, sometimes for hours on end, completely trapped, with my food staring back at me, mercilessly.

'Eat up, Pusscat, or stay there till you have.' Unfortunately I had no rescue hatch any more. The show dresser had been reinstated in the hall, heavily guarded by the Mafia.

As my eating habits went from bad to worse, I had many hours alone in the dining room contemplating the Michelangelo. A naked man, built a bit like Daddy, I thought, was nonchalantly draped over a rock, with his winkie hanging languidly over his thigh. He looked a little lonely except that right above him a thick arm, wrist and hand, rather like Brand's arm, reached down from the sky, or from out of the frame of the picture trying to comfort him. Why was the naked man, sunbathing on the rock, too lazy really to reach out and touch hands? The whole picture had me greatly puzzled, and its mystery would still linger on till bedtime.

I enjoyed that moment of the evening, after Mummy had left me all spruce and polished, sitting up in bed with *Struwwelpeter* upon the covers, impatiently awaiting Daddy.

She always gave me such a brief, business-like kiss. Sometimes I wanted to give her a great hug, for she smelt so fresh like clinging violets, but it wasn't to be. I watched her light my night-light, then give me her last smile speckled with relief. Her chores would soon be over, and she'd have time to natter with Daddy over a gin and tonic by the fireside. Knowing this, I'd stop her. 'Who does that arm in the dining room belong to – Brand?'

That stopped her in her tracks all right. 'Good God, no, Pusscat. That's God – that picture's a very famous picture by Michelangelo.'

I didn't think I liked God very much, because whenever Mummy and Daddy mentioned him, it was always when they were angry. 'Good God!' 'Oh, my God!' 'God Almighty!' 'Goddamn it!'

She tried her disengaging smile once more, but I stopped her. 'Who is God?'

'God is the father of Jesus.'

'Is Jesus the man who looks like Daddy, sunbathing on the rock?'

Mummy laughed a lot at that. 'Good heavens, I've never seen the likeness myself. No, the man in that picture is Adam, and Adam was the first man on earth.'

'Before Jesus?'

'Way before Jesus. Now don't forget to say your prayers. Goodnight, Pusscat.'

I decided to pray to Adam instead of Jesus, he looked so lonely on that rock, and after all he was first.

As Mother left my nursery I would ponder this. I had a great need to see the picture in its entirety, as if that would clarify some of my growing conflict over the whole Jesus, Adam, God business. Why did the arm cut off at the frame? If it was God's arm, then what did this God look like? I found out that it was on the ceiling of the Sistine Chapel in Rome, so I knew that one day I would go and find out in person what 'God' looked like.

Almost twenty years later, I was bathed in the sweat of a sweltering Roman summer, implacably lost among Roman streets, proudly christening our Lamborghini given to us (my husband Robert and me) by the film director David Lean.

It was a very important day for me. At long last, my first opportunity of going to the Sistine Chapel, and finally meeting the great man himself – God – beyond Brand's arm. My son Tom was strapped in beside me. Though only six months old, I'm sure he could have done a better job at driving around Rome than I was doing. For I was under the impression that our hotel was on a street called 'Senso Unico', so how come this stupid street, 'Senso Unico', wove its way all over Rome? With Tom crying in the blistering heat and the Lamborghini kicking up a fuss, I would have gone home if I'd known how to find a street that wasn't called 'Senso Unico'.

Spoilt bloody car! Having been designed for high speed and only feeling really at home at 120 mph on the autostradas, at 10 mph it was hissing and belching fumes of frustration, with the occasional thunderous fart, stalling every time I stopped and asked the way in Italian. After two hours of Senso Unicos and Italians unable to understand their own language, I'd had enough. We parked the frigging Lamborghini and took a taxi.

There we were at last, Tom in my arms, head craned upward, scanning that awesome ceiling for the missing piece of my childhood puzzle. I couldn't believe my eyes! Brand's arm! I started tracing childhood memories along that so familiar painting, up Brand's arm to my final destination – God himself!

I was horrified! God reminded me of some tacky, dated cliché of a thespian giving us his effeminate King Lear. Stung with disappointment, incensed at feeling duped, I lost all sense of the here and now, and dropped my son – CLUNK – head first on to the Sistine Chapel's marble floor. He didn't even cry, which was worrying to a degree. In fact he seemed to show no outward signs of deterioration, but, then, neither did I apparently when I fell off that swing, and look what happened to me – poor old Tom, perhaps it was God's will.

*

Not a moment too late Daddy came into my nursery. Smelling of sugar and spice and all things nice as he started flipping through the pages of *Struwwelpeter*. 'Now, settle down.' Daddy cleared his throat. 'I think that these pictures say it all, Pusscat.' He showed me a fat, strong-looking boy dancing by a table, with a full soup bowl upon it. 'That's the first day . . .'

> 'Augustus was a chubby lad,
> Fat rosy cheeks Augustus had'

In the next picture, on the second day Augustus looked much thinner:

> 'O take the nasty soup away—!
> I won't have any soup to-day—!'

By the third picture Augustus was almost as thin as me. The picture of Augustus on the fourth day, made me go goose-bumpy. He was as thin as the matches in the story of Harriet.

> 'Look at him, now the fourth day's come!
> He scarcely weighs a sugar plum;
> He's like a little bit of thread,
> And on the fifth day, he was – dead!'

In the picture after the one where Augustus was as skinny as Harriet's matches, there was a bowl of soup on the grass, with a wooden cross sticking out of the ground.
'What's that?'
'That, Pusscat, is a grave.'
'What's a grave, Daddy?'
'A grave is what they put you in when you're dead.'
'What do you mean, when you're dead?'

He looked at me sadly and said, 'When we die we get buried under the ground in a wooden box called a coffin.'

My heart began to beat very loudly. 'But how can we b-b-breathe under the ground, Daddy?' Bringing my arm – quick as a flash – up for tickles. Gently he started to tickle me into seventh heaven.

Up there, I started thinking about Augustus not eating, and the bowl of soup next to the wooden cross, and this thing called a coffin . . . What did Daddy mean about being dead and buried under the ground?

'How do we breathe in a coffin?' He stopped concentrating on his tickling job, and looked at me. 'We don't, Pusscat, because we're dead.'

I'd often heard this word dead. Mummy had said I'd be dead if I ate grass, if I didn't eat my dinner, if I galloped too fast, that I was sure to be dead before I was twenty-one. Daddy stopped his tickling. 'No – don't stop! Daddy, listen to my heart banging.'

He put his ear to my heart. 'Yes, it's banging away quite merrily, but it won't be when you're dead.'

My heart was galloping as loud as Mischief on the hard road, making my ears throb, and I couldn't feel Daddy tickling me any more. I could see him tickling me but I couldn't feel him . . .

'Daddy.'

'Hush now, Pusscat, it's getting late and you're over-excited, your goose-bumps have turned to ice – under the covers now.'

I could hardly talk for stammering. 'What do we do there? Just wait for someone to find us?'

Daddy laughed. 'No, only the worms come and find us.

When we stop breathing we can't feel or remember anything any more. So you see, there's nothing to be frightened of, is there?' Gently he tweaked my ears. 'Don't think about it, Pusscat, you have all your life ahead of you.'

'But I don't understand – what does "Death" *mean*?'

'Death simply means the end, that's all, Pusscat.'

In barged Mummy. 'Come on, John, stop frightening her with that damn book.' She pulled the covers up to my neck. 'Death means we finally go and join Jesus up in the sky.'

He closed up *Struwwelpeter*, put it on the table, and bent over to kiss me goodnight. Mummy brushed my cheek, then stroked out the light. Suddenly all that was left was Ted, Owly, and my night-light, flickering long, squiggly worm patterns all over the walls and ceiling.

Help! I'm in a coffin. I can't breathe – I can't hear my heart banging any more.

I lay there thinking of Augustus not eating, my heart stopping, dying which meant not breathing, being buried, the coffin, the worms coming and eating me away, and quite suddenly something more terrifying than the fear of death sneaked into my consciousness: simply, death had no distance, it was right there in my nursery. It was as if physically and psychically I lived through the death experience itself. It's certainly one of those memories that don't fade away.

I sat up, bolt upright, staring ahead of me, trying to remember how to breathe. My breath, like Chuzzer's, had gone walkabout. I don't know for how long I sat like that. However long it takes actually to experience dying and death. I used all my strength to haul myself out again by locking fast into Owly's eyes, flickering benevolently beside me.

I put my head back on the pillow, calmer now, because I knew then that death was a reality, that we all had to die. I knew, at the age of roughly seven, that death was an inevitable fact, because I had just been there.

The next night when Daddy had kissed me goodnight, and I laid my head on the pillow, I realized I wasn't scared about death, only of what would happen if I were to die before I was ready, before I was twenty-one. What if I were to die before I had sung 'Danny Boy' properly, before I could walk on my hands? What if I were to die before I had got my pony, or before Jukes and Chuzzer died? What if I were to die before I could hang by my knees on the trapeze, or had climbed up the rope-ladder to the tree-house? Or before I could tell King George, so that I left him in the woodshed waiting for ever with that heavy silver cup?

This started me off on a new and dreadful habit which went on for the next few years. I'd be convinced that I could no longer hear my heart beating. Once convinced, I'd sit up, and realize it must be so, because I couldn't remember how to breathe. What *was* breathing? How did I ever do it? I would sit there like a statue for an interminably long time, as long as I dared, then creep downstairs to the sitting room to find Daddy to give me a hug. On the first night this happened Mummy was very sympathetic, and just blamed Daddy and *Struwwelpeter*.

I got more and more frightened of the nights, knowing I was going to forget how to breathe. It was so strange, for as soon as Daddy's arms were around me, I forgot what I had come downstairs for in the first place. But as the trips downstairs became more regular Mother began to reach 'Wit's End', where Polly Trees grow. This being the case, whenever my attacks came upon me, I'd sit on the stairs where I was safe, happily wrapped in the sound of their murmurings.

My life changed considerably the Augustus night. Up until then, I'd the feeling that I was part of an 'overall master plan', that all my actions and thoughts were not mine alone, but were being watched over by a great Something. Maybe this Something was to do with the Somewhere that previously I'd yearned to return to. But I did not connect this place with God, Jesus, or Adam.

This Something periodically sent down tiny flecks of evidence reminding me of its attentive inscrutable all-knowingness, but after the Augustus night these flecks of evidence slowly, drib by drab, began fading away. The second to last fleck of evidence that I received from that Something came shortly after the Augustus night.

Through my life I've continually been embarrassed by the Hammer Horror wrinkles on my palms. With patience one is compensated for these little embarrassments, for gradually time catches up with them. But from puberty on, they wreaked havoc with my confidence. I would sit on my hands, or hide them behind my back. When doing hand close-ups in films, directors would politely ask if my stand-in's hands could replace mine. Fortunately when I was little these wrinkles merely intrigued me, and I spent hours fascinated by all their conflicting alleyways. On one occasion out of my wrinkled palm there popped a vision, or an imagining if you wish. I saw an ancient house, a church and a river running through unspoiled woodland. I felt it to be Home, because this Something told me it was. It also told me I'd have to grow as old as my palms before I'd find this Home of mine. As I looked deep into my palm that day I remember thinking how sad to have to be so old before coming Home.

Christ! I wish I'd known then how precious those flecks of evidence were. How lucky I was to be able to tap into that great Something.

Stupidly I'd grasped Daddy's news of death all wrong. He had convinced me that graves were there to trap us and prevent us from returning to the place I knew as Home. This death business meant that I was never going Home.

After the Augustus night I also began to lose the ability to see Drumwins, Drummoids, colours around people, and the ability to sense any overall master plan. My multi-dimensional world, any innate inborn wisdom that I had, gradually faded into the shadow, to be replaced by conditioning, concepts and facts, often false, that would smother everything that could have been.

Quite simply, Fear had made his great entrance and anaesthetized my awareness, gradually causing the fearless creature that I had been spiritually (or imaginatively) before the Augustus night to disintegrate. Fear was now in charge, because I'd been told that death was the end.

Oddly enough my flecks of evidence reappeared in abundance decades later, during that same period when Something told me to lean on silence, and my past came flashing back.

CHAPTER TWELVE

NANNIES CAME AND went, but I can't remember
their names for not one of them was worth the
effort of remembering. I didn't trust any of them,
and it was mutual.

I do remember liking one though, Dymphna from Ireland.
She was very young and pretty, all pink and perky, and she
spoke like Mauzie's mother. Dymphna and I had a little set-
to one day, Mummy was out and we fought in my nursery.
Dymphna was about to take Ted away from me. Knowing I
deserved it I punched her with all my might. This had little
effect so I tripped her up instead, she fell, and I picked up
Ted from where she had dropped him. Dymphna got to her
feet and threw me across the room – SLAP! – right into the
corner of Owly's chest of drawers, nearly toppling Owly off
his perch and cutting my forehead. It wouldn't stop bleeding,
though it didn't hurt at all, and I'd quite forgotten it by the
time Mummy came home.

When she saw my forehead she went skittering up the
Polly Tree and fired Dymphna on the spot. 'No, Mummy, it
was my fault!'

She bunged me in the car and drove me off to hospital to
be stitched up. I still have the scar. I was sorry though, I liked
Dymphna: she was honest, straightforward and had guts.
But they all had to learn that Ted and Owly must remain put.

Jukes and Chuzzer, on the other hand, got along fine with

the nannies, especially Chuzzer. It wasn't only his wheeze that did the trick. He had a way with him, being very beautiful and as perfect as Jukes in manner (when it suited him). He was clever too. He was brilliant at twanging the nannies' heart-strings, stringing them along, with different twangs for different nannies. His huge grey eyes looked out forlornly from his pained yet noble head, and the whole world melted.

Alas, I didn't have the knack of twanging heart-strings, and that was that. The only knack I possessed was knowing this, so I kept as far away as I could.

Mischief, the dark brown Dartmoor pony with a thick white blaze down his nose that I had been riding twice weekly at the Ingatestone Riding Stables, was now finally mine. I'd stood so strong and invincible that Mummy had eventually caved in.

He wasn't called Mischief for nothing, he was a fat load of trouble. If he wanted to go for a ride, that was fine, but if he felt like munching in the field, that was what he'd do, after I'd failed to catch him. Sometimes I would keep him in the stable so that I wouldn't have the catching problem, and as soon as I entered to tack him up he'd start his whooping cough. The vet was called on many occasions, but he could never find the cause of Mizzer's dreadful coughing.

'Don't ride him for a few days, just in case,' he would say, bewildered. Mizzer would prick his ears cockily, and return to his bulging hay-net, victorious.

Getting ready for riding was frustrating. Sometimes I'd

get as far as almost securing Mizzer's saddle to the girth strap buckle, when he would cannily blow out his gigantic tummy, thus preventing the essential union. We'd pant, heave and sweat, as we pulled in opposite directions, until I had no choice but to surrender, and wave goodbye to yet another day's riding.

Father bought eight evil white geese. He so wanted me to be his goose-girl and mind the damn things that he went to the extravagant length of bringing me back from Denmark a beautiful pottery goose-girl surrounded with geese. She's still here, with long blond plaits like Mauzie.

I was interminably teased by Daddy's geese (Gooses-men, as he called them). They had great order amongst their ranks. All eight of them would march in a line towards me, the two most wicked ones in the centre, hissing, forcing me into retreat by pecking at my feet, until they had me trapped in the stable yard where they formed a circle around me, leaving me no option but to leap over the stable door and into the tack room for refuge.

One day, trotting home down the Spinney, the goose battalion advanced with such resolute purpose that we couldn't get by. I kicked and kicked but Mischief wouldn't budge. Finally I gave him a mighty swish with my whip, something he'd never experienced before. It shocked him into a tentative advance. As he moved forward he was pecked on his fetlock with such ferocious accuracy that he leapt into the air. Upon landing he gave a buck, which sent him galloping off in hysteria and me smack on my bum, plumb in the middle of enemy lines. I tried to scramble up, but too late. The goose battalion closed ranks around me and slowly advanced, hissing and pecking at the air, until there was no air left to peck. One of them nipped me twice on my jodhpurs. Brand heard the commotion and came sauntering up to save me. You'd never catch Brand running – not in a million years. I don't think he knew how. Nor would he attend to the geese, he hated them more than I did. 'Dangerous bastards!' was all he would say.

I felt really grown-up when Father came riding with me at the weekends. He looked so dashing in his riding attire – cavalry riding boots, brown, worn and supple with silver spurs glistening, tweed jacket, soft cream cravat, and butterscotch breeches. He was always one with his mount, just harmony and collected power. Riding beside him along the quiet country lanes, I blossomed with joy, and I could have been as proud as Punch if it hadn't been for Mischief. He waddled along with his head in the hedgerow, sneezing, coughing, munching, while my kicks, whips and shouts had not the slightest effect. 'Come on, Pusscat, kick him on!' My thighs ached with all the kicking which somehow never hit the target, large though it was. And with his penchant for hedgerows, my efforts had as much effect as kicking Barn Mead.

'Come on, Pusscat, straighten your back, tighten your reins – shall we have a little canter now?'

I loved galloping up the straight stretch of bridal path, watching Daddy shoot ahead of me, splattering and spraying me with mud, water, twigs, sometimes low wispy branches. When Mizzer, puffing and panting like an old steam engine, at last caught up with Daddy, he'd be so over the moon with his accomplishment that sometimes, without warning, he'd collapse to the ground and have a jolly good roll. When Daddy wasn't there to save me, I'd get squashed like a wasp – but it was worth it.

As we trotted along through the woods, Daddy would point out huge craters. 'Careful, Pusscat,' he warned, as Mizzer and I were about to tumble in, 'those are where the doodlebugs fell.' This would rekindle my soft spot for doodlebugs.

With eyes stinging as they hit the light, so bright in contrast to the dense darkness of the woods, we'd find ourselves on Mill Green Common. Daddy would dismount, tether our mounts to a post and take me into Kate Camps's sweet shop for a Crunchie bar. Yes, Kate Camps sometimes kept a few on the counter nowadays.

Sometimes, with Daddy, the earth obeyed me by standing still. There we were, Mizzer and the grey mare munching grass, Daddy and I munching Crunchie bars as nimble flickers of sunlight danced across his silver spurs, to the chime of distant church bells. This, I thought, was what life was all about.

'Let's be off, Pusscat,' he said, interrupting the chimes. Going home was a totally different bag of pony-nuts. Mizzer would shoot along, faster than a doodlebug, passing Daddy's grey mare as he headed flat out, with masses to spare, along the lane. Once again I was as effective as an ant upon a shooting star. Mizzer knew this, as well as he knew the way home.

Daddy stammered fiercely behind me, 'Steady, Pusscat, never gallop on the hard iron road – pull in those damn reins!'

I hadn't a hope in hell of obeying Daddy's now distant bellowings. Besides as the hamlet of Fryerning went scuttling by in fast motion, I was gripped by a gurgling excitement. This sensation, which always comes to me in dangerous situations, I later identified as euphoria. It would get me into a heap of trouble in the years ahead.

After Daddy caught up with me and grabbed Mizzer firmly by the reins, he would point out nature's secrets to me, teaching me the names of all the trees, wild flowers and hedgerows while demonstrating those that were edible. Hazel he called bread 'n' cheese, young oak leaves he'd call ploughman's lunch, sorrel he'd call sour grass (I became such a sorrel junkie that Mummy would often find me on all fours in Mizzer's field. 'There's worms in grass. You'll never see twenty-one – mark my words!') Elderberry flowers he'd call publican's blonde. Invaluable knowledge. In summer time I can fill my belly out riding – I'm a cheap date.

CHAPTER THIRTEEN

I DON'T WANT to go and spend two weeks with Granny. I don't like Granny, and Ilford even less. Mother says I have to go, I say I won't. It turns into the usual battle of wills, but there's something I'd noticed about grown-ups – they always win in the end.

Mummy is to take Chuzzer to a sanatorium in Switzerland because he can't breathe any more in England. Jukes is old enough to stay at home – lucky old Jukes, he always gets what he wants. Pooker's going to Switzerland too. (I always knew there was going to be trouble when that little blonde bundle of joy popped out of Mummy's tummy. How did she pop, I wonder. I wish I'd been there. I think she climbed her way out of Mummy's tummy button. Jukes climbed out of Mummy's tummy button too, though me and Chuzzer climbed out of her titties, leaving her tummy button free again for Pooker. Quite disgusting it all is, I'm not going to have stupid babies crawling out of my titties – oh, no!)

Heavy rain is falling as we approach Ilford's ugly grey suburbs, there seem to be no gaps between drops. I'm clinging on to Ted for dear life. I wasn't allowed to bring Owly or Micky with me. Micky was a lurcher, given to us by the gypsies. Daddy decided to get Micky after Mummy was frightened by a tramp staring at her from behind the bamboo as she was putting out the washing. Micky had pooey breath, but I loved him with all my heart, even though he wasn't mine. No dog of mine would live on a beastly chain in a kennel howling to be let off. 'That's what guard dogs do, they howl,' said Mummy. 'They protect us.'

As we turned into Granny's road, called Hastings Avenue, it amazes me how Mummy could possibly tell the difference, each road being exactly as horrid as the last. 'I want you to promise me that you'll behave yourself.'

'Why should I?'

'Granny did knit you Pip, after all.'

How could Mummy bring up Pip at a time like this? Has she no shame at all?

The only friendly thing about Granny's house was the way the light caught the coloured glass in the front door. It reminded me of Kate Camps's great jars of coloured sweets. How I wanted to be on Mill Green. The banisters weren't bad as banisters go, though not in the same class as Lady Petre's. Granny forbade me to slide down them, naturally, because I enjoyed it. Enjoying yourself is harmful to adults. 'Come into the kitchen, Wren, you go into the sitting room, Pusscat, and stay there while I talk to Mummy.'

I hated that dark sitting room, it smelt just like Mauzie's dining room – fish 'n' chips and Uncle Willy's socks. To think I had to stay for two whole weeks. I looked around me. All the chairs wore strange lace hats. An enormous wireless took centre stage, everywhere felt dusty but looked as shiny as a new pin. The atmosphere was nothing like it had been in Grandpa's day. He was such a kind, jolly man. But he was dead, poor old Grandpa, being nibbled away by all those worms.

That afternoon my nightly horrors arrived ahead of

schedule. I was so frightened. What if I lost my breath in the night? There would be no Daddy to run to, only Ted. I grabbed Ted and went to find Mummy in the kitchen.

'Hello, Pusscat, you can let in Trixy now, from the garden.' I couldn't believe my luck. In came a beautiful little brown dog with bat ears like mine, but frayed around the edges and a saucy fox's plume for a tail. 'That'll keep her quiet,' said Granny, as if I couldn't hear.

'You can come and drink your tea now, Pusscat.' She knew very well I hated tea.

'C-can I have some milk?' Granny was about to purse her lips, so I quickly pipped her to the post.

'P-p-please.'

'I'm afraid you'll have to wait till tomorrow.' She turned to Mummy. 'That stammer hasn't got any better, Wren. What are you going to do about it? I mean,' she looked at me, 'we can't have you stammering when you grow up, now can we?'

'Why not? *I* don't mind,' I stammered.

'Yes, we know that,' said Mummy, getting up and brushing her smart tweed skirt free of cake crumbs, 'but you haven't got to listen to it. We have.' Trixy gobbled up the crumbs with glee. 'I'd best be off. Must be home before dark.'

Ted and I were thinking that we'd take Trixy to bed with us. 'Granny, can Trixy sleep with me, please?'

'No, Pusscat, Trixy's bed's in the corner over there, see?' There it was, a nice basket with a red rug in it. What would I do?

'Well, goodbye, darling, you be good to Granny now, and no nonsense, do you hear?'

Somehow I survived my first night in Ilford. Mostly I was able to survive the days too, and the meals – thanks to Trixy. We went on mammoth walks together down rainy streets. Everyone seemed to be coughing, crying or ill in Ilford.

I loved playing Peeping Tom in the early evening, for Ilford folk forgot to draw their curtains at dusk. But there was never much to see, only unhappy people drinking tea. I remember thinking how apt the name *Il*ford was. I was catching a touch of the *Ilfords* myself, I was feeling ill. Perhaps I was getting polio? Mummy had forbidden us to go swimming at the Chase swimming pool in Ingatestone any more, because of the polio scare. She said, 'Children who swim in public pools are dropping like flies.' This was a dreadful shame, since I loved swimming in the Chase swimming pool.

Granny held my hand even tighter than Mummy, as we ran to catch a tall red bus yesterday, while it was moving away; perhaps that's where Mummy got the idea of crunching hands from. It was my first time on a double-decker, or indeed any bus.

'Can we go upstairs, please?'

'No, stay here, Pusscat, I can't climb the stairs.'

'I can! Oh, please, I've never been on anything so exciting.'

'All right, but come straight back.'

Climbing the stairs was fun, I got tossed about, like in the sea at Thurlstone. There was only one man on top, rather old, sitting up at the front. The man looked very sad in his yellowing grey mac. I wobbled and bumped my way down the aisle. As I was about to sit on the seat across the aisle from him, the bus jerked and I fell against him.

'Sorry, I'm very sorry, sir.'

'That's all right, miss,' he said, with a sad yet hopeful look in his watery eyes.

Retrieving my balance, I straightened up and took my place on the opposite front seat. It was great fun watching Ilford fly by. I remember wishing the time would fly by as quickly. I'd been in Ilford for less than a week, yet it seemed like for ever. I'd almost forgotten what Mizzer smelt like, Micky's breath too. Wouldn't it be a lark to have Berty my rainbow cock up here on top of the bus with me, he'd have a lot to crow about all right!

I turn to look at the man beside me. He has little clumps of hair sprouting, like Pooker's from his shiny egg head. He gives me a sad grin, and starts fishing his hand into his mackintosh pocket – maybe he has some wine-gums, or a Crunchie bar in there?

No such luck, all he brings out is a lonely-looking winkie-waddle. He looks at me as if he's very proud of it. I don't want to hurt his feelings and say that Daddy's is much jollier. Even the boys' winkies are perkier than this poor lost worm. Indeed even Adam's winkie, lying lazily across his leg on the dining-room wall, was a braver affair.

He doesn't seem too pleased with me, so I say, 'It's fun, isn't it, up here in the front?' He doesn't answer me, but gestures for me to take another look at his winkie, which seems to be getting tireder and tireder. Maybe his winkie is cold on the top of this bus? If I can't even feel my nose, is it any wonder his winkie is all shrivelled up? Why doesn't he tuck it in all nice and warm?

'Lovely,' he whispers, guiding my eyes down to land

once more on his sad and sorry winkie. He's so proud to have me watching his winkie, that politely I keep looking. He strokes it as if it's made of precious mink or something. It looks so tired that I yawn in sympathy. I wonder why yawning is so catching? I'm always catching Mizzer's.

The man is furious with me. He shakes his head, leans across the aisle and digs me in the ribs with his elbow. Then I realize – of course! I forgot to put my hand over my mouth when I yawned.

A bell rings out of nowhere. I don't know what it means but the bus seems to be stopping. I get up in case Granny is getting angry with me. He gives me such a pleading look, like Trixy before I put her lead on.

That occasion in Ilford was the only time that a strange gentleman has ever exposed himself to me. I have been on hundreds of tubes and buses, but I have never received another such honour.

I sometimes watched Granny of an evening. She would sit so still in front of her wireless, with Grandpa's seat opposite all crisp and empty. I remember thinking that Granny must be so alone without Grandpa, with no one to tickle her or scrub her back in the bath, or mash her potatoes for her. She used to be such a sparkly lady when Grandpa was still alive. She had an unusually beautiful singing voice that bore no trace of the rusty harsh edge of her speech. She had been trained as a singer. My mother said that Grandpa fell in love with Granny when he heard her singing one day and mistook her for her voice.

She sang in the bathroom, or sometimes when she hung out the washing in the garden. I loved to hear her, it made my tummy go all warm inside.

'Twas on the Isle of Capri I first found her,
'Neath the shade of the old walnut tree,
I can still see the flowers blooming round her,
As we met on the Isle of Capri.

Another favourite was 'Come ye back to Mandelay, where the flying fishes play.' I longed to see a fish fly.

Crossing off the days was another happy moment. Only six more and then I'd be home again.

One night I couldn't find my breath anywhere, on and on my no-breathing went. I tried to keep my mind off it by thinking how Chuzzer had to cope with this situation every night. I fervently wished Chuzzer would just pop up from behind the bed – or Jukes come to that. It was no use, I couldn't keep my mind off it. How was I to rediscover the knack of breathing? I sat bolt upright in bed, looking out at the sick night skies of Ilford. It was as if I had a steel rubber tyre around my chest, pressing all the air inside me further and further inwards. The grandfather clock in the hall didn't help either. It kept chiming the night into my very bones.

I knew I was going to die because, however hard I tried, I was unable to recapture the knack of breathing. It was the worst ever. I clung to Ted but he didn't seem to care. Why should he? He was breathing away quite comfortably.

I could take no more.

I left Ted in bed and crept along the corridor. I stood outside Granny's door for a while because I was too frightened to go inside. Finally I plucked up the courage to knock.

'Go to sleep, it's four o'clock in the morning!'

'I'm sorry, Granny, but I can't breathe.' I barged into her room, and there she was, all wrapped up in a woolly coat with bits of old rag tied all higgledy-piggledy in her jet black hair.

'Don't be stupid, Pusscat, if you can't breathe how can you talk? I'll take you to the park tomorrow, if you're a good girl.'

'Can I sleep with you, Granny?'

'Certainly not – now, off with you!'

Actually, I was glad about that. The idea of waking up next to Granny's smudged lips and I'd lose the breathing knack for ever. Perhaps she has to keep her lipstick on in case Grandpa returns in the night – she'll wear down all her lipsticks, if that's the case.

I couldn't return to my room, so I crept downstairs, and made straight for the kitchen where Trixy leapt into my arms. I yearned to carry Trixy's basket upstairs to my bedroom and cuddle her all night, but I didn't want Granny's fury upon me for it was much worse than Mummy's when it got going. As Trixy washed my face all over, my breath began to return. Her licks gave me quite an appetite, so I reached up and polished off the small box of Puffed Wheat that we'd bought the day before, and put it back on the shelf.

With the five o'clock chime of the grandfather clock, and a nice full tummy, there I was tucked up with my head and shoulders in Trixy's basket, her soft bushy tail across my face. Breathing easy, at last I sank into a lovely deep sleep.

And that's where Granny found me next morning. Her leering face burst into my dreams, a fiery dragon hissing for more flesh. 'What in the name of heaven are you doing in Trixy's basket? How dare you disobey!' She towered above me, with those funny bow rags flopping about in her hair, and her violent red mouth shooting great gobs of fury all over

Trixy and me. So terrified was I that I peed. I could do nothing to stop it, besides, I found the warm trickle rather comforting.

As I sat, half in and half out of Trixy's basket, frozen to the guilty spot, Granny's fury gradually ran out of steam. She turned to the sink to fetch the kettle. She reached for the porridge saucepan with one hand and with the other fished down the Puffed Wheat.

'Pusscat, where's the Puffed Wheat?' I remained glued to the warm wetness. 'C'mon, where have they gone?'

'I'm sorry, Granny, I've eaten them.'

'You little thief, you must always ask me, before you steal things, is that clear?'

With no Puffed Wheat, I now had to face the old Porridge Battle – if it wasn't for Trixy I would have run clean away.

'Now, come and eat some porridge, put some flesh on to those wicked little bones. Look at your hair. I'll comb it after breakfast, before the policeman sees you.' Mummy, too, was always on about the policeman seeing me. What would he do to me? I always run away when I see one, just in case.

I dreaded Granny combing my hair even more than porridge. I picked up my spoon, wondering when Granny would get up so I could put the plate on the floor for Trixy. The only problem was that Trixy didn't like porridge either.

Suddenly Granny gave an almighty gasp and dropped her spoon, splosh, into her porridge. She got up and started staring in the direction of Trixy, or rather my puddle right next to Trixy's basket (where I'd left it). She gave me a quick look and said, 'Trixy, you've never done that before, you wicked little dog!' She grabbed hold of Trixy and pushed her poor nose into my pee, then picked her up by the scruff of the neck and carried her into the garden. My heart thumped worse than it ever had thumped before.

I strained my neck to see Granny beating the living daylights out of Trixy. I saw her cringe, I heard her giving the saddest bewildered yelps, and my own heart crashed against my ribs. I heard Granny screaming. I left the table and ran to my bedroom where I slammed the door, hoping to shut out the guilt. But it wasn't that easy, for my guilt had followed me in, I felt it hovering all around me. I buried myself under the blankets, and sobbed.

Why didn't I own up? How could I have ended up being more cruel than any of them? How could I have stooped so low as to let Trixy take my punishment for me? I was stifled with shame.

My stammer got worse. Granny couldn't understand what had got into me. I had to pluck up courage just to look Trixy in her hopeful, loving eyes, having put her through such humiliation and torture. It was her forgiveness that I found hardest to bear, for there was no doubt in my mind that she knew what had taken place. How could she not know with Granny thrusting her nose into my smell? While my head was bowed in shame, Trixy's eyes were forever looking into mine with adoration and compassion.

My guilt clung to my shame, congealing thick like Marmite, in the air, the house, the walks, the park. Finally I stayed in bed, with a bad Marmite cough, for the last four days of my stay. I coughed and counted the chimes of the grandfather clock. How slowly the hours went by.

*

I'm now going to play Grandmother's Footsteps and take two great liberties with Old Father Time. One step forward first.

I learnt much later that the reason Mother went into the kitchen with Granny on that first day was for Granny to tell her that she had cancer of the stomach. That stay in Ilford was the last time I saw Grandma, she died very soon afterwards.

Although Granny missed Grandpa enormously, leaving a great void in her life, I suspect that while he was alive she took it for granted that her powerful temper would continually be embraced by Grandpa's patient and considerate nature. He was one in a million, a gentle, easy-going kind of a man, yet never lacking strength. I think she realized after he died that perhaps she had taken his precious spirit for granted, thus finding herself living out her last days riddled with remorse. She wasn't a cruel woman, just one of the millions who realize too late that they never fleshed out their lives sufficiently to round them off with any dignity. So she turned the regret inwards, slowly deafening herself to the grandfather clock echoing through the hall, relentlessly ticking away any remnants of salvation.

While Grandmother's stiff regretful back is turned, I'm going to take a huge leap forward in time, to collect the end of this little tale. I'm now living on the Old Road, by the sea in Malibu, Los Angeles, twenty-three years after the Ilford Saga.

One day, Hanna, my Guatemalan daily help, told me she had a friend coming to live in LA from Guatemala, who she wanted me to meet. Because I respected Hanna's domestic attributes (a lot more than my own) I listened to her request.

He was called Alviro Geraldo and because he was a psychic, with very special powers, she said with pride, 'If you try him out, just once, you could help him so much even introduce him to some of your friends?'

I had never indulged in such things, and I certainly didn't believe in those shady, suspicious – spooky, even – areas of the paranormal. At that time I was still under the misapprehension, because my father told me and naturally he was never wrong, that death was the end and I had no problem with that. (Early childhood memories were still buried at this time.) Being an atheist suited me fine, not only because it was easier somehow, but because blind belief was of no interest to me. Only proven facts, something tangible that I could witness before my eyes, would force me to question my atheism. The prospect of meeting some quack of a psychic didn't fill me with the remotest enthusiasm. I expected he would turn out to be some sort of fraud or con man – after all, they all were. But because of my respect for Hanna I agreed to go.

I arrived at the appointed hour at the modest bungalow where this Alviro Geraldo was staying in downtown LA. When Gladys and I entered – Gladys McTavish was my Skye terrier – I was surprised by Alviro's massive head which almost toppled off his delicate petit frame. His English was appalling.

'Please, don't be frighten, come an' sit down.'

I wasn't aware I was frightened, so his comment annoyed me rather.

'Please, why you hangry?'

'I'm not angry, I'm just—'

'You very very hangry – please si' down.'

I felt threatened, not angry, rather like Berty when a new

cock entered his domain. I chose a chair on the other side of the room. Gladys took up her position at my feet.

After some polite small talk, he suddenly looked up and said, 'Your Gra'mama say sorry.'

Here we go I thought. Even a fool knows we all have or had a Granny, and she's probably sorry about something. 'Sorry for what?'

'Sorry becau'e she pull your hair so bad.'

I wasn't impressed.

'Why you comma here? You no lika me?'

'I came here at Hanna's request, I don't believe in mediums or any of that psychic hogwash.'

'Then no possible me help you.'

That somehow pissed me off. 'I thought I was going to help *you*. I'm not in need of any help, thank you.'

'You very proud woman.'

'I wouldn't necessarily call a sceptic proud.'

'Ah!' he said, looking straight at my knees. They were, for some reason wobbling just a fraction. I tried changing my position, which calmed my knees and made him smile.

Suddenly his face changed dramatically. He swung it sideways, like Danny my drake, alert, as if listening for some worm in the earth. 'One day, you very littel, you go stay with Gra'mama. Dis you no like – you no like dis one bit – Gra'mama an' you no good friends – you only lika de dog.'

Well, that was an easy one too. There I was, sitting across the room with a dog at my feet. I could have done as well myself. I bent down to give Gladys a cuddle, more to hide my wiggling knees than anything else. Alviro smiled gently, so I decided to do an introduction. 'This is Gladys.'

'No, no, dis dog no call Gladys—'

'Yes, that's her name—'

'No, no – no dis dog of Gra'mama name "Trishy"—'

'No,' I said firmly – and meant it.

'Yes – di dog name Trishy!'

My knees were playing up rather badly now, so I crossed them the other way, clearing my throat. 'No, Granny didn't have a dog called Trishy.' I was buggered if I was going to give him an inch.

'OK. Dis dog – you love very much – I tink dis dog . . .' He sat, waiting for inspiration from his beloved floorboards, or perhaps Granny was there whispering to him from down under. 'Dis dog – ah – dis dog not called Trishy. Disa dog called "Tricky" – yes, dis dog Tricky—'

'No,' I was adamant, 'this dog you speak of wasn't called "Tricky" either.'

'OK. We forget di name, OK? So, you lova di animal very much!'

He delivered this with triumph. 'Obviously,' I said, stupidly pointing to Gladys, who was in the same direction as my wobbling knees.

'You very nervoos woman!'

'Obviously.' Exposed, my knees could wobble to their hearts' content.

'You sometime laugh so much you pee-pee. You sometime so frightened you make pee-pee also. On dis day you maka pee-pee next to Tricky. Gra'mama frighten you, an' you make pee-pee.'

This was getting out of hand, I wasn't liking it at all.

'You tink Gra'mama tink Tricky do pee-pee – but she tell me now dat she know it you who maka di pee-pee – Tricky alway too frighten to maka pee-pee in di house. So she punish you by takin' Tricky in di gardin – hit Tricky many time. You look . . . so ashame. You see Tricky cry, you so ashame, to dis day – you always feel too much respect for di animal. You lova Tricky too much.'

I sat there stunned. I pretended not to be, I pretended to take it all in my stride, but then my false composure finally caved in, it had become redundant, for I knew I hadn't fooled him for a moment.

'Trixy, not Tricky,' say I, all hoity-toity.

'OK. Tricky woman, Trixy!'

'How the hell d'you know all that? I'd forgotten it all long ago.'

He smiled down at those blasted floorboards. 'Si, si, si, you ha' forgot, but Gra'mama no forget nothing. She so sorry, si, si, Gra'mama so sorry.'

'But you went back in time, I thought psychics told the future?'

'Time, very strange. Time do many things – possible go back or forward, all the same thing, time is everywhere. Dis is why time so tricky for di psychic. Time like putty.'

'I don't understand . . . putty is all soft . . . pliable.'

'Yes, like time. Time also,' he searched for the word, 'pliable, many games possible to play with time. An' time play many games with all of us – especially with the psychic.'

From that day, my respect for Alviro Geraldo grew and grew, as indeed did his reputation, turning him into one of the most sought-after psychics in California. He gave me my first nudge towards facing the creeping realization that perhaps my father was wrong.

CHAPTER FOURTEEN

RETURNING HOME from Granny's was a high point, almost worth going to Granny's for. Barn Mead welcomed me with open branches. How pleased I was to see all my friends again! I could tell that they were pleased to see me, too. They all came up, clustering around me, led by Berty the cock, always first up to say hello, not surprising since I'd known Berty all my life.

As soon as I had unchained Micky from his prison cell he went over the moon with glee. He came straight at me full pelt, such a bullet of ecstasy that I couldn't help falling over in a heap. Having licked me to death with his pooey breath, we danced and danced, playing chase all over the stable yard. Mizzer whinnied to me from the paddock and all my feathered gang squawked their chorus of appreciation. All was indeed well.

Micky went faster than light as he leapt over the vegetable garden, all I could see was a trail of dust. I decided to play our game of hide-and-seek and hid from him in the greenhouse. I don't think he saw me go in, perhaps he lost my scent. Finally I took a peek out of the glass, and he saw me – the game was up! I ducked down quickly – alas! too late. Micky came flying through the window with triumphant joy, CRASH!

My clothes were suddenly being splattered with blood. I couldn't see what was happening at first, then I noticed

Micky had cut his front leg on the glass. Blood spurted out of it like Mizzer's water tap. It all got worse very quickly. Whatever had possessed him to leap right through a pane of glass like that?

'Come on, Micky, we'd better go and find help.' But he couldn't walk at all. He began whining and licking his leg, which looked a terrible mess. I tried carrying him, but he weighed a ton. 'All right, Micky, you stay here.' I ran to get help. 'Mummy! Brand! Mummy!'

'Pusscat, come in and get washed.' She saw me. 'Good God! Where's all that blood coming from?'

'M-M-M—' My stammer overcame me.

Mummy shook me, then changed her mind and took me into the kitchen. 'Now what are you trying to tell me?'

I couldn't stop stammering. 'M-M-Micky has cut his leg very badly.'

'Thank God for that, I thought you were going to tell me something much worse.'

'Mummy, p-p-please help!'

She did finally telephone Brand to come up, and called in the vet. I managed to escape her iron grip, and ran back down to Micky, with Mummy screaming at me, 'You come back here and eat your lunch – Pusscat! D'you hear?'

I rocked Micky in my arms for what seemed an eternity. There was so much blood, it was all over the two of us. I kept hugging him as he licked my face, sharing each other's blood and tears. Whereas neat pristine little Trixy kissed me all around my mouth, never going inside, Micky liked to plunge his great tongue right in, as deep down my throat as he could reach – a pity really, given that unfortunate breath, but that didn't stop me loving him dreadfully. We grew so close down there in the greenhouse that day, closer than I'd been to anyone – except Daddy, of course.

The vet came. While I was taken away to eat my lunch, Micky was shot. His leg was smashed into little pieces, so the vet said. Why didn't they let me cradle him in my arms while he died? I never saw him again.

It was an Indian summer evening, warm and mellow, I wanted to get home quickly from school and go for a long ride, so I took the shortest route home cutting across the Beggar Hill meadow. I wasn't allowed in this field because of the enormous black bull. Once Daddy took me through the same field to the T. P. Pond (tadpole pond). 'OK, Pusscat, take my hand and make a run for it – now!' As Daddy took my hand, I turned to see the bull heading straight towards us with mighty intent. We just managed to get under the fence in the nick of time. 'Never come through this field on your own, Pusscat.' Daddy looked quite white with shock. 'Promise me?'

It intrigued me. Why was everyone scared of this bull? One day I decided to try a test. I entered the field at the top end. I found that if I ran he'd charge me. Approaching him slowly was the knack. Admittedly he gave me a savage glare as I came closer, but I refused to be put off, and walked with great purpose up to him. He stood there mesmerized at my nerve. I stopped to give him one of *my* better savage glares, then turned my back on him and walked on homeward very slowly indeed.

I wasn't particularly courageous (besides, what is courage

if not foolhardiness bordering on the stupid?) I'd simply done my homework, taking time to look, to study that bull's eyes from the road. I discovered that when I gave him fresh sweet grass from the verge, he scooped it from my hand with such gentleness that I concluded he was just a silly sloppy old fool, who liked indulging in a game of 'He' from time to time. After all, it must be very boring standing alone in a field all day long.

Animals taught me very young the importance in life of bluffing it out. Also that adults have been programmed to fear certain types of creature. Just because Bull=Red =Danger, that poor old bull spent most of his life unloved and deserted. Sharks too get rotten PR, while we 'humane beings' continue attacking them while invading their territory.

Fortunately I managed to catch Mizzer with a juicy carrot, and once we were all tacked up I decided to go and visit Nel who lived down the lane. Although she was nearly four years older than me we were great friends.

'Don't be late for supper, Pusscat,' Mummy shouted from Pooker's nursery window.

Arriving at their farm, I could smell the aroma of ripe apples, there is no smell to equal it. I'd like to have been an apple farmer, just for the smell. I always got a warm greeting from Nel's brother Malcolm, who was a little older than me, and her little sister Alison. 'Hello, Pusscat,' said Alison, 'will you stay and play?' Nel arrived from deep within the orchard looking tired and sweaty. She worked with her father a lot, because they didn't have any other help.

I dismounted, and handed the reins to Nel. 'I'll stay and play with them.'

'Are you sure, Pusscat?' asked Nel, taking the reins and mounting up.

'Quite sure, but I must be home by six o'clock.'

Alison took my hand eagerly and off we ran, Alison leading the way straight towards my favourite apple tree, its branches bending over with plump Victoria apples (a large yellow crisp apple, similar to a Victoria plum, both tasting sour and sweet at the same time).

Malcolm appeared. He was holding his little ferret close to his chest. The funny thing about Malcolm was he looked just like his ferret, rather pointed and skinny, with little narrow eyes that darted all over the place. He was brilliant at school, so they said. No wonder with those bright, slitty eyes never missing a trick.

'Want to play "doctors and patients" with Malc 'n' me?' enquired Alison coyly, greedily biting her way through another huge apple.

I'd never played that game before, but I didn't want to let them know that.

'Go and put that beastly little ferret away, Malc, and let's teach Pusscat how to play, OK?' Suddenly, quick as a Flash – by name and nature – their collie stole the apple from my hand, which was a real pity, because it was delicious.

As Malcolm went off with his ferret, he did a quick look back over his shoulder. 'Alison can play the nurse and Pusscat can be the patient.'

'What do I have to do?'

'I'll show you,' said Alison. After tossing half her apple away, she became most business-like and took off her top, displaying her chubby torso. Doing a little dance she started tweaking her nipples. 'There's milk in there,' she said, with great authority.

I remember thinking, how amazing that she could be so sure about something so completely wrong, but I wasn't in the mood for arguing, especially while she was wiggling her hips around, humming to herself.

I liked Alison, but that day she seemed in a funny mood. On she went, quite undeterred, concentrating very hard on her trouser buttons. As she strained to pull them down out popped a bottom as chubby as the rest of her. It was dimpled, like her ruddy cheeks, which often went purple, as did her hands in the winter. 'Come on, Pusscat, pull them off for me.' I did as I was told.

At that moment Malcolm arrived – minus ferret – and saw Alison about to take off her flowered knickers. He shook his head in boredom. 'Alison, put your clothes on. Nurses don't take their clothes off, only patients.'

Alison continued humming and wiggling her now naked bottom around. 'I'm just showing Pusscat what she'll have to do.'

'Well,' said Malcolm, 'hurry up.' After he had taken an apple off the tree with a brisk professional twist (I never got the knack of the brisk twist, so kept getting told off for ruining next year's growth) he sat on the ground with his back to her.

Alison, now free of any hindrance took great delight in her nakedness, coming close by me and then quickly turning around, spinning like a top. This I found quite interesting, because I'd never really looked at a girl's slit before, I'd seen my little sister's, so minuscule it hardly counted. I'd seen my own, passing the bathroom mirror, but never paid it any attention, it didn't interest me. But for some strange reason, Alison's slit was a completely different kettle of fish.

Sitting there beneath my favourite apple tree, with Alison wiggling her bum and parading her slit in front of my nose, I suddenly found myself tingling with some new little gurgle deep inside my tummy. 'Go on, Pusscat, have a good look at it,' said Malcolm, with those little beady eyes of his dancing everywhere, even behind him. Alison came up so close that I was afraid she might hear it too, so I backed away.

Malcolm found this very funny. 'I do believe Pusscat is squeamish,' said Malcolm, twisting another apple off the tree with great authority.

'I'm not squeamish!' Now, I wasn't sure what squeamish was.

'Go on, Alison, show her.' Alison came up to me for the second time, and leaned her slit towards me while opening it up with both hands, so I could see the bright pink flesh inside it.

'Down, Flash,' I said to the collie, to give myself a breather.

Then Malcolm stood up, and turned Alison round. 'Bend down, Alison. I think this patient's trouble is in her other hole,' he said to me. Malcolm bent Alison forward with great ease, and Alison didn't kick up any fuss whatsoever. 'You see, Mrs Smith, your daughter needs an operation, look.' Malcolm started to pull open Alison's slit, which was amazingly close to her botty-hole, where upon he very skilfully placed his finger near to the edge, Alison squirming with glee all the while.

Now, I'd never seen a botty open before. I'd seen Micky's and Mizzer's botties and that lion at the zoo, but I'd never

ever seen a human one. I found it quite amazingly neat, such a tiny hole, though not nearly as pink as Alison's slit. Malcolm seemed very taken with it. 'You see, Mrs Smith, I have no choice but to operate.'

Alison wiggled with delight. 'Oh, yes! Go on, Malc, show Pusscat how you do an operation.'

'Be quiet, Alison, Pusscat's going to be the patient today.'

Flash went flying off to the far end of the orchard, so I took this as a good excuse to change the subject. 'You'd better go and fetch Flash, your Dad doesn't like him chasing Mr Gamer's cows.'

Malcolm came over and put his hand on my shoulder. 'That's all right, Mrs Smith, Mr Gamer's cows aren't in there this week.'

I was well and truly stumped. Alison started giggling. 'I think Pusscat is frightened of playing.'

'I'm not frightened of anything,' I said, my knees almost buckling beneath me.

Malc was now very close. 'Don't worry, Pusscat, Alison was pretty shy at first, weren't you, Ali, eh?'

I mainly remember the great conflict churning up my insides that day. If we're all born innocent, why wasn't I simply instinctively revelling in it just like an animal would? Why so much embarrassment, so much guilt, for what? I'd never been told not to do such things, and I'd often seen Mummy bathing the boys in the bath. I'd felt no guilt when the man on the Ilford bus got his winkie out – it mattered not a jot. So why, in the orchard that day, was I in such a state? And why was I so determined to see it through to the bitter end?

Malc did a quick check both ways and took his stance

centre tree trunk. He then unbuttoned his flies as if plucking an apple. Perhaps he was going to produce a ferret? No such luck, nothing but a winkie. Here we go again, I thought. Although standing against the tree, all ridiculous, he was totally in command of the situation. He began stroking his winkie, as if it was also made of mink – like the man on the bus.

'Have you never seen a penis before?' I didn't like that word at all, it sounded disgusting. But perhaps it was the right word in Malc's case, because his winkie began to grow ever so slightly – amazing – like one of Jukes's conjuring tricks! I'd never seen anything like it.

'I've seen lots and lots, thank you, and they all look the same,' I lied.

Malcolm turned his little hot eyes to me. 'Have you ever touched one?'

'Yes, hundreds of times.'

'Well, now you can touch mine, if you want to.'

I didn't have an enormous desire to touch Malc's growing winkie, but I didn't want to seem rude, so I did quickly. I didn't like it.

Malcolm guessed I wasn't impressed. Luckily his winkie shrank back to normal and he put it away, changing the subject with a brisk rub of his hands. 'OK, Mrs Smith, the waiting room's packed.' He gave me a little ferret look. I noticed his eyes were bright and sparkly and his face was quite red.

'Does Nel play these games?' I was stammering badly.

'She taught us,' said Malc simply. 'Please undress now, Mrs Smith.'

Alison saw that I was shy and moved in bossily. 'I'll help you, Mrs Smith.' She unbuttoned my jodhpurs and began to pull them down. I refused to lie on the grass. I tried to keep my knickers on but Alison just wouldn't hear of it. Malcolm watched everything with his beady eyes flashing.

'You c-c-can have a quick look, Doctor, but then I have to go.'

As I pulled my knickers down – with Alison's help, of course – my heart started galloping fast. 'Hmm,' said Malcolm, coming forward to get a closer look, 'that doesn't look too good to me, I think you're going to have to lie down.'

'No, D-D-D-Doctor, I think you can do what you have to do standing up.'

'Would you please turn round then, with your face towards the tree.'

I can remember being very relieved as I turned to face the apple tree because they could no longer see my blushes. But what was I really thinking? Was I gripping it so hard in the hope that they might stop?

'Open your legs wider, Mrs Smith, please,' said Malcolm impatiently. I found myself obeying. There he was beneath me, his head on the grass looking straight up between my open legs. Then slowly, his hands crept up my thighs.

Why did I have such a wildly beating, guilty heart? Half of me knew what I was doing was bad – why? At the same time, something inside me was becoming all nice and warm. I have no problems with that, for those feelings were purely instinctive. Even when I caught a glimpse of Malcolm rising up on one elbow to get a closer look up my slit from the ground, I certainly wasn't altogether hating it. Yet I turned my face back to the tree, burying myself into the prickly bark, pretending that I wasn't getting excited, pretending even that I wasn't there.

When he moved even nearer, sliding his hand higher up my thigh until it reached the brim of my slit, the feelings grew so complex, so overpowering, that I finally knew I'd had enough.

'Hmm,' said Malcolm, as I quickly put my clothes back on again, 'we'll have to have another look at that next week, but I think it's healing nicely.'

The whole experience had a hint of a Victoria apple. Sweet and sour. Nasty but perhaps a little nice too.

There never was a next week. I remained quite friendly with Alison and Malcolm, but we never played those games together again. I didn't tell Nel about it, though I wanted to on many occasions. By Nel's reaction I'd have known how naughty, or how ordinary, what we had done was. But if Nel had turned out to be very shocked, it might have frightened her away – and I dearly loved Nel.

CHAPTER FIFTEEN

ONE MORNING arriving at Nel's house early, I went upstairs to find Alison and Malcolm having cuddles in their mother's bed. She had always seemed so aloof and cold but there she lay, her hair and nightie all tangled and hay-wire, with the two of them snuggled up, softly cushioned amongst her ample breasts. It shocked me, not because it was shocking but because it was so lovely. I had never experienced such an early-morning light-hearted freedom – freedom from keeping up appearances, chores and daily routine. 'No time for cuddles – must set an example to the servants.'

Mother was never seen in her dressing gown – let alone her nightie. She was always up and dressed, ready to start the day by eight o'clock sharp, so I'd naturally presumed that mothers simply didn't do that sort of thing. How wrong I was, and how saddened, especially after Alison told me with a shrug that they had cuddles most days. The experience shifted my relationship with my mother into a new perspective. I began to make dangerous, negative comparisons.

Only once in my life did I catch my mother before the day had taken away her sleepy dust, for not one of us questioned the rule of not entering her bedroom without first knocking. One bright spring morning, with the early sap rising, my curiosity overcame me. I timed it so that my father was still having his morning soak in the bath, and I mustered up the courage to creep into my mother's bedroom without knocking.

There she was, a statue of vulnerability, standing in front of her three-sided mirror with her back to me, silhouetted against a blue sky puffing up little white clouds in the ample window beyond.

She was naked. Her back was towards me, pale and gleaming, but her front view reflected in the mirror was cut off at the waist. However her breasts in the mirror were perfect. I knew nothing about breasts then, so I had nothing to compare them with but I just knew they were perfect. And when I grew up and saw other breasts, there were never any to compare with Mummy's at that moment. Perhaps it was a trick of the light, for I recalled no trace of sagginess (her breasts having fed the four of us) – quite the contrary, they looked voluptuously tilted.

She stood completely still, her eyes looking into her mirror eyes, too far away to be bothered with self-regard or, indeed, vanity. It struck me how close we were at that suspended moment – as if it were the first secret we had ever shared. As if catching my thoughts she clicked back into the present, and walked over to her underwear drawer; as she did so, the light from the east window played the puffy white clouds into brief drifting shadows floating across those upward-tilted breasts, making her nipples dance.

With her back again towards me I noticed two enchanting dimples at the base of her spine. As she bent forward to her underwear drawer, full of feminine secrets, I knew that was my cue to creep out again, secretly – just like the moment I had witnessed.

*

There were three different ways home. My favourite led into a glade that joined the bridle-path where, looking snug and cosy, the Romany gypsy encampment stood. An old van and a crumbling rusty car with no wheels sat close by. Children played almost naked some days, squelching around in the mud with several horses with feathered feet and four lurcher dogs. One of the lurchers looked like Micky but he wasn't too friendly, and sometimes he wouldn't let me pass. Mother made me promise not to enter the encampment, telling me gypsies were dangerous because they tended to be unreliable.

I knew these smiling people weren't dangerous, just that Mummy didn't like them because they had parked themselves right next door to her friends the Gore-Browns, lowering the tone of the neighbourhood.

The gypsy children were wary of me at first, running away whenever I appeared, but after a few visits they sat on the ground and stared, picking their noses and feet and poking around in each other's hair, like chimps. Ted, the eldest boy, would sometimes come out and talk to me. He was the one who had given us Micky. Ted was truly dashing, cuddly like my Ted at home, but with glossy black curly hair, not crinkly and fuzzy like mine. He was so dark and handsome, that he didn't so much charm the birds off the trees as dazzle them until they fell at his feet in a great dizzy pile.

Later, when I was about twelve, I got a kind of inner awakening watching Ted at Ingatestone fair, controlling the merry-go-round with masterful ease, his black locks gathered in with twine, white teeth gleaming, sweating beneath tattoos anchored in deep turquoise. I used to tingle as I watched those turquoise anchors changing shape according to the whim of the tanned and glossy muscles beneath, flexing in time to 'Looking for Henry Lee', which boomed in fits and starts from the primitive loudspeakers. (Strange – because I've never fancied large muscles since.)

All the young girls of Ingatestone village felt the same way, for they would all gather in a tight bunch next to Ted's roundabout. I got a whiff of thickly cloying cheap 'Outdoor Girl' perfume as I swooshed by on my painted steed. A busy circle all giggling, smoking and wobbling on their newly acquired high heels. All pointing their new Maidenform bras, harsh make-up and grotesque beehive hair constructions firmly at my Ted. But the fact remained, they were all much riper and more ready for plucking than I was at twelve. Ted did seem quite fond of me, often stepping between the horses as they circled round and round, making his way to sit behind me, holding me around my waist as merrily we jiggered up and down in time to Johnny Ray, 'Crying in the Rain', 'Cherry Pink Mumbo' or Ruby Murray and 'Softly softly turn the key'. Mingle that heady stuff with Ted's sweet garlic breath tickling my ear, those first naked sweat smells and Brylcreem blasting my nostrils. How could I not melt?

One day walking home from school, Ted put his arm around my shoulder and invited me in for tea. 'Sorry to hear about Micky,' he said sheepishly, 'but he was always a bit of a scallywag.' I pulled away, otherwise I would have cried for I was still in mourning.

What a perfect place to live! Everything in the caravan, although well worn, gave me the sense of cherished messiness. How I wished we lived in a warm and friendly caravan painted so many different dazzling colours, with no worry about tidying up or denting Mummy's stupid boring cushions. Why, I wondered, was Barn Mead painted such pale cold colours? Mummy could learn a few tips from the gypsies.

It was a potent, foreign experience having tea with Ted and his mother, Ethel. She was small and held the power, like Loo my little brown hen. Such a heady mixture of smells wafting out from behind a secret opening, covered in sparkly coloured hanging beads. 'Can't go behind there, lass – private it is,' said Ethel, wagging her large dirty index fingernail at me, with the tea brewing up even more exotic aromas by this time.

I spent many an afternoon in the warmth of Ethel's flamboyant den. It's such a shame grown-ups can't sit quietly without drinking tea. I never dared ask for milk, just smacked my lips to be polite. The tea was probably a mixture of washing-up water, cobweb juice and dead Gore-Brown dog, and that's why Micky's breath smelt as it did.

As I climbed the last hill home I usually bumped into God. God was the biggest, whitest dog I had ever seen. I knew he was God, and so did he, and indeed so did all the rest of the dogs in the neighbourhood. I was later to discover that he was a Pyrenean Mountain Dog. Often King George would have a natter with God. I think they enjoyed each other's company, both being so majestically regal 'n' all. I made a vow with myself, with King George as my witness, that when I was old enough I would buy a Pyrenean Mountain Dog of my own.

One of these journeys back from school sticks firmly in my mind. I climbed the last hill home and made my way down to the stables to feed the birds when I felt something peculiar in the air. Why weren't they all crowing for their supper? Perhaps Brand had already fed them? No, of course, it was Brand's day off . . .

Something most definitely was wrong. I gathered speed. Silence, except for a bit of half-hearted hissing from a battalion of hang-dog geese. I ran across to my chickens' play-pen and then I saw them – a bleeding battlefield of gizzards, heads, feathers strewn all over the place. I wandered around just looking. I don't remember feeling anything at first, just bewilderment – how could it be? How could it be? Each of them, without exception, was headless. Then the vomit rose – great clumps of it – and since I wasn't in the car, I didn't feel the need to hold any of it back. For the first time I was free to be as sick as I wanted, free to begin to exorcize the pain.

I saw Berty all battle scarred with no fine perky head aloft, I saw Gus's bright yellow beak hanging from a head which in turn was hanging from her bonny brown body, with long wormy bits hanging with blood. I saw Danny, my dearest drake, his head quite some distance from his body. I went and retrieved it. Gradually I found the head of each and every one of them, and placed it back where it belonged.

Gerty my reddest rooster, clashing with her own blood as her feathers started to congeal. My little bantams . . . such teeny heads they had had . . . I hadn't realized. Loo had put up quite a fight by the looks of it, she was more bloody, and messy than the rest. All their eyes were transfixed with incomprehension more than with fear, as if unable to understand what had taken place.

What kind of a devil could rip my friends apart in this way? It must have been a madman. I was never any good at jigsaw puzzles, but I had no difficulty in finding all the matching parts that day. As I finished replacing their heads and tails, it dawned on me that every bird was complete. Whoever had committed the crime that day had stolen nothing. Bewildered I went over and held Berty's head and began rocking him to and fro.

That's how Daddy found me, cradling Berty's head in my arms. I didn't notice him at first. 'Damn fox, Pusscat, damn fox.'

'A fox? But he wasn't hungry – he didn't eat anything.'

'No, Pusscat, it just got trapped and ran amok.'

'What does that mean?'

'It means the fox panicked, couldn't find a way out of the play-pen, so went berserk.'

Then a nasty, bitter taste rose up in the wake of my vomit, something worse than hatred, a feeling similar to the one I had had after I had saved Chuzzer's immaculate conception – the desire for revenge.

'Come along, you're not going to be able to mend them I'm afraid.' With such tenderness Daddy took me in his arms. That did it, the flood gates opened and I cried and cried. I couldn't stop, couldn't get over the waste, the futility of it all, the fine noble head of my rainbow cock – there'd certainly never be another Berty, not ever. 'Never mind, Pusscat, we still have our Gooses-men.'

CHAPTER SIXTEEN

S O THERE I WAS, at the age of eight, ANGRY, wanting my revenge. I was no better than a great many of the planet's population. I needed to kill. I needed to kill all foxes! I took up fox-hunting in earnest and joined the Essex Union Hunt. Often it seemed that the actual kill was too fast, the hounds too precisely accurate, the foxes did not suffer enough – I wanted it slower. Mizzer, on the other hand, was slow, so witnessing the kill was a rare event. Usually the damn fox got away, it was all too easy to lose the scent. I wasn't getting my retribution quick enough. But with sufficient determination and a lorryload of fury all things are possible.

I became obsessed not only with foxes but with the whole ritual. I loved getting up at four thirty, dressing quietly so as not to wake the rest of the house. Hauling my way into my new cream jodhpurs and brown boots, tussling with my cravat and gold pin. Brushing up the velvet of my navy blue riding hat. There was always the problem of whether to stuff my great ears under my hat, which made them throb, or expose the damn things, and let them freeze, flap, and be done with it. I usually chose the latter, but tried not to make the fatal error of returning to check out the overall effect.

I wasn't allowed to go alone in the beginning, so Nel accompanied me to the first few meets on Kipper, but it didn't take me long to get the hang of it. I loved hacking to the meet through the undamaged day with its luscious fleshy smells of late autumn; the frail half-light leaking into a sleepy dawn chorus. All senses a-quiver, crisp with untouched hope. I can almost smell it from here.

The meet gathered on the village green. A mixture of all sorts, though it was easy to guess the old money, for they carried an easy, elegant air, whether it be astride or side-saddle. Others, the *nouveau riche* feeling the need to prove themselves worthy and to get in with the old money, always sat a little more tentatively upon their new sleek acquisitions.

Some really tiny fearless children sat astride beautifully well-kept little ponies, all with such a natural inbred confidence that a second look was necessary, before realizing they were, in fact, on the leading rein. Nel and I would usually join up with Peregrine, because Peregrine and his pony Tinkerbell, a little pudgy piebald pony, were as scruffy as we were.

I suppose it's natural to remember the time I got blooded more clearly than others. Amidst steamy pirouettes and the pungent pong of sweat and supple leather, the Master arrived. A symphony in pink, looking in the pink – perhaps pink with drink, but certainly pink with frustration due to his strawberry roan gelding's refusal to move on. He dug in those pointed spurs with almost cruel purpose before checking that his steed was in the midst of that necessary P for pink. Naturally he plummeted to a deeper shade of embarrassment pink, for no spurring on earth was going to detract the strawberry roan from his moment of serious pleasure.

Quickly looking around to see who saw him pinking up, worse still, spurring on a peeing steed, he said a few good mornings. Suddenly the now hugely relieved strawberry roan pranced forward and, not a moment too late, the Master gave the nod. The huntsman blew his horn, the hounds were invisibly and silently given their command and the hunt moved off in a flurry of impatient true-blooded hunting pink.

Within no time at all the hounds had the scent, and the whole hunt turned left off the lane, through a five-barred gate – and we were off! Mizzer moved like the wind when he wanted to. Peregrine, Tinkerbell, Nel and Kipper must have been somewhere behind me, because that Tinkerbell was most definitely overweight and Kipper was a clodhopper.

A ditch came looming up and Mizzer jumped it like a champ. 'Gone to covert!' was the next thing I heard, although I was too busy clinging on to Mizzer's withers to be able to know exactly what else was happening.

I couldn't believe my eyes: there were Tinkerbell and Kipper way up with the leaders! I kicked Mizzer on, longing for some lightning, but Mizzer was doing brilliantly – for him. I'd never been so fast in my life.

The next thing I saw was that damned Tinkerbell flying over a hedge! I wasn't sure about this hedge. I'd never jumped anything as high before, let alone a hedge. Mischief decided he didn't like it either. He stopped dead, giving me no time to decide whether I was in agreement or not. I went over – unfortunately alone. CRASH! Falling off into soft mud was a piece of cake. Just as I was brushing off the mud with a clump of dock leaves, a lady appeared out of nowhere. She was riding side-saddle, all dressed in black with a black veil. She bent down gracefully to hand me Mizzer's reins. 'Are you all right? That was quite a fall.'

'I'm f-f-f-fine, thank you,' my stammer unending because of the shock.

She was very pretty indeed, with a neat silky blonde bun at the nape of her neck and mounted on a bay mare – how do these women stay so prim and proper out hunting?

'You were very brave even to try. I headed straight for the open gate.'

'I never saw a gate,' I said, mounting simultaneously to impress her.

'Come, follow me, I know where they went,' she said, and took off.

I quickly stuffed my ears inside my hat, because they were freezing something chronic. I liked the way her black skirts billowed about in the wind. In fact, I thought she was absolutely smashing.

We lost the scent of three or four foxes. Two crossed the river, some went to ground, others went to covert. Wretched to think that so many get away, any one of whom could have been my gang's murderer.

I was about to join Nel and Kipper and head off home when the huntsman blew his horn and we were off again. This time the hounds were smelling blood. So indeed was Peregrine because he flashed by me. I heard great excitement ahead, but however hard I kicked Mizzer the reaction was minimal – he'd had it. I saw everyone gathering in a tight little bunch at the crest of the hill. 'Come on, Mizzer, one last push!'

We arrived just in time to catch the Master flicking blood over Peregrine. Barn Mead would have crumbled with all the thumping I gave Mizzer at that moment, as I tried to push him forward to await my turn – but he wouldn't budge. Perhaps it was because of this, flailing thighs thumping up and down, frantically determined to reap their revenge, caked, besplattered and sweating, that the Master, smiling to himself, decided to swipe me too with the blood from the freshly dead fox carcass.

It was a strange sensation as the blood, still warm, hit my freezing face. Did I hear a loud chorus of grateful squawks from all my dead friends as retribution echoed through the air?

'Don't wash it off till dawn,' said the Master, bringing me back down to earth with great formality. I didn't deserve to get blooded on that particular occasion, because I hadn't witnessed the kill. I'd cheated, simple as that. I wonder if my gang knew I'd cheated, down there among all the worms and moles.

Jogging home through the early dusk, I had a taste for blood and made a vow. I'd win my pads, my mask and my brush, the only way to satisfy my revenge. Then all would be over. I looked down to see my bloody cravat blending nicely with the setting sun. There was to be no washing tonight, the blood wasn't coming off till dawn. I would fight that battle to the end, however much Mummy protested.

CHAPTER SEVENTEEN

THERE WAS NO doubt my stiff upper lip slipped a trifle after the death of my flock. I was left with only Mizzer. Daddy became concerned because I spent all my time doing pathetic manic handstands or attempting to get Mizzer to sit like a dog. Mizzer knew very well what I wanted. Once when I gave the command to sit he made one of his lethal rolls, which I took to be an important step in the right direction. It's near to sitting, after all.

With a great deal of reluctance Mother finally caved in and bought me a new partly sheepdog mongrel puppy. I called him Puffin, and he became my whole world. Daddy found him utterly irresistible too, and greeted him with such whole-hearted glee when he returned from the office, that Puffin would repeatedly slop Daddy's whisky all over the shop, as he skimmed across the room propelled by his swirling fluffy tail.

A sad little tale though, because after only three months, Puffin got run over while I was at school. Mummy had let him wander out into the road. She must have had her head in the skies, the kitchen, her bedroom, on her mail, on Pooker – but not on poor Puffin.

Even though my friendship with Puffin was short-lived, it didn't lessen the excruciating numbness that affected both Daddy and me. It was the first time I saw him cry, but I'm not sure if it was for Puffin or for me.

A wonderful pink pig arrived called Charlie who helped me to let go of Puffin. Anyone who says, 'You filthy pig', or claims that pigs are dirty, ought to have the privilege of sharing a night with one of them, as I did on many occasions.

I'd slip out of bed and into my dressing gown, pocket an apple or two from the fruit bowl, stuff the torch into my other pocket and stealthfully creep out of the house without making a sound. Fortunately those were the days when doors didn't have to be locked. When I arrived it seemed as though he'd been expecting me, for he'd give me an Owly glance upwards, then a shuffle sideways with a grunt, as if to say, 'Come on, then, if you're coming. Hurry up and close the door, you're causing a draught.'

Eager to obey, I'd make a little nest of straw for my pillow and cuddle up. Hard to describe, that strange mixture of smells – the Mill House grain shed, Ted the gypsy's caravan and something very sweet, similar to condensed milk, or Pooker's nursery.

Charlie had green eyes like Daddy's, with the same wicked twinkle. Scrutinizing their depths, I was astonished to find a truly ancient being to be reckoned with (later the elephant and gorilla would affect me in the same way except their eyes were brown). Everything wobbled as Charlie snored, grounding me. He had warm squashy bits, clean and welcoming, and I clung to the safety of his breathing rhythm – slow and easy – as we drifted off into dreamland together.

One morning I was down at the stables messing about with Charlie and grooming Mizzer, chattering to them as usual, when Mother arrived. I didn't like her trespassing in my domain one little bit – it was always bad news. She would sometimes spy on me without my knowing, which I found unfair especially if I was in deep conversation with the animals, or talking to the trees. And whenever I sang to them, she'd go up the Polly Tree. I wondered why something so harmless upset her so.

'Only witches talk and chant to trees and animals,' she said, awkwardly ill at ease with her surroundings.

'What's a witch, Mummy?' By the looks of things in general, witches were not too good at all.

'A witch has strange powers, which she draws on from nature.'

'Is that bad, then?'

'Yes, very bad. Talking to trees and animals means that either you are a witch, or—'

'Or what?'

'Mad as a Hatter.' She was the one looking Mad as a Hatter.

I knew something serious was afoot. 'Pusscat, I want you up in the house this minute,' she said in her coldest voice. She took me firmly by the arm with her usual grip.

'Your wickedness will be the death of you, you won't live to see—'

'I know – to see my twenty-first birthday – I know!' I was getting sick of Mummy telling me I wouldn't live to see twenty-one. How could I ever forget, for Christ's sake? All I wanted was to enjoy what I had left.

She dragged me over to the beautiful sideboard in the dining room. It was close to my heart, both for its warm fruitwood colour, and because it held, on its shiny surface, the great friendly fruit bowl. I was the fruit lover in the house.

Then I could see what all the fuss was about. Someone had recently carved half-inch notches at two-inch intervals all along its majestic front. I knew I hadn't done it, but if I hadn't, who had? Apart from Mummy and me there were masses of suspects. Agatha Christie would have had a field day. To say Mother was overstaffed would be an understatement. She employed Nora, the Scots cook, Carmelina and Luigi, an Italian couple, who lived in, the maid, Brand the gardener, the daily help who came in every other day, plus another gardener as well as Brand, who doubled up as chauffeur. No wonder I lived down in the stables, there was no room at the inn for me, Nel or Margery (the cowhand's daughter).

'Don't you bring that lot into my kitchens!' I didn't know until later, that kitchens were the meeting place, the hub of a house, the very centre. This sideboard incident wasn't the first time I had been wrongly accused, but it sticks in my mind because it was the day our first television was to arrive, and we were particularly excited.

When Mummy had finished scolding me she took me up to my room, gave me a jolly good hair-brushing and locked me up for the rest of the day. Carmelina, looking very hang-dog, brought up my meals. I heard the television man arriving, the general buzz of excitement drifting up the stairs. I so wanted to be down with the rest of them but I knew I was being punished, though I couldn't for the life of me remember committing the crime. Even now the injustice wafts occasionally into my nostrils when I'm putting on the telly. In Mummy's defence, there were many times when I was the guilty one – in fact, probably most times. But not then.

I know I was stubborn, a fussy eater, plain, common (in Mummy's eyes), a loner, dirty and rebellious. My choosing to live down in the stables sent her up the Polly Tree. But she had me trapped in a no-win situation, because she wouldn't allow me in the house till evening either.

Had I so wished, I had the pick of the county to play with. Mummy would have happily driven me, or had me driven to any one of the posh homes littered about the Essex countryside, so eager was she to have me play with her kind of children, but I never showed the slightest inclination to do so. She found my attitude incomprehensible and the split inevitably widened between us, with little hope of reconciliation for quite some time. Yet I still had so much love and respect for her.

It was a gloriously warm spring day, and I was going up to the house to ask my little sister to play with me. She was growing into a real sport, because the previous week, she and my brothers were watching telly, and I persuaded her to jump from the sofa to the armchair; she overshot the mark, landed on the floor and was knocked out cold. Mummy was most upset, though not as upset as I was because *I* thought Pooker was dead. Pooker took it very well. When she came to she'd forgotten all about it. She was shaping up – I'd have her riding in no time, jumping too. Full of such thoughts I came up through the vegetable garden towards the house, approaching my boundary of the giant oak tree. What was all that commotion at the far end of the croquet lawn? How easy it is to tell an important occasion from quite some distance away. It's as if familiar people with familiar body language quite suddenly become false, studied. Something was happening in the rose garden. What could it be? A lot of people gathering, the whole family except me – fiddle-de-dee!

A little distance from the house, I saw my golden sister's hand held tightly with my Mother's . . . I saw my Father, I saw a stranger – from the house leaped my two brothers. My mother looked more like a goddess than a queen, everyone so spruce, uncommonly clean, with my two brothers a perfectly dashing pair, the sun shimmering in everyone's hair, Daddy a Ronald Colman with a hint of Tarzan. But who was that stranger, that other man? Mummy's roses, most beautiful, were the best in all the land. But who on earth was the stranger – what's that in his hand?

The shock of remembering forces me into rhyme. At first I thought that the stranger was holding a gun. It took me quite some time to realize it was a camera, I suppose because I thought it impossible to be having a family portrait in the rose garden without me. As I watched them coyly posing, and heard the camera's click echoing across the croquet lawn, suddenly I knew with crystal clarity what lay ahead. It was as if something crept up behind me and banged me on the head.

That bang, the length of a second maybe, let in the light, opening my vision to another dimension, enabling me to take a peek at my destiny.

(It was the last fleck of evidence that I'd receive from that Great Something for a while. I could be wrong about the Great Something. Perhaps it was Old Father Time shuffling through space, recruiting my awareness for a second, in the hope of shifting me to see things from a more enlightened perspective, be it only a smidgen's worth. Or maybe time and the Great Something are one. Whichever, I believe these flecks of evidence are a common experience for most of us. We brush them aside in case they're imagination, self-delusion or, worse, in speaking of them we'll be considered mad.)

But that sunny spring afternoon in the rose garden left me with not a whisker of doubt. The smell of roses wafted across the lawn, sweet as my future.

It wasn't a boast, it wasn't a threat, it wasn't a dream, nor was it an ambition: it was a fact. I was going to be a film star. Simple as that. Oddly enough, I didn't much like the idea, so I spent the next few years denying myself that certainty. Focusing my dreams on the safety of horses and animals. Nowadays, having thoroughly digested the truth of everything being within me and me being within everything, I regret having wasted so much of my life stubbornly refusing to accept these 'cosmic' proddings.

I asked Mummy many years later why I was left out of those family photographs. 'Oh, darling, making you dress up would have been too much of an effort, you have no idea what a fuss you kicked up every time I asked you to go anywhere, it just wasn't worth my while.'

CHAPTER EIGHTEEN

MY CHILDHOOD began with a Fairy Tale, then faded somewhat into a Fairly Tale, and then, at the age of eight was disintegrating into a Common Tale, because I was getting angrier. Not merely at the death of Micky, Pip, Puffin and my feathered friends, but with school too.

Even as I neared the end of my last term at Miss Ingrams', the school experience was doing its utmost to scar me for life. I grew ever more doubting and frightened, unable to grasp anything except the general consensus of opinion that I was stupid. I was walking up my own dark cul-de-sac, powerless to grasp any opportunity to prove them wrong, except by rebellion.

This got me nowhere except standing with aching legs in murky, unhelpful schoolroom corners, where there was to be even less opportunity for growth or knowledge, let alone any hint of self-esteem. Too much undermining, because of my stammer and dyslexia, too much optimism crushed behind the dark ages of the school gates. Yes, I was ANGRY, all right.

I moved on to a school in Chelmsford which was, on the surface, just another decent little county school. It had a motto above the main hall: 'I am, I can, I ought, I will.' I knew I *was*, I knew I *could*, I knew I *ought*, I knew I *must*, but how to get at it, how to break through the blindness in my head and reach down to where my potential was screaming for release was another matter. If it hadn't been for that motto, I wouldn't have kept afloat.

My two years at St Anne's School in Chelmsford were a farce, if only I had been in a laughing mood. No such luck. My head was held high with arrogance, hiding fenced-up fury. My teeth perpetually ground out anger, which gave birth in my dreams to a mass of rabbit nibblings all along the rim of my top sheet. For some reason, Mummy believed I was doing it on purpose, but how could it have been on purpose when I was totally unaware I was doing it? This continued for many years, off and on, whenever I was fuming inside.

English reading classes were my bleakest dread, for I couldn't read and, what's more, my stammer as well as my ears had made me the laughing stock of the school. In order to save myself from these weekly humiliations I had to time it just right. I would excuse myself – seep out unobtrusively to have a pee – just as the girl before me was about to begin her turn at reading. On one occasion, though, on returning to my place, the teacher said, 'Ah! Sarah, perhaps you would kindly read for me now? Please start at the third paragraph from the bottom.'

I just sat, stuck to my seat, staring at the page, completely at a loss as to what a 'paragraph' looked like. And was third the same as three? 'Come on now, we're all waiting.' I could feel the eyes of the whole class upon me, but then it all went black and silver. 'We're waiting!'

'I c-c-c-c-c-c-c-c-c-c-c-c-can't,' I said, finally.

There was an embarrassed hush right through the classroom. 'And why not?' she demanded, leaving me no choice but to answer.

Here goes, I thought. I won't tell them it's because I can't read, I'd best tell the other half of the truth. 'Because of m-m-m-m-m-m-m-m-m-my st-st-st-st-st-stammer.'

Everyone hooted. 'Shush, be quiet all of you. Sarah, stay on afterwards, I want to talk to you.' That was the only help I'd ever received, up till then. Mother was given the name of a woman who apparently had worked wonders with stammerers. I knew something needed to be done. I was now almost nine years old, and my stammer was not improving – well, it was, I'd had so much practice it was now perfect!

The lady lived in a sweet little cottage. She was slight, small and silvery. I found her shyness as comforting as the cottage itself, which was overloaded with pot-pourri. 'Speak the speech, I pray you, as I pronounce it to you trippingly on the tongue.'

She gave me a speech to learn – Elizabeth Barrett Browning's *cri de coeur* to her father. I've always been able to summon it up; it trickles out so easily, gliding up the silky pathway of Memory Lane, linking up directly to the calm tip of my non-stammering, non-tripping tongue. How could it ever be forgotten? It was the first time in my life that I was able not only to memorize something by heart, thanks to Daddy's and Nel's patience of an evening, but when I recited it back – SLOWLY – as if by magic I didn't stammer at all.

Stammering is caused, she explained, by thoughts leaping ahead of the ability to turn them into words. 'There's a simple explanation,' she said. The brain has two sides: the intuitive, creative side, and the logical side. Like a chest of drawers, with a creative drawer and a memory drawer. When a speech is learnt off by heart, it gets put into the memory drawer, and when the already constructed sentences are pulled out of the memory drawer they automatically get regurgitated at a smoother, more coherent pace.

Thank God for that little lady. Unfortunately most schools focus on the logical side of the brain, which is such a pity, since it straitjackets almost two-thirds of our creative capacity. Dyslexics have enormous difficulty getting access to information embedded in the logical side of the brain. I hope nowadays that the school system has more understanding, and therefore patience with this.

I didn't stammer when I sang either, though my singing dreams were fading because of everyone's attitude. Mummy did kindly take me to a local singing teacher, who said, quite simply, 'Forget it.'

During that last term at St Anne's, I had to sit the Roedean School entrance exam. Mother kept telling me it was the best school in England, and I kept on pleading with all my might to be allowed to go on to Chelmsford High School, but she said I wasn't clever enough and there was a great shortage of day schools in our area.

'I'm failing the exam!' I said.

'Oh, no, you're not!' said Mummy with a mysterious glow of confidence.

On the day of the exam, a teacher put me in a small room with a window overlooking some lovely horse-chestnut trees and gave me my exam papers. As I sat there, always stuck, half-way up the horse-chestnut tree, she'd barge in, lean over me, and from time to time give me little hints. If these failed to ignite, she'd give me little nudges which conveniently tumbled into a few answers. Obviously Mummy was determined to win the Roedean Battle, by fair means or foul. I went along with the plan because she promised me that if I got into Roedean she would one day buy me a palomino, like Roy Rogers's Trigger. I chose to go against my intuition because of Palomino Promises! Corruption had set in.

CHAPTER NINETEEN

SUMMER HOLS arrived at last! Mizzer had a new trick; he could rear up and stand with his front legs on a barrel. Mummy's Palomino Promises turned into a little Pekinese puppy challed Chan. Chan was not a lap-dog, more a riding or bike dog, for everywhere that Mizzer went Chan was sure to go, in my arms, or sometimes alone. Even when Mizzer reared up on to the barrel he managed to keep his balance. And he loved sitting admiring the view from my bike basket – a real goer was Chan.

I had a new impossible trick I was practising: doing a handstand on Mizzer's rump while he was standing on the barrel. I have to admit that I found this trick a bit of a bugger but I kept persevering.

I'd sworn Nel to secrecy about knowing I was going to be a film star. She looked at me dubiously through her curry-comb and said, 'If that fails, Pusscat, why not join the circus?' This seemed an absolutely wizard second choice, especially since Daddy had suggested it too. So I was determined to have two strings to my bow, especially as Nel didn't seem to think that I was ever going to make it as a film star. 'You have to be really beautiful to be one of them,' she said regretfully, while kicking Mizzer on to jump a home-made wall. So I practised circus tricks every day. I could hang by my knees on the trapeze, later by my feet. I practised somersaults, cartwheels and handstands till the cows came home.

I wanted to stand up on Mizzer's rump while cantering, but I couldn't get him to keep cantering on, and balancing on a pony's rump while trotting is very hard. So I made a long bamboo whip, with which I could threaten to sting him gently if he slowed down. When he slowed down to a trot yet again, I gave him the tiniest little flick of a sting on his flank. His response was very clear, and to the point: he wanted me off, and succeeded – every time.

I got fed up with all the falling off. After really hurting myself with a crack on the back of my neck, I decided to practise falling off on purpose until I could do it without hurting myself. Although I never mastered that particular balancing trick with any grace, I can at least fall off with some. (All this practising falling off wasn't wasted: twenty years later it came in handy when I did my own stunts in a cowboy movie in America.)

That summer polio was the word heard on every nervous whispering lip, on the buses, at school, at parties, especially at the Chase swimming pool. Polio was successfully infiltrating both fear and panic into most family circles. Rather like Aids today, it was becoming an epidemic. The Chase swimming pool gradually became emptier and emptier – perfect! Mummy didn't like me going, but she also liked me out of her hair, which put her in two minds over this polio scare.

I was becoming quite a good diver, possibly from having fallen off Mizzer so many times. After falling on to hard ground, dropping into water seemed like falling off a log. So with nothing whatever to fear, and even the occasional belly-flop turning into a piece of feather cake, I naturally became really daring. There was nothing too clever about this, except that I managed to impress Daddy sufficiently for him to introduce me to all the diving possibilities – back flips, swallow dives, handstand dives and hundreds of belly-flops!

My first nasty experience was after a neat, almost splash-less swallow dive. I was alone in the pool. I pushed up the way I always did it, by using my hand against the bottom, or the side, when my right hand got caught behind a fat pipe, which ran the length of the bottom of the pool. I was quite unable to break free. In the panic that followed I even tried ripping my hand from my wrist – after all it was my right hand that was stuck, I would never have to write again. (Daddy lost the battle for a left-handed tennis-playing daughter, though not altogether because Pooker turned out to be left-handed too – wouldn't she just?) Although I make fun of it now, at the time it was desperately lonely and ominous down there, but I think I was too young to see how danger-ously close to death I was. While tugging away at the blasted drain, I became aware of extra air coming from somewhere within my body. When the possibility of death did eventually sneak into my head and I thought to myself, this is it, I'm about to die – Mummy was right all along, I managed to find another little pocket of air from somewhere. I knew I had my brothers to thank for my extra lung capacity, due to all the drowning practice I got in the bath.

Suddenly I felt a tingling, a warm release (not the silent P in swimming either!). I felt a shadow move across – there was someone else in the pool. I saw a man doing the crawl above me in jazzy trunks. Surely he might see me? I prayed fervently to Adam that he would see me.

My prayers were answered. He saw me on his next dive. He followed my arm down from my shoulder to where the fingers were trapped. He then prised the pipe sufficiently apart for me to yank my hand free. Ouch! The pain made me so dizzy, that for a moment I forgot how to swim. The man was most helpful and kind. He life-saved me to the edge and started kissing me, deep in my mouth. I wasn't sure that I liked the kissing very much, but I felt better quite quickly. I kept thanking him, but he was more keen on giving me a lecture on how I must never ever swim alone again, and would I promise him?

When I got home I couldn't tell anyone of my near-drowning, because I wouldn't be allowed to go to the Chase ever again. 'What have you done to your fingers, Pusscat?'

'Oh, M-Mizzer trod on me by mistake as I was cleaning out his feet.'

'It looks mighty swollen – I'll have a good look after supper.' End of that little Chase Tale.

But I have one more little Chase Tale. Chuzzer, back from his wheeze cure in Switzerland, was away at prep school with Jukes, Summerfields, in Oxford. He wrote Mummy and Daddy a letter saying that he could now 'dive like a knife!' This was excellent news from my point of view. Before he went to prep school, he had hated swimming. Hooray! Now I would have someone to swim with during the long summer hols. (Jukes would never come with me, especially since Daddy had given him his film camera and the latest gadget, a wire recorder. This was the first form of recording machine, before the tape recorder was invented. It was exactly the same, only you recorded on to a thin silver wire rather than tape. Jukes was very nifty with these new fangled gadgets and machines; revelling in all the latest inventions. He was forever roping me in to help with his stories, poking the microphone under my nose. 'It's vital, Pusscat. You'll become famous, your cockerel will represent Pathé News, think of that!' Without bragging my animal noises were pretty realistic, so Jukes was keen to record them. Although my cockerel noise, thanks to Berty's instruction, was hot stuff, I could also do pigs, hens (broody or otherwise), goats, sheep, dog bark, cats, donkeys, birds, cows, and yodel.

'Shall I sing "Oh, Danny Boy—"'

'Thank you so much, Theda Bara,' said Jukes, quickly pulling away the mike before I could finish. '"The pipes the pipes are calling."' Turning to me while switching off he said, 'That's your best Pathé News so far.' I asked Jukes who Theda Bara was, but I don't think he knew.)

Finally after a great deal of badgering I got Chuzzer in the mood to bicycle with me for a swim at the Chase. Being with Chuzzer were the best times for me, I'm not sure why. Maybe it's because, when he desires – it's all tied up with his damn wheeze – to be a good companion, he has no equal. He was the sun for me, and when he shone it was powerful stuff, putting all else into shadow.

As we arrived at the pool, I noticed three old ladies, knitting, in the shade at the far corner. Apart from them, there wasn't a soul to be seen. We both went to change. When I reappeared Chuzzer was bouncing like a true professional, testing the board's spring. I was quite floored by his keenness to get going. Then, with one final leap in the air, he did the most magnificent swallow dive. Indeed he could dive like a knife – I had just witnessed it. I had to admit that his swallow dive was a great deal more elegant than mine. But this was always the case with Chuzzer, he was a natural athlete, and if it hadn't been for his wheeze, why, the whole world would have been his oyster.

As I stood at the edge of the pool, contemplating the fact that he'd left hardly a trace of a ripple, the penny didn't drop so much as tinkle slightly on the outer rim of my brain. Why hadn't Chuzzer reappeared yet?

He's showing off, I thought, he'll suddenly appear right up at the shallow end just to surprise me.

But he didn't. I peered into the water, straining my eyes to see beneath the thick mist of chlorine – and there he was flailing in the misty depths, right up the deep end. 'Help!' I shouted across to the three old women. 'G-get help, my brother's drowning!'

They turned to each other, back to me, and then simultaneously took up their damned knitting again. 'Help! Please go and get help – my brother's drowning!'

Surely Chuzzer wouldn't be able to dive like a knife without being able to swim? It wasn't possible, was it? What if the 'drowning toad' – his nursery prank – had turned into a much more wicked, more sophisticated prep school trick?

No – I knew it was for real.

In I plunged. But when I reached Chuzzer I couldn't find his head, or his tail, or anything. He was swirling around in a frenzied ball of panic.

When he did see me, he kind of leapt on top of me. I couldn't do a thing – redundant as a flea beneath a prancing bull elephant in musk. He had chosen my head as his means of getting to the edge. My whole face was beneath the water, while Chuzzer panicked, paddled and fought his way back to safety. Absolutely horrid. I could neither get him off, nor breathe air in – I had surely had it. I couldn't see anything, only feel this great weight above me, and the blinding pain of aching, near bursting lungs.

Then suddenly the gigantic weight began to lift. It was canny Chuzzer climbing to safety. Having used me as a buoy or a raft, he had triumphantly managed to paddle himself back to the edge of the pool.

On the edge at last we both just flaked out motionless, like two beached whales, unable to function. I couldn't breathe but it didn't matter, I was too far gone to care.

Some time later, the shock took over. We tumbled into the most unstoppable bout of giggling I'd ever experienced. 'Dive like a knife! Swim like a brick!' How ridiculous it all was! And how absolutely absurd it must have looked to those three old ladies knitting in the shade, if they had bothered to look.

Chuzzer never would discuss what happened that day, the episode was put into no man's land. I think he was inwardly grateful, just too embarrassed to talk about it. He was certainly swimming adequately on our next holiday.

This time to Rappallo in Italy, with Daddy's American partner Bill Brassert, and his son Lex Barker who either was or had recently been Tarzan – there have been so many. I dreaded these family holidays abroad. All I wanted to do was to stay at home with my animals. I know it sounds ungrateful, I know I was damned lucky to be going to somewhere as beautiful as Rappallo, but all things are relative and for me it was catastrophic. I was off to boarding school in ten weeks' time, and my whole world was on the verge of collapse.

Rappallo was indeed beautiful, but as I looked out of the hotel window upon the small sun-blessed bay beneath, with the crumbling ochre buildings rippling the water orange signalling the oncoming sunset, all I could think of was the gymkhanas I was missing at home, the horse shows I could have entered Mizzer for.

Swimming out in the tempting turquoise stillness of late afternoon, I had a rather too intimate entanglement with a huge octopus – it probably wasn't as big as all that, but at nine years old it seemed quite large enough. However much I shook it, it clung. I didn't want to start screaming, because only cry-babies scream, and also because I was well aware that I was trespassing in its territory. (This kinship I had with animals – all creatures, in fact – should not be mistaken for some compassionate super-awareness, that it might be in danger of cracking itself up to be. It was simply that animals were considered inferior and so was I. Humans continued underestimating our intelligence, so it was always a case of us (the creatures) against the rest.)

It's tricky guessing the sex of an octopus, but by the way it was climbing upwards, I think it was a fella. As I watched him entwining his tentacles around my upper thigh, suddenly I reached a point – *my* boundary – beyond which I could not let him trespass. I could bear it no more, I began to scream. 'Help!'

Tarzan lazily raised his great torso from his towel, and sauntered self-consciously, shading his eyes from the glare, towards the water's edge. He waved to me, to let me know I'd been heard and that he was about to dive in, when he had second thoughts, paused, looked at the time, and then backtracked to toss his watch on to his towel. He blundered forward a second time and suddenly stopped again.

I could have been swallowed up by this time, if the octopus had fancied me sufficiently. What the hell was Tarzan up to? He returned to his towel, folded it around his watch (it was a beautiful watch, admittedly), then – not a moment too soon – he transformed himself into the Tarzan of old. Yes, Tarzan plunged forward into a sort of dive-cum-belly-flop, and crawled out to save the damsel in distress – save her from the dragon's jaw. How about that? I didn't realize how powerfully an octopus's suckers suck. After Tarzan had finished pulling the monster off, I was left with strange reddish purple marks that took ages to fade completely.

When Tarzan had finally ripped away the last tentacle, he got the octopus by its neck, and began to swim off with it.

'Where are you going?' I panted, trying to keep abreast of him.

'I'm just going over to that rock.'

I wasn't quite sure what he meant, until I saw him bash the poor octopus's head again and again against the side of the rock, until it was nothing but pulp.

From then on I was unable to identify Tarzan with the hero I knew. I had mistakenly put him on a pedestal. I'd seen one of his films, and it seemed to me that he understood and protected the creatures in their own habitat – if not Tarzan, then who? For surely Tarzan was in the jungle as an equal to the beasts whose habitat it was? And here he was bashing an ocean creature to pulp in its own habitat. 'Mea culpa,' mea pulpa!'

That was the day I experienced, for the first time, something that, as I grew up, would sadly become the norm. My heroes tumbling off their pedestals and turning to dust before my very eyes. Yet it was my fault for putting them on the pedestal in the first place.

Soon after we returned home I began to feel rather ill. I caught Mummy on the landing coming out of her bedroom with Pooker. 'Mummy, I think I've got polio.'

She looked daggers at me. 'Well darling, you only have yourself to blame if you have. I warned you about the dangers of catching polio in public swimming pools.'

'But I haven't been to the Chase since we came home from Italy.'

'Doesn't matter, it takes some weeks to surface,' she replied over her shoulder, as she descended the staircase in her *Sunset Boulevard* kind of way. I ran downstairs behind her.

'Feel m-my head.' I grabbed her hand and placed it on my head.

She let it rest there for a wafer of a second. 'If you ask me this polio of yours is a touch of the Roedean Terrors. You have no temperature so off you go.'

Three days later I was lying in bed with my first headache, sticky fever and feet turned to clay. Dr Stevens sat on the end of my bed and leaned in close. 'Open your mouth, and say "Ah".' As he peered down my throat, he automatically opened his own in sympathy – the sight was far from pleasant, so was the smell.

Mummy stood over us, with her arms crossed, leaning on one hip smoking a cigarette. 'Well, Dr Stevens?'

'I'd like to test her knees, Mrs Miles.'

Out of bed I got . . . I remember being quite taken aback at how difficult it was, not helped by the panic beginning to surface, thanks to Dr Stevens's repeated shakes of the head.

He tapped my kneecaps with a metal object. 'Can you feel that?'

'Yes, Dr Stevens, I can feel you tapping my kneecaps.' He kept repeating it until they were quite sore.

'What's the matter, Doctor?' said Mummy, her voice more high-pitched than usual, as she puffed away on her cigarette.

Dr Stevens cleared his throat. 'I'm getting no sign of any reflexes. Can we go out for a moment, while I get my other bag from the car?' In his defence I must admit that Dr Stevens was a rotten liar. I could hear them both whispering at the top of the stairs.

I knew even before they returned that it was polio, and wondered if I had willed it on myself, because I was sure I had polio on many other occasions too, but they were merely crying wolf. But what *is* crying wolf other than bringing towards us that which we fear the most? Because I believe thought is the seed of all things, I've learnt that it's best to pay careful attention to what I am thinking at all times, otherwise – I am, I can, I ought, I will get polio!

Pooker was now in my nursery and I was in a tiny room at the opposite end of the house next to Jukes's palace. I didn't mind too much because my box room faced south, and I could see Mizzer in his field. I like small rooms anyway, they are more protective. Naturally Owly looked down on me, sharing my terror.

It was a strange time, lying there waiting for the polio to go the whole hog or gradually fade away. There were, apparently, quite a number of polio cases where it failed to take its cruel paralysing final grip.

'You'll pull through, Pusscat, I know you will,' said Mummy one day, testing my reflexes. 'Just keep praying to Jesus.' If my reflexes continued to give no response, the outlook was bleak, but no one knew, not even Mummy, if or when rain might stop play.

I was trapped both to the left and to the right, two great octopuses ready to entangle me, and suck me under – Roedean School or paralysis for life.

I didn't do any praying as such, because I was in rather a muddle over all that sort of thing. I still placed the image of Adam before me when I wanted something, but I was beginning to have many doubts, thanks to Jukes who kept telling me that Adam never existed. School had taught me a little about the Jesus chap that Mummy seemed to hold such store by. Daddy, on the other hand, didn't believe a word of it. 'Nonsense, Pusscat, if you want to get religious about anything, then look out of the window, at the trees, the hills and the sunset, that'll be the nearest to God you'll ever be likely to get.'

'But why does Mummy love Jesus, then?'

'Pusscat, Jesus is fine for Mummy, in fact all religions are fine, if you need them. But one day, when they've all managed to fight each other into extinction, my trees, hills and sunsets will still be here.'

'But don't you ever pray?'

'Not really. I just feel full of gratitude for the beauty around me. That old oak tree, for instance—'

'Daddy, the rope-ladder's still frayed.'

'I'll get it fixed this weekend.' I gave him a look. 'I promise,' he said.

There was a long pause, and we both knew what it hid. He gave me a great big hug. 'Pusscat, I'll bet that old oak tree will get you well in no time at all.'

Daddy wasn't a gambling man, usually turning out the loser, but on this occasion he won the bet and I recovered completely.

CHAPTER TWENTY

MY MOTHER was all dressed up in her new bottle green suit, with velvet collar and cuffs and a cloche hat. She was the Belle of the Station Ball. The other mothers looked smart, but Mummy – quite simply – was a star.

I was trying not to burst, too. There were many girls crying upon their mothers' breasts, but I was not going to join them. It was hard, though, with the new uniform, the smell of the station, the impending separation, the unknown, the strange girls, all of whom I was sure were going to be much too upper crust for the likes of me.

Every item of my school uniform was so large that the hems had to be turned over double, ending up near my tummy button on the inside. That day we were all in our woollen travelling dresses of different colours; mine was itchy maroon, and my neck and arms were driving me mad.

For lessons we wore navy blue tunics, with a white shirt and tie, which at least didn't itch. But with everything we had to wear the obligatory great cloak, sweeping the ground, made out of very heavy material. My twelve-inch hem made me bottom-heavy, I felt I might fall over with every step. 'It looks fine, Pusscat, and it'll last you.'

But there was a plus side to these overwhelming clothes: my school hat, thank God for it! I'd managed to tuck my hair and ears firmly under it, so in that department all was fine.

Father

Mother

The first picture of me

But do I belong here?

A picnic with our governess Miss Cripps, Chuzzer and Jukes

Mother takes the biscuit

Me and Chuzzer – I thought I'd pushed him in the pond

Below: The house where I was born, Mill House, Ingatestone

Father and Mother in the garden at Mill House

With Jukes and Chuzzer – I've got a Crunchie bar in my knickers

Above: Mischief

Right: Jukes with Micky

Charlie

Chan

Above: Me with Uncle Willie and Mauzie on Kitty – lucky Mauzie

Above: Brand

Barn Mead

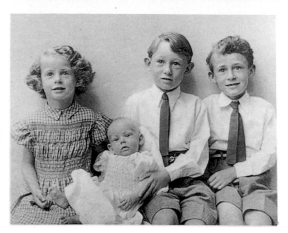

Top: I want the waterwings

Above: Got them!

Left: Enter Pooker

The girls began to get on the train. Mummy saw this, and I think wanted to be off before the flood gates burst forth. But she needn't have feared – I wasn't going to let them. I was biting the inside of my mouth very hard; the pain of that, combined with the itchy woollen frock, helped to keep my mind off the parting.

Mummy was most graceful and kind to me that day, probably because she was so relieved to be getting rid of me at last. But I'm sure I recognized a look between us as the train began to move, a quick flash of mutual respect, as if she was proud of me for maintaining my stiff upper lip. It might have been relief at seeing the back of me but I don't think so, for most of the other girls were sobbing by now, and I wasn't – not yet.

But it wasn't just that. I do believe I saw something else come between us in that moment, something deeper than merely mother and daughter. And then it was gone – and so was she.

I bagged a corner seat next to the window and gazed out of it, chewing on my mouth, willing it to bleed, as I chuffed down to Brighton all alone. Watching the greyness of the city disperse into the crisp cleanliness of the countryside, I was reminded of another lonely train journey. I was about seven years old and Daddy had put me on the train from London, in a carriage with a nice friendly lady, who promised to see that I was all right. I knew Mummy was going to meet me at Ingatestone when I arrived.

Chuffing out of Liverpool Street through the East End there were masses of high concrete buildings being built at that time and they always struck me as sad and ugly. I asked Daddy once why they were there. 'They have to get rid of the slums, Pusscat.' Looking hard at the slums, albeit from a railway carriage, I was struck by the earthy atmosphere, a bit like Ted's gypsy encampment, and as I watched the children playing in the streets it got me pondering why Daddy thought the high rises could possibly be better.

At Ilford the lady collected her bag and said, 'This is my stop. Now don't forget, you have Romford, Brentwood, then Ingatestone.'

When we stopped at Romford I knew I still had plenty of time to go to the loo before Ingatestone, so off I went. I bolted the door, like Mummy always did, put paper on the seat, like Mummy always did, and washed my hands afterwards. Pulled the plug and went to open the door. I couldn't. The door was well and truly jammed. I was locked in the loo. Out of the window I saw we were pulling out of Brentwood. I began to panic. Next stop, Ingatestone.

I went back to the window – it wasn't the opening kind. My panic grew. I banged on the window, I banged on the door, I screamed and screamed.

Ingatestone came and went and I was trembling like a tadpole. What was I going to do? Where was the train going to stop? At the other side of Kingdom Come? HELP!

But there was no one to hear me. I sat on the lavatory, way past weeping.

We chuffed into Chelmsford – why had no one heard my cries? I screamed blue murder at Chelmsford station – but to no avail.

When the train stopped at Colchester I tried my powerful lung capacity again. I let the whole world know that I was trapped. I banged on the windows with all my might, tears streaming, knees wobbling.

'Are you all right in there?'

'HELP!'

'No need to panic, miss,' said a kindly voice, 'this train stops here – Colchester's the end of the line.'

'Get me out! Get me out!'

'Calm down and listen. I'm going to push the door inwards. When I say pull you pull the bolt as hard as you can. OK?'

'OK.'

Miraculously the door opened, and a very tall man in uniform came in and studied the lock.

'It's these old trains, the doors are all warping, we'll have to see to that. I'm so sorry, miss. Come with me and we'll sort you out.'

I was put in the Station Master's office, where there was a warm fire. The kind man brought me a cup of tea and a biscuit and the panic gradually began to subside.

I didn't know our telephone number, only the name of our house. After a very long wait, two hours at least, Mother came through the door, and let me cry on her tummy.

My mouth was bleeding, I had to go to the loo. I pushed my way past mounds of navy blue uniforms, and bolted myself in – checking the lock first, this time. Then, sitting on the seat – paper down first, as Mummy always taught me – the flood gates opened.

I stayed there for the rest of the journey.

Getting off the train at Brighton, there was a real buzz of excitement from the older girls, gossip ringing out as they swapped their summer hols stories. I followed the crowd, hardly aware of what I was doing.

'New girl, are you, for the Junior House?' said a sad-looking skinny lady.

'Yes,' I replied regretfully.

'Yes, ma'am.'

'Yes, ma'am.'

'Follow me, and don't be too down-hearted, it'll be fun when you get into the swing of things.'

Little did I realize, sitting there in the school bus looking out on Brighton sea front for the first time, what a major part this town would play in my life in the years to come. I noticed Royal Crescent and thought how handsome and elegant it was. Laurence Olivier would come to live there. A bit further on was Lewes Crescent, which was to become my parents' next and final home.

Suddenly a shiver went down my spine. There, on the cliff above, a great fortress stood so arrogantly, as if it knew it ruled the waves. It looked icy cold, implacable in its grim austerity. It must be a prison, I thought, because although the walls were high enough, barbed wire had been added. Poor prisoners, I mused, as the bus proceeded to brake, and make a left turn into its formidable gates.

With the realization that this was indeed Roedean School, a grey numbness began to seep into my bones, from which I knew, while I was there, I would never escape. Not only did it take a relentless grip on me during this Roedean period, but it must have numbed out my brain as well. For try as I may, I can only remember fragments, which I find most irritating. I've often noticed when the pain of life really becomes unbearable, I switch off.

The Junior School was separate from the main building, but just as unfriendly. I was shown into the long passageway of the dormitory, to my tiny wooden cubicle, with nothing but a bed, and the sea. I looked through the window. What could have been sadder than the English Channel out of season on that cold rough afternoon? No trees at all. How could anywhere on earth not have any trees? I stood there grappling with the fact that this was to be my home for the next six or seven years.

No animals either. Then suddenly it all made sense. Mummy wanted me as far away from trees and animals as possible. Obviously my habit of talking out loud must have concerned them sufficiently to warrant a transplant. How they had succeeded.

Still, I had Ted, so I put him on the pillow on top of my nightie. Taking my hat off was quite a moment, my cover would be blown and they'd all see my ears. I concealed them with my hair as best I could. Then, taking a deep breath, I went down the main staircase – spiffing banisters! Best to wait a while, I thought, as I followed the other girls to find the hall for prayers.

At that first assembly in the great hall, I looked around the hall to see if there were any faces that I took to. There weren't, but I can remember looking at the girl's hair directly in front of me, and wishing mine was like hers. It wasn't like any hair I had ever seen before. It had a purple gloss that shimmered in the evening light, even more than Ted the gypsy's, remarkably luxurious deep dark chestnut.

What is that whiff that permeates even well-kept public institutions? In the beginning it almost knocked me out. It's hard to believe that soon I wouldn't notice it at all: a daunting smell made up of dusty old books, disinfectant, cabbage and ripe games shoes.

The glossy girl in front turned towards me. She must have been foreign, I thought, like a Red Indian with a fine profile, haughty and proud. She was what I called beautiful. She happened to be in the same dormitory, and was the youngest of the three de Barros sisters, Virginia, Carol and Lilith. They were famous in school, the 'Brazilian Beauties', and had a millionaire father who was some famous big-wig in Brazilian politics. We became good friends and still are to this day.

I sat behind her in class too, so that I could gaze at her hair, the only pleasure I got in those foul classrooms. Although we all called her Lilith, her two sisters called her Lilita – I liked Lilita best. My nickname at Roedean was Smilo. I liked this name. SMiles are good for putting up a bluff. I have a large mouth beneath my stiff upper lip, which tends to make me look rather merry. I try to tilt the corners up to prevent the dark moods from taking too much of a hold.

We were settled in the gaunt classroom; it was Latin. Latin was good the first day for the mistress said, 'Does anyone here know any Latin?'

Since nobody stood up, 'Yes, ma'am,' I said.

'Well, let's hear it, then.'

All eyes were upon me. 'Amo – amas – amat – amamus – amatis – amant.' It was my party piece – Jukes had taught me.

'That's excellent, now what does it mean?'

'It's the verb to love,' I replied with great confidence.

She peered around the room. 'Anybody else know any Latin?'

No one did so, for the first and only time, I was top of the class. The verb to love, my party piece, remained the only Latin I ever was able to learn, everyone very soon passed me by. Perhaps Jukes should have been my teacher.

Thank God for sports, for without them I would have run away time and time again. The playing fields became my home, the essential release from all my pent-up classroom frustrations. I liked lacrosse best. It's a Red Indian game, and the only game that exists where there is no rule against killing your opponent. With the lacrosse stick cradled close to your chest, right in front of your face, quite a lot of damage can be inflicted, if you're sufficiently accurate, that is. No wonder it's forbidden at the Olympics.

I became very useful at all the sports on offer – lacrosse, rounders, netball, cricket, though the Junior House didn't have a cricket team, which I found infuriating because of my rather nifty googly-ish bowl. Netball was a great game, perhaps a little tame, but the need for quick-witted accuracy appealed to me so much that I found myself captain, but not for long. I only wanted to score goals, not cope with the never-ending responsibilities – thanks a ton. My tennis, too, came on a treat. I have all the strokes and I'm strong and fast, but I lack the temperament, so Daddy said, unpredictable under pressure. As soon as I'm ahead, I cave in. Typically British – pathetic!

I've had a skin problem since birth. Unless I'm constantly sloshing myself with grease my lips, heels and hands crack severely in winter. On two occasions I had to go to have the cracks sewn up in hospital because they refused to heal. Jolly inconvenient, loving the outdoors as I do. Before breakfast every morning we had to run a couple of miles up and around the old racetrack at the top of the Downs. Up there the wind howled so ferociously I couldn't even feel my lips splitting.

There were endless idiotic rules. A classic example: if you had orange juice, you couldn't have milk to follow. For some reason you had to have tea. I found this rule unacceptable, since milk and orange juice were all I could take pleasure in. I went to Miss Pike, the house mistress, to ask her why this was the rule. She replied that it wasn't my business to enquire about the rules, but to obey them. Silly spikey Pikey twat! Another rule was that *ladies* never scoop up their food with their fork; no, even peas must be balanced on the top. I'd never heard of such a silly rule, so I made use of it. I'd try very hard to balance my peas, but they'd go all over the shop. Over me, down my woolly itchy dress, over the table, the floor – everywhere. Eventually, because of my messy eating habits, or indeed not eating at all, I was sent to the kitchen for punishment.

This turned out to be the 'in' place! So much cosier than the dining room. The maids were kind to me, I felt a rapport with them and they with me. They'd give me titbits and as much fruit as my heart desired. Naturally I behaved worse than ever in the boring dining room, flicking my peas everywhere, just to get back into the kitchen. I also learnt from a maid that the reason we weren't allowed to drink orange juice followed by milk was because it all curdled inside the stomach giving us cramps. Stomach cramps? Codswallop.

Wherever we went, it was always two by two in a crocodile. Left out of the school gates and along the coast to Rottingdean, past St Dunstan's School for the blind. How lucky I was. Although I was grossly unhappy at Roedean, at least I wasn't blind, nor even paralysed, come to that.

I liked going for walks so I could spy out the lie of the land and plan my escape. I'd already snuck off to have a wee reconnoitre around the outer perimeter. The outlook was very bleak indeed – high walls and barbed wire, with the great gates permanently closed unless in use. Roedean had been used as an army barracks during the war, and apparently there were secret passages going down to the sea front. If only I could have dropped back from the rest of them, to explore on my own. Unfortunately crocodile form didn't allow this.

Lilith and I did, however, find underground passages that ran beneath the school, leading into a secret underground room. We called this 'Hatus', which is, I believe, a 'voodoo' word in Brazilian. Hatus reminded me of Mauzie's lofts – I expected to find suitcases full of money. In time we permitted other girls to join, and it became the in place. You were simply a nobody unless you were a member of Hatus.

I often went down to Hatus, it was the only place where I could be alone. I still needed this, not only because of natters with King George, which I was still in the habit of having from time to time, I'm ashamed to say, but because of my need for silence.

Our trailing cloaks did the work of a dozen maids, as we marched forth every day from the Junior House, across to the Senior School and the chapel. Those canny mistresses were killing two birds with one stone. Two by two, clippity-clop, swish-swish in our neat crocodile, sweeping great areas clean and smooth – our wake fit for a king.

The school chapel was linked to the Senior School by echoing cloisters. I found it fearfully intimidating passing through the Senior School, though it all looked very impressive, if you were up to that sort of cleverness, but personally I was very relieved to be only passing through. To me it was as daunting as its smell, which later would boomerang back into my nostrils, whenever I visited a university; a smell of élitist academia, the dreaded stench of intellectual accomplishment. The chapel itself was pretty spectacular, presided over by the headmistress Miss Horrobin, known as 'the Horror'. She was a vulture hovering ready to pounce, as she loomed over us from her pulpit, shrouded from head to foot in black, topped off with a mortar board. There was a beautiful choir, which I longed to join but that would never happen. I had been put to the very back at singing practice, and told that I must sing as quiet as a mouse – naturally.

Some of us practised swooning, so that a mistress would help us out of chapel as quickly as possible. They had to be jolly authentic swoons, though, to pull the wool over a mistress's eyes. I never managed to pull that one, probably due to my appalling overacting but those talented few with first-class swoons were well rewarded, being gently escorted back to the dorm where they were free of the sermon – lucky devils!

One day I was called from class to see Matron. I was always being called to Matron because of my splitting skin, for it was her job to see that it never reached the sewing-up stage, but I'd never been called away from class before. This wasn't good news at all, I thought, climbing the stairs.

Matron was decidedly disgruntled. She shoved my top sheet under my nose. 'What's this?' she said.

'I don't know, Matron.' Damn! I'd returned to my old sheet nibbling habit – what a bore.

'It can't continue.'

'I didn't know I was doing it, Matron.'

'Get a grip of yourself, we can't afford to have all the sheets peppered with holes just because you don't know what you're doing. Do I make myself clear?'

How can you stop doing something that you only do in your sleep?

I became too frightened to go to sleep in case I started nibbling. I'd change the sheet top to bottom. I tried pushing the sheet away, placing my cloak over me instead, thinking that my teeth couldn't possibly gnaw their way through that thick material, and woke up to find little holes all across it. Why was I doing such a stupid thing? Why couldn't I stop myself?

Endless nights spent with the bed stripped bare, tossing and turning, angry winds deafening me and the loose window panes rattling. No way of protecting my neck from the piercing draughts, except by pulling the bedclothes up to my chin, but then I'd nibble. I didn't care, better to shiver than have punishment from Matron. I wanted to go home, I wanted Charlie, Mizzer and Chan. I missed Charlie most – his safe smell, his warm wobbly bits.

Once, through my nightly shiverings, I heard moans and a strange rhythmic bouncing coming from a cubicle. I went to see if everything was all right. I crept around the curtain. The girl was obviously in some pain, grunting and squirming about. Naturally I moved closer to see if she needed any comforting. She promptly leapt out of her skin.

'Ah! What the hell are *you* doing?'

Why was she so furious? Had I shocked her or something? I remained baffled by her embarrassed fury for quite some time.

In the changing rooms downstairs the lavatories were divided by wooden partitions. One day, after games, I was sitting on the loo, pondering, when I noticed some writing high up on the wall. I stood on the loo seat to get a closer look. It read: 'I stuck my finger up Mary's quim, and she liked it.'

What was a quim? I would have liked to have asked someone, but there was no one I knew well enough to confess my ignorance. Was a quim like Alison's slit? Was it a botty hole? Why did she like it? If it was like Alison's slit, maybe I was meant to have liked it too?

Some time after the quim incident, a senior girl sang me the Roedean School song:

'We are from Roedean, good girls are we,
We take a pride in our virginity.
When we go down to the beach for a swim,
Everyone remarks on the size of their "Quim".
Up school, up school, right up school!'

Most of the girls had a crush on someone. I didn't want to be left out, even though I couldn't find a single girl whom I considered crush-worthy. There was no one as beautiful as Mummy. However hard I tried to get into crush mode, it was doomed to be a half-hearted affair. What on earth was a crush, anyway? What did it mean? I plucked up the courage to ask Lilith, hoping not to look too much of a fool. She thought I was having her on. After all, I'd been at the school as long as she had, so how come I knew nothing about crushes?

'What d'you mean?'

'Well, what do crushes do?'

Lilith laughed. 'Crushes don't do anything, idiot, *you* do it to them!'

'What do you do to them?'

'Oh, Smilo, don't you know yet?' tossing her glossy hair.

'No, tell me!'

'Well, anything you want, really . . .'

'Such as?'

'Well, you make their bed, or give them your sweet ration.'

I couldn't believe it! After all the erotic guesswork I'd been up to at night (while trying not to nibble away at my sheet) and it was down merely to being a slave? Nevertheless I took note. I'd keep it on hold until I was older, then perhaps view this crush business with wiser eyes.

Lilith and her two beautiful sisters from Brazil were more physically advanced than we were. They were downright sexy, even before their teens. One spring afternoon Lilith and I were sitting on the warm grass bank watching a tennis match, when Carol, Lilith's sister who was already in the Senior School, saw us and came over to join us for a chat.

As she slid down on to the bank, her tunic rose right up (she always wore her tunic shorter than anyone else in the school). My eyes popped out of my head, for there, between her well-shaped thighs, was this silky chestnut hair trickling its way out from the corners of her excessively brief briefs (she never wore school knickers either). That one time I caught Mother naked her lower half was cut off by the mirror. I'd seen little fluffy bits over parts of Daddy in the bath, but although he was a man, he had nothing remotely as bushy as this.

They began giggling, and Carol said, 'Hey, Smilo, you're as red as a beetroot, what's up?'

'Nothing, Carol.'

'Do you mean to say you've never seen pubic hair before?'

Now at that time I hadn't even heard the word 'pubic' let alone seen it. I didn't live in Brazil, did I?

'Do all Brazilians have pubic hair, then?'

This, for some reason, made them both double up. 'We all have pubic hair, you silly billy!' said Carol, happy to show me more. 'It's just that mine has started to grow before yours because—'

'Because you're precocious,' said Lilith drily.

I thought at first they were having me on. I would *never* have that strange bunch of stuff between my legs. I was from Ingatestone, Essex, after all.

'Lilith's jealous, Smilo, because she hasn't started proper breasts yet. Look.' Innocently, without lewdness, Carol gently lifted a breast out from its lacy nesting place. 'You see, we all have them to look forward to.' Some senior began urgently waving in Carol's direction. 'I'll be late – I must fly. Bye.'

So much to take in. It was a very pretty breast that Carol had shown me, not in the same street as Mummy's, but there we are. We can't all be Mummy, can we?

The idea of one day wearing my own brassière began to peck at me, giving me my first brief thrill, linking me to some kind of womanliness. I liked these things called breasts. I had really wanted to touch Carol's, play with them . . . give them a good squeeze – but I didn't know her well enough.

I began looking at the senior girls' breasts. I liked biggish ones best. Not too big, but something to get hold of, if I were a man, that is. There was one prefect who would have been the very essence of primness if it hadn't been for her ample breasts swaying to and fro as she pointed her finger at me. Her reaction to me was one of acceptance mixed with disdain, a gnat she couldn't quite swat. On occasion I must've made her life a bit tiresome. But I couldn't help that, I was too busy wondering how it would feel, squelching and tweaking those beautiful breasts. I'd purposely get under her nose just to watch them gently wobbling, encased in their olive green school frock. She was called Lynda Bates, known as Batey. She is the only girl I can recall with any clarity. It wasn't just her breasts that intrigued me, it was also her sense of purpose. It's easy to say all this after the event, but there must have been some reason why I can remember her so clearly when, apart from Lilith (whose frock colour I can't recall), everyone is a blur. I think it was because Batey was in touch with her identity. She possessed something vastly enduring, apart from ambition, and a piercing confidence shone through her pebble specs. She placed her best foot forward, did Batey, and grew up into Lynda Chalker.

CHAPTER TWENTY-ONE

Three weeks from the end of my first term – I was still only nine years old – the Junior House was putting on a play about St Francis of Assisi. I wanted to play St Francis because of his love for animals, but an older girl pipped me to the post for this juicy role. She was called Anna de la Croix, so I suppose her name had a lot to do with clinching it. But she was tall, admittedly, and very manly, which also must have helped. I did manage to get myself a part in this production, as a beggar. Being skinny was finally paying off. Actually it turned out to be a good part. The nearer we got to the great day, the more excited I became at the possibility of not being a total embarrassment after all.

At St Anne's my stammer always prodded me into non-talking parts, so this was the first time I was going to speak on stage – and, what's more, in front of Mother and Father. Thank God my stammer was much better, although still not comfortably reliable. When I became nervous, embarrassed or angry it would surreptitiously creep back, jolting me out of any hint of complacency.

It's impossible to describe to those few who have never known it the terror of a gathering audience echoing in an auditorium. Experiencing it for the first time gave me my first serious taste of collywobbles. They have simply got worse over the years. I know many actors feel as I do, yet have the courage to overcome the all-consuming panic induced by that noise. I have not been so brave. I've had to turn down a great deal of work that I would've liked to accept, because of my naked fear of the pre-curtain auditorium din roaring at me – the beast that must be tamed. Otherwise, like in the zoo that day, it would piss all over me or have me for dinner. Perhaps it's because I've never had the discipline to tame myself. Or because critics have chosen to have me for dinner, which hasn't helped my confidence. Or perhaps it's no more than vanity – I'm so vain that I can't fully submerge myself in the role? What an appalling revelation.

I crept around the curtain and instantly picked out Mummy and Daddy already seated. I saw a large audience eagerly awaiting the afternoon's entertainment.

The cast managed to get through the forty-five minutes almost without a hitch, though there was one dodgy moment when St Francis dried. Fortunately I knew his part and was able to hobble past as the beggar, whispering the forgotten lines up-stage, so hardly anyone knew what had happened. I think I was more proud of that than anything.

As the curtain fell I must admit I thought it had all gone rather well. When I came forward to give my individual curtain call, the clapping swelled so unexpectedly that, quite without thinking, I leapt triumphantly off the stage to give Mummy and Daddy a hug. CRASH! SNAP! OUCH! My ankle went.

I was rushed to Matron, who said I had to go to hospital for she was pretty sure it was broken. Mummy couldn't believe I could have been so stupid. 'You'll never learn, will you, darling?' she said in front of Miss Pike. 'Look before you leap.'

Spikey Pikey, the old boot, was being professionally nice. Or was she genuinely pleased with the whole proceedings? 'Your daughter takes to acting like a duck to water.'

Daddy ruffled my hair. 'Must learn to test the ice first, though, eh, Pusscat?'

Mummy and Daddy said that they'd best be going, there was nothing they could do. How well I remember waving them off that day, for it was the first time in my life I'd accomplished something that we were all proud of.

I *had* fractured my ankle. It was very tedious, since the netball and lacrosse fields in the winter terms were my life's blood. In hospital they chose, after much debate, to use thick bandaging to force my foot outward (I'm knock-kneed and pigeon-toed) rather than the usual plaster-of-paris, for it was essential to turn the ankle. They decided this should be done each week by Matron. If my ankle began to turn inwards, Matron could readjust the bandages.

In those final three weeks of term I never got it rebandaged. I kept telling Matron it was fine, and proved this by shooting around the netball and lacrosse pitches so vigorously that she assumed all was well. It wasn't, but I was damned if I was to go OG (off games) because of a stupid broken ankle. Five years later Mummy suggested I get it broken and reset as it had grown a lump on the side. I didn't need to, because I broke it again, anyway. In fact, both ankles would end up broken twice. But the lump is still there.

CHAPTER TWENTY-TWO

S OMEHOW MY first year at Roedean came to an end. At Waterloo station I fell into Mummy's arms, I was so relieved to see her. She let me nestle against her for about five seconds, which was pretty good going, I thought. 'C'mon, darling, the train was late, and we have to get across to Liverpool Street station to meet Daddy.'

There he was! He twirled me round and round. Oh! I had nearly three months ahead of me of pure heaven!

When we arrived home, Nora the cook was looking more dour than usual because dinner was waiting. The boys were already there – so much bigger – watching telly in the sitting room. Chan came to sit beside me on the floor, licking away the months of agony. I looked at Pooker, all grown-up in her pretty blue dress and spotless white socks, her golden locks long now. I noticed that I didn't feel jealous any more, just a warm sense of gratitude mixed with a kind of pride. Why pride? I'd done nothing towards the perfect little personage so self-possessed in the huge arm-chair. I don't think anyone on earth was as happy as I was that evening.

I overslept the next morning. This was serious because Mummy and Daddy insisted on breakfast at nine o'clock sharp, so I was dressed and downstairs quick as a flash. Entering the dining room, I noticed that everyone had pretty well finished their bacon and eggs, so I went to the sideboard, and helped myself double quick. 'Sorry I'm late, Daddy.' I sat down to eat it.

'I'll let you off lightly this time, Pusscat.' Daddy raised his *Times* in front of him.

Not wanting to keep anyone waiting, I scoffed my breakfast. I wasn't fond of bacon unless it was really crispy, which it wasn't, but being the first day home, I didn't want to make a fuss, so I stuffed it down as best I could. Proud of my empty plate, I took a swig of milk to wash the taste away, with some scrumptious toast and marmalade. Suddenly my two brothers broke the silence and sang: 'You've eaten Charlie! You've eaten Charlie!'

I looked at them, I looked at Daddy behind his *Times*, I looked at Mummy still beneath Adam and God, behind the *Daily Telegraph*, I looked at Pooker, who wasn't interested. It couldn't be true – could it?

'You've eaten Charlie! You've eaten Charlie!'

I thought of my friend in the stables, I thought of that fatty soggy flesh I had just managed to swallow, I thought of my nightly cuddles, and I tried to puke it all up again all over Mummy's lace table-cloth, but nothing happened. I just sat there, unable to move, unable to puke, unable to comprehend.

Mummy finally appeared from behind her *Telegraph*. 'Really, boys, that was totally unnecessary.'

As I looked at them, everything seemed to freeze – no, to move into a very creepy sense of *déjà vu*. Daddy remained behind his *Times*, Mummy slowly and reluctantly put down the *Telegraph* and, taking Pooker by the hand, floated across the dining room, just like I knew she would. I even knew what she'd say next. 'Come on, Pooker, let's go and find Nora.' She did.

It was as if I'd dreamt the whole nightmare before, many times, and that any minute I would awake. Then I threw up.

'Come now, Pusscat,' said Daddy, raising his eyes above his *Times*, 'I didn't dream you'd react this way. A pig's a pig, you know, it's got to be eaten in the end.'

That first day, which should have been so light, so happy, had changed beyond bearing – dark, darker than school, even. I went down to see Mizzer, who whinnied and let me nuzzle into his familiar smell, so consoling, that smell. I didn't look into Charlie's stable – I didn't need to, I just felt the ghastly void. I whispered, 'I'm so sorry, Charlie, I would never have let it happen to you if I had known, please forgive me.' It was his eyes that I would miss most, even more than his wobbly bits.

I went out to the old oak tree and put my arms around its great bark. Trees have always helped me to dredge up good feelings, subduing terrible moments, easing the pain away. Besides, I hadn't hugged a tree for over three months. I looked at the rope-ladder that reached up to the tree-house, but it was more frayed than ever. Daddy had promised to mend it so many times.

I could feel Daddy just beginning to teeter on top of his pedestal; a very serious state of affairs. Surely my hero, whom I loved, worshipped, couldn't possibly topple off it?

I spent the rest of the morning behind the oak tree. I wanted to hide from everyone, even Mizzer and Chan, to mourn my pig in my own way. I had a little chat with King George. He agreed with me that it was very cruel. He said he would never do a thing like that to his own children.

'Pusscat, what are you doing down here all alone?' I

jumped. I thought Daddy was at the office, then I realized it was Saturday.

'Go away – I think you're horrid!' He paid no attention, just kept on coming towards the enemy, as if he wanted to win the MC all over again. Why wasn't he heeding my fury? 'Go away! You let me eat my best friend!'

'Pusscat, he wasn't your friend, he was for us all to eat.'

'I should have been told he was bought for breakfast. You knew I spent some nights with Charlie, you should have warned me!'

'And then what?'

'I would've made sure not to love him so much – I *hate* you! Go away, I tell you!' He didn't.

'Pusscat, I love you.'

'Oh, yes? What about your promises?' indicating the frayed rope-ladder. 'You've done nothing but send me to a school with no trees, no animals. You've broken your promise to mend the rope-ladder, and you happily sat there letting me eat my dearest pig.'

Ouch! I remember my legs being on fire that day. Wandering around talking intimately to King George, I'd completely forgotten about being among the most lethal stinging nettles in the garden. Daddy noticed, and jumped at his chance to change the subject. 'Why do you let those nettles sting you?' He began rolling up his trousers. I could see his black suspenders, which he undid to roll down his socks. Like Owly Daddy's suspenders gave me comfort: he'd been wearing them all my life. 'You see, Pusscat, it's all a question of mind over matter. I'm going to walk through those stinging nettles. As I brush past them I'm going to tell them "No!", command them not to sting me. Are you listening?'

'I don't know what you're talking about.' Daddy could be so stupid sometimes. 'That's what nettles do – sting!'

'They are alive, just like you and me, which means they can give and receive energy. I'm going to command them not to sting me. Are you watching?' Off he went, right through the longest nettles in the far end of the garden. 'If you think you will be stung then you will. If you think you won't, then you won't. The power of the mind can move mountains, Pusscat, as long as you believe it.'

With his crinkly hair and moustache he looked like Charlie Chaplin, wading through the nettle bed with his pink legs and flapping black suspenders.

'How do I know you're not being stung like billyo and just covering it up by being brave?'

'You can tell by my legs.' He came wading back, stroking his calves this way and that through the nettles. 'See, not a single sting!' I looked into his eyes. Was he lying? 'Not my face, Pusscat, I didn't put the nettles near my face, did I? Don't look so doubtful – you have a go now.'

There was nothing to lose, I didn't believe a word of it and I was already badly stung, but a few more wouldn't make much difference. I walked up and down those nettles, quite determined that they would not sting me and, d'you know, they didn't. I was much more surprised than I let on. I have used this 'mind over matter' a great deal during my life and it works nine times out of ten (with stinging nettles!). The tenth time is always when I doubt – or when fear creeps in. Lack of doubt is the key, an implacable doubtlessness, mind.

My father taught me something important that day, more useful for my future than anything I had learnt all year at Roedean. Lucky old Daddy! There he was about to take a tumble off his pedestal – and there beneath my ancient oak tree he got saved by the bell.

CHAPTER TWENTY-THREE

POOKER, WHO HAD just turned five, was blessed with a quiet confidence, so I was determined to get her riding Mizzer well enough for me to get my palomino at last. It wasn't that I didn't love Mizzer, but he was too fat to get anywhere at the gymkhanas. Besides, what fun it would be to go riding with Pooker.

One day we were coming home – me on the bicycle, her on the leading rein – when a great lorry came thundering up the narrow lane. Mizzer did a vicious buck and whipped the leading rein out of my hand. Poor Pooker took off at a full gallop up the lane, the lorry following in their wake.

I finally caught up with them both. The lorry was long gone, Mizzer – typically – was at his most content, munching the luscious grass from the verge, with the leading rein straggling through the rich grass. Pooker gave me the sweetest of smiles, as if she had not an inkling of any past danger.

'Mummy can I have a palomino pony?'

'What on earth for?' Mummy was in her element when busily wafting through her newly created rose garden. We had been at Barn Mead only a few years, but she had transformed the place, with little signs emerging here and there of its oncoming splendour.

'Because Pooker deserves to have Mizzer now. You should come into the Spinney and watch her.'

Mummy looked stunned. 'You haven't been taking Pooker along the lanes, have you?'

'Of course I have. I was going on the lanes all by myself at five, let alone with an elder sister on a leading rein!'

Mummy looked at me suspiciously. 'I don't want Pooker hurt—'

'I don't want Pooker hurt either. I love Pooker.'

'All you want is a new pony – you can't pull the wool over my eyes.' Mummy was such a tyrant!

But she did come to the Spinney one afternoon, and proudly watched her daughter walk, trot, canter and go over a little jump which I had erected for the occasion.

'Well done, Pooker, you are a real little rider now. Congratulations!' Mummy patted Mizzer, rather like the Queen might do, and turned to leave.

'Can I have my palomino now?'

Mummy turned towards me as if I had asked for the Taj Mahal. 'Pusscat, if you get a good report his term – I can't understand why it's taking so long – then we shall rethink the whole affair.' And off she strutted.

I had intercepted my school report. It was hidden at the bottom of my sock drawer. Because of the Charlie interlude, I was determined to get my own back on the lot of them. I had no reason to open it, since I knew only too well what was in it. I didn't want to ruin the summer holidays before needs must.

*

We played a lot of Cowboys and Indians that summer. Jukes and Chuzzer were pretty serious-minded cowboys, really out to get their revenge on the native. All togged out with the gear – cowboy chaps, hats, holsters, guns and bullets, and then there was me, the Indian with only a pigeon feather. It was great fun, though, for I always knew I was safe, being the tree-climbing champ.

One particular afternoon, loaded with guns, Jukes couldn't run fast and Chuzzer was having trouble keeping his hat on. They simply couldn't catch me. I was as light as my feather and swift as an arrow – which I didn't have. When I saw them both huddled together in a pow-wow up by the trapeze, probably reloading their guns, I decided to take refuge behind the summer house. I leapt out of the copper beech to shoot across the rose garden. They spotted me mid-dash and came charging across the croquet lawn, guns firing left, right and centre.

I was a goner. I gave a scream, put my arms up in the air just like in cowboy films, doubled up and fell over dead. (No one takes longer to die than an actor!) It was a rather realistic death, because I really thought I'd been shot. Funny, the power of imagination, because I was convinced my thigh was throbbing. Just as I got up, trying to shake off such imaginings, I saw blood on my hand, looked down and there it was, spouting out from my thigh.

I *had* been shot! It didn't hurt too much – or was it just numb? I pulled down my trousers, there was a hole in my thigh.

Jukes came up, white-faced. 'So dreadfully sorry, Pusscat,' he said politely, looking into the revolver's barrel with disbelief. Quite smart, being shot with a revolver. He had put in home-made bullets of compressed cardboard, quite ignorant of how lethal they could be with a gun of that power.

Mummy drove me off to hospital in Chelmsford. Although the doctor removed the bullet efficiently, I was secretly proud that it left its mark. This circular scar made for a useful pause in proceedings as I grew older. One could say it made quite an impression.

He swore he'd never fire a gun again. A week later, there he was aiming at some poor flying object over the garage. Boys will be boys. (Bang bang!) In his defence, it was an accident. He shot me, a swiftly moving target, from a distance of thirty yards and Jukes was no marksman.

He was off to Winchester next term, where his school motto would be: 'Manners Maketh Man'. Piece of cake – Jukes was home-free.

Usually Daddy came home on Friday evening with a new film for us to watch, mainly comedies. They were silent black-and-whites, mostly, Charlie Chaplin and Buster Keaton, but for me Laurel and Hardy were the best. There's still no one to hold a candle to them – their genuine innocence, their brilliantly uncluttered timing, bouncing off each other, creating gold nuggets of genius and generosity – pure comic perfection.

By this time Jukes was perfectly capable of setting up the reel-to-reel himself. One Saturday night he threaded the film importantly through the spool. 'OK, Chuzzer, you can dim the lights now. Charlie Chaplin, ladies and gentlemen,' said Jukes, with such professionalism.

But on this occasion it turned out not to be Charlie Chaplin, but a man and a woman naked on a bed doing very strange things together. Daddy rushed over and stopped the machine, mumbling, 'The shop's made a mistake – idiots! Sorry, everyone, I'll take this back Monday morning, and give them a piece of my mind.'

I thought no more about it, until Jukes reminded us, years later. We went into fits of giggles, as we recollected Daddy's absolute shock after he entered the playroom.

I believed his story, then. It's only now, as I sit here at midnight tapping away, that a worm of wickedness enters my brain. What if Daddy had brought two films down from London for the weekend, and got them muddled up? I quite like the idea of Mummy and Daddy, with their whisky and gin and tonic, creeping down to the playroom once we were all tucked up in bed.

No. However hard I try to continue down that saucy path, I just can't see them doing such a thing but, then, children never can, can they?

Although puberty creeps up on us all, my generation's parents didn't seem to have heard of it. There was no evidence anywhere that there was any such thing as lust or sex, certainly not around my parents. Perhaps they had submerged their own youth's secret needs in the drawer marked 'conveniently forgotten', under denial or regret. Since they didn't understand their own sexual awakenings, was it so wrong that we didn't understand ours? How well I remember many a shifty silence saying, 'Manage on your own.' Having nothing to go on but pure animal instinct was lucky in a way. No Aids, so no sexual instructions from the media battering my senses day and night, destroying the natural process of discovery. No, I'm not a hundred per cent sure that my parents were so very wrong, for I'm glad the mystery was left intact.

Lately we've become obsessed with our physical body. And to my mind the emotional body, too, has begun to lean dangerously over into indulgence. It might not be untimely to shove just the tip of our spiritual toe into the 'Doorway of Equal Balance'. After all, we've tried everything else, and we can't do any worse than the last hundred years, can we?

Getting the physical, mental, emotional and spiritual into perfect harmony is what most of evolution is about. There seem to be no short cuts either, just daily dedication, as I try to break the chain of every generation's mistakes, plus all my own.

I return to my green shoots of puberty.

One evening, that Roedean summer holiday, I heard a banging going on in Jukes's bedroom. I thought the two boys were playing 'Ee-Ees,' though it seemed more like the rhythmic noises that I'd heard on many occasions coming from different cubicles at Roedean. I still hadn't a clue what it was all about. Curiosity pulled me next door. I stood silently in Jukes's doorway, which was ajar, watching him. Chuzzer wasn't there, Jukes was playing 'Ee-Ees' alone, and although I couldn't see any detail it looked terrific fun.

After a moment or two, I returned to my room, where I

started wiggling around as best I could. I tried very seriously and energetically to emulate Jukes's rhythm and excitement. I didn't know what the hell I was doing, but I swore that one day I would master this . . . this . . . whatever it was. I didn't know where to put my hands, so I laid them flat on my tummy and applied a little pressure. Heaving away, up and down – off I went. Gradually, as time went by, wriggling about a bit, I managed to get myself breathing deeply. I was sure deep breathing had something to do with it (it has, of course, everything to do with everything).

Although my efforts remained fruitless for quite some time, I never gave up. I can be a tiny bit tenacious at times (those sort of times). My stubbornness coupled with the Three Deadly Ps – Patience, Practice, Perseverance – plus Daddy's lesson about mind over matter, had its effect. About two years later something happened. Bob's your uncle! A warm fleeting tingle crept in. I liked this speck of a feeling a lot. As the months went by I became quite an expert at connecting myself up to it. In time the feeling grew to be something more than a mere speck – and I loved it! Bloody well should have 'n' all – after all the hard work I put in. Hard work like that has to culminate into triumph in the end, I believe.

Strangely enough I never put my fingers anywhere but on top, and I never came thinking sexy thoughts. My actions were purely instinctive, maybe even innocent, since I knew nothing. I found the after effects utterly relaxing, enabling me to go to sleep much more easily. Thanks to this better, brighter feeling of peace and well-being, I found I'd stopped nibbling my sheets. So where's the harm in that, pray? (But we're leaping ahead somewhat.)

Mummy thought there was terrible harm in it. Apparently 'Ee-Ees' was a wicked, unforgivable sin. Jesus had no alternative but to punish all participants particularly severely. And what punishment it was. Jesus cursed you by sending you blind and making all your hair drop out! Mind you, I'd always had my suspicions about Jesus anyway. After all, He'd only given me twenty-one years to live. As I lay there doing 'Ee-Ees' I used to wonder if all my hair could possibly fall out before I turned twenty-one? With such short life expectations, perhaps I might die with my eyesight intact, and a full head of hair – pubic or otherwise.

CHAPTER TWENTY-FOUR

BACK TO SCHOOL once more (quite some time before 'Ee-Ees' hard work finally paid off) and nothing got any better.

One night as I lay in my cubicle at Roedean, with the familiar rattles and draughty moans whistling through the windows, I became aware of a little lump over my heart. I used to wear two vests under my Viyella nightie, so it must have been quite a distinctive lump. I couldn't examine it in the mirror without turning the light on, which was forbidden. So I spent the night listening to my thumping heart, and wishing for the lump to go away. I didn't like it, even though it wasn't hurting. It seemed somehow alien to me.

As soon as I fell asleep it was next morning, and I felt it again. It seemed bigger than ever. I took a peek at it in the mirror – my nipple was hard and swollen. But I knew it wasn't the beginnings of breasts, for surely they grew together, didn't they? I was looking forward to a couple of Mummy's beauties sprouting forth, but not this strange lonely lump which taunted me in the mirror. I thought it best to keep quiet, not go to Matron, in fact not to tell a living soul. But as the months wore on, the lump got bigger and bigger. I looked at other girls' titties in the changing rooms. I wasn't able to see a single one growing wonkily, they all grew in perfect unison. Obsessed by this, I would look at nothing but girls' breasts, longing to see just one lop-sided pair.

Half-term was longed for by most. Although I longed for it too, it was home I really wanted, but it was too far away to go to. Seeing the parents was terrific, of course, though it wasn't like seeing Mizzer or Chan. It was a real hoot, watching Daddy's vintage Rolls sweep up the drive apparently with no one behind the wheel. Poor Daddy, he loved his old Rolls, as we all did. But he had to have a pile of cushions under his bum to see out of the windows at all, and after a long journey, they'd become somewhat compressed.

Once, we were all driving along Ingatestone High Street when his cushions actually slipped and he disappeared sideways into what could have been a serious catastrophe. Luckily, being athletic, he managed to regain both the wheel and his somewhat shattered dignity, narrowly preventing the Rolls from making a rather quaint entrance into the local chemist's shop. There were only a couple of onlookers to witness this charade, but in a small community, one is sufficient.

For half-term in Brighton the parents stayed at the Royal Crescent Hotel. Fortunately Chuzzlewit had recently come to school near me in Rottingdean. He may as well have been in Mandelay with all those flying fish, for I hardly ever saw him, but I used to fantasize our escape together. I'd run across the moonlit Downs and rescue him, and we'd both gallop off into the sunset. Rarely did Chuzzer's and my half-term sychron-ize. How did we get through those fraught, false, usually rainy weekends? I didn't relish them and I knew Pater and Mater didn't either – outings stiff with the correctness of everyone purely doing their duty. They tried to give us a good time on the obligatory pier, the dolphin aquarium once, but never again – poor dolphins. We usually ended up at the Ship Hotel for tea. Having lunch at the Royal Crescent Hotel, I saw a man I recognized from the telly. Quite a moment that, when you notice your first celebrity – even if it was only Robert Beatty. But what's the use of meeting Robert Beatty with only one breast?

When Chuzzer was with us we played at not treading on the pavement cracks, like most children. We'd give each other dares. If Chuzzer wasn't with me, I used to tell myself that if I didn't tread on a single crack, I needn't go back to school. I love Brighton's pink paving stones, all different shades of pink.

A wet Sunday in Brighton, with no Chuzzer and the rain whipping up the sea and obscuring any hope of a horizon. Mummy decided we should go to the cinema to see *Wuthering Heights*, starring a man called Laurence Olivier.

I didn't think much of Merle Oberon, or Laurence Olivier come to that – until he went to the window near the end, looked out across the moor. His whole being was straining, searching, hoping for some sign; some symbol of reconciliation for their two eternally linked but cruelly severed souls. It was the way he cried, 'Cathy – Cathy!' At that moment something snapped inside me; something that hitherto had been taut yet numb, became a feeling, soft and pliable.

We trailed out slowly into the light. I always found that so disorientating, the moment of stumbling forward, fighting off the shift back to reality, clinging to the fantasy to avoid that moment of readjustment to the cruel harsh light and the horror of returning to Roedean prison. I was caught in this struggle when Mummy said, 'He's so like you, John, sometimes, especially when he smiles.'

Daddy failed to take this as a compliment. 'Umph! I must practise a more genuine smile, if that's the case – what d'you think, Pusscat?' I wasn't sure what to say, but since Mummy had mentioned it, I suppose there was a likeness between them . . . yes, I suppose there was.

I saw a magazine for sale as we left the cinema. On the cover was a moody but very romantic picture of Laurence Olivier. I pleaded with Mummy to buy it for me.

'You can't go back to school with *Silver Screen*, it'll get confiscated.'

'No, it won't, I'll hide it. Lots of girls have magazines like this one.'

'I'll buy it for you, Pusscat. It'll remind you of me,' said Daddy, looking at Mummy, 'apparently.'

So, thanks to Daddy, I finally won the battle. But I think it was more to keep me quiet at the darkest hour of all, driving through those gates, up past the Senior School, to the final goodbyes at the door in front of Spikey Pikey.

I stuck Laurence Olivier to the inside of my locker door, and I would ask to spend a penny as often as possible so that I could go down to the locker room and submerge myself in reverie – what a strangely haunting face!

*

A few weeks later I began to feel very odd. It turned out to be measles, so there I lay alone in a darkened room in the sanatorium. Measles was nothing compared to my lump. This was still my main worry, as I tossed and turned wondering if it were better to have none than one.

Finally I could bear the titty saga no longer. When everyone was at lunch, I crept along to Matron's medical cabinet, located of pair of scissors, ran back to the bathroom – and there in front of the mirror I attempted to cut off the lump. It was much more difficult than I imagined. I hacked away, but I was unprepared for the blood – it reminded me of my bullet wound.

I wasn't making much headway when I heard someone coming. I leapt back into bed with everything prickling and stinging like billyo – guilt, measle spots, titty wound. I hid the scissors under the pillow, beside the picture of Laurence Olivier taken from my locker door.

'Hello, Smilo,' said Matron, 'and how are we feeling this afternoon?' As she came over to examine my spots, she couldn't help but see the blood. 'What's all this?'

Because I'd been caught 'red nightied', so to speak, I decided to come clean. I told Matron of my fears.

To my amazement, Matron became very gentle and kind to me. Bathing my wound, she explained that some girls' breasts did grow at a different pace, but there was nothing to worry about because they usually ended up equal in the end. 'You should have spoken to me about it, you silly girl.'

After applying some foul-smelling ointment, she put a large piece of lint and cotton wool around it, and a plaster. 'I'll look at it again in the morning, we mustn't let it become infected,' she said, looking at the blunt scissors and shaking her head woefully. 'It may leave a scar.' Matron was right. It did leave a small scar but it was of no consequence, for I finally got two breasts in the end!

A news bulletin came through on the wireless. King George VI had died peacefully in his bed. I was devastated, I'd been unfaithful to him. I had forsaken him for my dark and brooding Olivier. I couldn't take it in. He was the first human being I'd ever been in mourning for. Getting over it was a long and lonely process because there wasn't a living soul I could turn to. Who would understand my devotion to that miscast and kindly king? My first love was dead, stammer and all, and I only had Laurence Olivier to wipe away the tears.

The Easter holidays – the shortest in the calendar – came and went. Two precious weeks were wasted in Jersey with chicken-pox. No sooner had I returned and tacked up Mizzer than it was back for the long summer term.

Roedean and I were drifting further and further apart. I knew it wasn't Roedean's fault any more than it was mine. It was just a hideous incompatibility. My life was going down the plug-hole in a relentless and, to my mind, unnecessary misery. I was blessed with a large capacity for happiness, so a sense of injustice began at first to niggle and then to rankle, badly.

Towards the end of term we were told my Miss Horrobin, that the Queen Mother was coming down to pay us a visit, and what a privilege, what an honour it was for the school, to be receiving such an important guest. She explained how we should not approach the Queen Mother directly, but that if she approached any one of us, we should do a little curtsey, then say, 'Ma'am', answer her question, then another 'Ma'am', then another curtsey. For the next two weeks, the whole of the Downs became a bobbing sea of 'Ma'ams' and curtseys – for a change I'd done enough homework!

I kept thinking how sad for her to lose her king. I didn't even know him yet it broke my heart, so what must it have done to her? Poor lady, I pitied her. Even before she arrived I felt a bond between us – after all, we had both loved the same man.

When the great day arrived, we were all lined up outside the Senior School. The juniors were nearer the front, and I found myself very nicely placed in the centre of the main steps up to the school. Her great shiny car pulled up, and out she stepped, so trippingly, so delicately serene. I was immediately drawn into the simplicity of her natural majesty, transfixed by the periwinkle beauty I saw before me. She surpassed my wildest dreams of what a queen should look like.

With regal grace she made her way slowly towards us. She stopped at the girl beside me, and gave her a wonderful smile. 'How do you like it here?' she gently asked, while Spikey Pikey hovered in the background.

Curtsey. 'I love it here, Ma'am.' Curtsey.

The Queen Mother smiled and moved on, looking down at me, my ears taking up most of the view, I'm sure. I was mesmerized by her china doll skin. Were they periwinkle or cornflower, those dazzling eyes of hers, matching her witty feathered hat catching the breeze? 'And how do you like it here?'

I remembered to do a neat little curtsey, just like I'd done a million times for her husband, and then, just as politely as Jukes:

Curtsey. 'Ma'am – I hate it, Ma'am.' Curtsey.

She gave me a wondrously warm and Owly knowing twinkle. As she did so, she lifted her gloved hand, wagged it at me in a most friendly fashion, and laughing gently, said, 'Oh?'

What had I done? She'd heard all right, but she couldn't very well stay and discuss it, could she? But she didn't have to because that 'Oh' spoke volumes. As she glided on, I felt we had shared a moment of truth.

Next Sunday in chapel, after the sermon, Miss Horrobin said out of the blue, 'Will Sarah Miles come up here, please.' Gradually it began to dawn that Sarah Miles was me. I stood up. 'Come here.' I walked up the aisle to the front, a very long way. I looked up at her, the great black crow looming down from her pedestal of power. I was frightened enough of the woman as it was, without adding a pulpit and tassle.

'Your behaviour, my child, continues to show not the slightest sign of improvement. When are you going to learn to pull your socks up?' I bent down and pulled them up. A wave of laughter rose from the gallery. 'Come to my house after chapel, I want a word with you.'

It struck me later, that I could've warmed to Miss Horrobin as she sat there in her house, simply dressed, with no tassle or pulpit. 'Sit down, please.' I sat down. 'It has come to my attention that you told the Queen Mother that you hated the school. Is this so?'

'Yes, ma'am.'

I wondered who had played Judas.

I stood firm, refusing point blank to apologize. After all, I was telling the truth. 'But you see, Miss Horrobin, I do hate it here.'

'It's not just your lack of remorse, you understand, it's your whole attitude since the day you arrived at this school, you've been nothing but trouble. I'm really left no alternative but to expel you.'

'Do I leave now?' I asked, trying not to sound too eager. She must have caught the frisson of excitement in the air.

'No, you'll leave at the end of the term.'

I'd become an expert at counting off the days.

CHAPTER TWENTY-FIVE

MATER AND PATER were, understandably slightly miffed, but I think they saw it coming. Daddy and I were playing tennis on the first day of hols. 'Better to be expelled for telling the truth than for lying, I suppose,' he said. 'I wonder if your mother's great-aunt sneaked on you?' I hadn't thought of the Queen Mum as Mummy's great-aunt.

Daddy's tennis was lethal. He was a superb player. He used to play frequently with Stephen Potter who wrote the books *One Upmanship* and *Gamesmanship*. To see these two out on the court, turning the knack of cheating into an art form – not the kind of tennis I should have been learning at all. Daddy used to say, back in the fifties, that tennis would one day become a boring game of mere muscle power, and then it would return again to a game of cunning intellect – 'Thus,' he said slipping another dirty shot to me, which clipped the net, and sent the ball off in another direction.

All too soon we were off for that damned summer holiday, this time to the secluded home of an Austrian artist, Marc Sontag. He lived right at the top end of Majorca, near Cala Rajada. How I longed to be let off the hook. Was it too much to ask to remain at home? Ironic, really, the way most people love holidays, and can't afford to go on them, whereas I had to go on them when all I wanted to do was simply to stay at home. (I still do.)

But Majorca was different from anywhere I had been before and I found myself in an undiscovered heaven. I think it was mainly due to the incredible lightness that I'd felt ever since I'd watched those doom-laden Roedean gates release me from my torment and fade behind me for the last time. The whole holiday embalmed me in a womb-like softness, unreal yet always present. I didn't question it, I just learnt to surrender gratefully. I was often alone, I wandered down to the beach through cool dark pine trees, where warning shafts of scalding Cala Rajada heat would pierce my naked feet. Leaving the shadows behind, I'd gallop over scorching virginal beaches, to tumble headlong into a cool aquamarine sea. It was dreamy lying there, bobbing up and down, as if I were lying on Batey's breasts. Caressed by benevolent waves, I discovered (only periodically, mind) the knack of surrender, a total confidence that only comes with trust. Thus the days drifted by.

In the evening the sound of crickets, the aroma of pine and salt, mingling with the scents of rainbow flowers, and the juicy, mouth-watering cooking smells couldn't fail to bring on a new kind of sleep, filled with no dread of Spikey Pikey, or holes in my sheets, or galloping gales. A truly wonderful no-more-Roedean sleep.

A perfect holiday except for one moment when things got a little dodgy. We were off for a drive around the island, Father at the wheel of a rented car, doing a fair lick on those twisty Majorca roads. Mother was beside him, spectacular in pale blue with a straw sun hat, smoking a cigarette. Both were defending their corner through a hint of alcohol, only a hint, mind. Quite out of the blue Daddy took the whole family, at great speed, straight over a twenty-foot drop.

I remember most clearly flying through the air and, because time was suspended, it gave me ample time to think about my oncoming death. There was no fear. Inside the car everything was cocooned in stillness, except for Mother's cigarette smoke intertwining with the brim of her hat. It seemed to swirl around for ever before – BOUNCE! BOUNCE! BOUNCE!

We all landed with an enormous jolt in an ancient olive grove. Daddy's eternal luck held out for us that day. The car shot on with great momentum, choosing to hit – out of all the mature trees that were available – an immature, pliable sapling. CRASH! We were travelling at quite high speed. Had it not been a sapling, which bent to embrace the impact, there would surely be no Miles family left to tell the tale.

I wasn't sure why everything went into slow motion, only that it certainly did. I remember a chasm of silence as we all sat there unable to move. Slowly we scrambled out of the car, and checked each other out. No one was badly hurt. Chuzzer, or was it Jukes?, had a bloody nose, but what's a bloody nose? Bloody Hell – it was a miracle. All I can remember after that was the whole family collapsing in shock some two hours later, a delayed reaction in a friendly Spanish café. We all started to giggle, uncontrollably, unable to stop, like me and Chuzzer at the Chase swimming pool, the utter relief I suppose.

Having now had my fair share of close brushes with death, I feel that this slow time-suspended dream sequence that takes place isn't simply my imagination. (Science would argue that the brain cuts out for one's own protection, but that hasn't been proven.) On these time-distorted occasions I feel protected. As if Something's embracing – even cradling – me. I'm relieved it isn't my madness alone, for I've met many other people who've felt the same experience when close to death. (And from those who have died and returned.) I call these near-death experiences 'God's cradling', a cradle made of time, space and light.

Leonardo's concept of God, the ancient thespian with the long, white beard on the ceiling of the Sistine Chapel has had a good run for its money. It's time to move on.

Home again. Jukes wanted to be confirmed in Winchester Cathedral. Why not? There was one slight problem, though: you can't be confirmed without being baptized. Due to Daddy's reluctance for such nonsense, it wasn't ever on the cards until Jukes kept repeating his request.

(I don't know when Daddy finally got his divorce from Pat, nor do I know when Mummy and Daddy tied the matrimonial knot. Whenever it was, it was tied tightly in a secret knot. But since we didn't know they weren't married, it made not a halfpenny-worth of difference either way.)

Poor Daddy, unable to dissuade Jukes from what he considered a nightmare, managed to dig up some old rector friend of his to perform the dirty deed down in Hampshire. What a farce! All christened together – all over and done with in one fell swoop just to make Jukes happy. We were dressed up, posh and uncomfortable as could be. Looking as if butter wouldn't melt in our non-religious mouths. Jukes had grown quite religious, but then who could blame him, going to Winchester Cathedral every day for prayers? The spirit of the place couldn't help but dig deep into his bones.

We arrived in the pretty little parish church, all in a line waiting to have our heads dunked in the christening font. 'I christen you Chrisopher John, I christen you Martin Richard—'

Suddenly all hell broke loose – 'I will n-n-n-n-n-n-n-not be called Richard!' fumed Chuzzer, and he meant it. Quite an argument ensued, but Chuzzer held his position like the true warrior he is. (I'm glad he stuck to his guns. Richard is a difficult word for stammerers to say, neither Chuzzer nor I can say it to this day, so to have him christened Richard would have been a bugger of a bore.) 'I christen you Sarah Elizabeth, I christen you Vanessa Anne.' Jukes could now go and get himself well and truly confirmed, but I doubt very much if Jesus would have approved – Daddy thought it a fiasco.

CHAPTER TWENTY-SIX

MEMORIES OF my next school, though rather misty, aren't encased in barbed wire spikes like Roedean memories. They remain similar to the building itself, a rambling Elizabethan muddle, chaotic yet mellow. As we entered the school gates and drove up the drive of Crofton Grange School, in Hertfordshire, I felt nothing of the hopelessness I'd felt on first entering the gates of Roedean, even though it was the Easter term and the other girls would be settled in already. (I had a whole term at home because Mummy couldn't get me into Crofton at the beginning of the school year – perfect bliss!) I felt a certain amount of safety knowing it was only an hour away from home, and although animals were forbidden, there were certain compensations such as no uniforms needed. The school was situated within wonderful ancient parkland, some of the best climbing trees I'd seen.

Mrs Baines, the headmistress, came to greet us with her two Border terriers, who were to be for ever bonded to her considerable wake. She didn't seem quite all there, Mrs Baines. Though certainly a beauty in her day, she was now rather plump, with white hair, and she was as far removed from the likes of the Horror as it was possible to be. She had a gritty sly look though, as if she knew she was missing a few marbles and was checking to see who'd picked them up.

'What beautiful trees,' I volunteered with enthusiasm.

'Aren't they?' said Mrs Baines, adding, with a curiously vague firmness, 'But climbing them is forbidden.'

Oddly enough, having no uniform made me slightly uncomfortable. I realized why uniforms were perhaps a good idea, after all, for without them you could sort out the rich from the poor with no problem. Mummy was still wedded to her, 'But you'll grow into it, darling', routine. When, pray? In another lifetime?

All the girls were milling, chic as could be, around the upper lawn in front of the ha-ha, looking rather dishy, as if in training to be débutantes. I felt out of place already. I noticed one girl who looked as unkempt, chaotic and unsure of herself as I did. She was tall, with wonderful thick mousy hair and specs. Her movements were quick and rather staccato as she made her way over to a beautiful, confident, classy lady.

'That's Jasmine Bligh, the television announcer,' said Mummy, checking her lipstick in her hand mirror before entering the fray.

Beauty, I have discovered, is either drawn directly to beauty, or directly away from it, according to whether men are present. Since there were no men to threaten status, Mummy and Jasmine made a beeline for each other.

Her daughter was also called Sarah. We were thrown together that first day, not only because of our beautiful mothers, but because she, like me, was also a new girl that Easter term. Sarah Pale Johnson. I called her S.P.J. We found ourselves thankful to be put together in a dormitory for four. The dorms were different from Roedean, not being boxed into cubicles. Some dorms were larger, some were very small with only two beds. I wanted one of those one day, though it

The Festival of Britain: 'You'll grow into it, darling'

Half-term boat ride – why can't I be riding Mizzer?

Roedean, the prison

The prisoner. My first performance, as the beggar in *St Francis of Assisi*

How I longed for the holidays! Pooker is riding Mizzer, I'm on Prince Charming

For once he lives up to his name

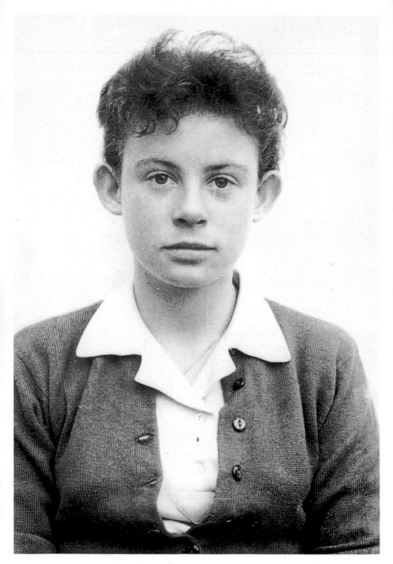

I'm going to be a movie star

Above: My getting-into-RADA treat,
a cruise to Tenerife.
Where's the action?
Not at the Captain's Table

Above: Skiing with Jukes in
Austria

Mother and Father hatching the plot to palm me off on Dr Mary Adams

Left: In the bath without Sylvia (© *Michael Ward*)

Below: My new Prince Charming, Willy Fox (© *Flair Photography*)

Sir Larry's new star

EIGHTEEN-YEAR-OLD Sarah Miles was still at acting school a year ago. Now she is to be Sir Laurence Olivier's co-star in his new film *Term of Trial*. She plays a 15-year-old schoolgirl who falls in love with schoolteacher Sir Laurence.

French actress Simone Signoret is also in the film, but Sarah said last night: " Mine is the biggest part. I can still hardly believe it.

" Only last Christmas I was a student at RADA, then I went into rep at Worthing, and now this. I must admit I'm a bit worried about the whole thing.

" It has been quite astounding. I didn't even have a test. Somebody saw me acting at Worthing and the next thing I'd signed up for this part. I'm not really interested in films—I prefer the stage. Still, the money's good."

Was she overawed at the prospect of acting with Sir Laurence? " Terrified," said Sarah whose home is in Chelmsford, Essex.

Black-haired and belligerent, but somehow I got the part

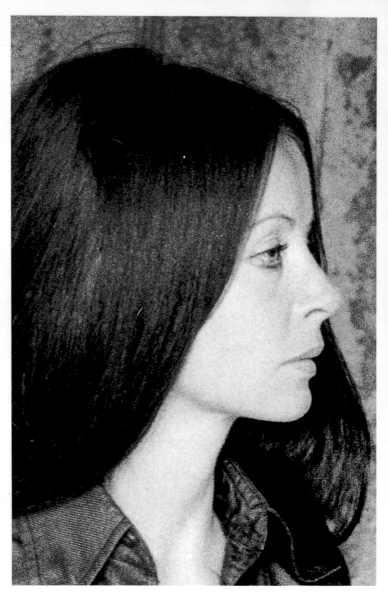

Perserverance paid off – look at the hair

would be damn tricky for Ee-Ees. But with practice, we all managed to be discreet and to turn a deaf ear. I never spoke of Ee-Ees to another girl. I began checking my hair in the mirror daily. So far, though, my eyesight was holding up well.

A few of the senior girls, and there were some ravishing ones sprinkled here and there, were up to something in the ha-ha at night with their boyfriends from Haileybury School up the road. Most of us knew this, but no one blew the whistle on them, especially since we didn't really know what that something was.

The school hymn, 'O strength and stay, upholding all creation', was sung to the same tune as Danny Boy. This gave me such a powerful surge of homesickness every Sunday evening, that Mrs Baines, quick off the mark for someone so slow, leapt forward and asked me kindly to sing quietly. So what else was new?

There were two really beautiful females at Crofton Grange. One, a pupil called Min Musker, a close friend, was a creature from the wilds; prowling round, her ambling amber grace was quite mesmerizing. Deep olive skin and a sullen untamed look that zapped you from beneath dark and flashy eyebrows. Min went on to marry John Aspinall where, no doubt, in company with his private menagerie she was less conspicuous.

The other was Miss Clap, the games mistress. I often wondered whether either of them were worthy of my sweet ration. In the end I decided not. I would probably have made Miss Clap's bed, if she'd asked me to. She was superbly co-ordinated, with silky white-blonde hair, glossy as her radiant skin. The most glorious, bright-eyed and bushy-tailed gym mistress one could ever hope to meet – perhaps I could get her to make my bed?

In Miss Ashby, the art mistress, I also found someone who could inspire me. I couldn't paint for toffee, too much competition at home probably. Jukes isn't half bad, Daddy was pretty good and Chuzzer is quite brilliant, but Miss Ashby gave me confidence to feel I could do it too. There was an under fourteen school competition in which a great many schools were entering. 'I want each member of the class to put their best foot forward,' said Miss Ashby. 'I want to see Crofton among the winners.'

Because of my passion for horses, I'd learnt to draw them fairly adequately so I decided to combine my horse-drawing talent with my unfailing love for gypsy Ted. My 'Gypsy Encampment' painting was finished. Trees, horses, a camp fire around which stood the caravan, Ted, Ethel, dogs and children. The dogs were a mess, they had to go.

It not only qualified, but it won me first prize.

I had never won anything before and my eyes popped out on stalks. I can't believe many schools could have entered this competition because, between you and me, my painting wasn't that good. What was good was being able to impress Miss Ashby. How rewarding it was to feel what girls like S.P.J. – who was very clever – felt almost daily, just once in my school life. Things were looking up: two mistresses that I respected enough to want to impress.

I was usually bottom of the class. S.P.J. was always top. What was most unfair was that she could easily get me giggling. It was a wicked giggle, silent and lethally infectious. A mere quiver of nostrils (apart from Mummy's, hers were the only nostrils I'd seen shaped like willow leaves) was the only hint of her inward hysteria bubbling away like a discreet volcano. That wretched quiver was enough to get me many a black mark: it was too subtle for the teachers to see but off I'd go, completely out of control.

'Will you please leave the room, Sarah, and stay in for detention tonight.'

'Which Sarah?' I'd ask hopefully. 'There's only you, Sarah, giggling.'

And so it was for several terms, till Sarah, my partner in crime, was taken away to another school in Berkshire. I was sad because I didn't know she was going to leave. I missed her as well as our giggling bouts. But most of all I missed not being able to copy the answers from her exercise book.

Since fame goes hand in hand with falsehood, I'm glad I've kept the friends I made at school. For some reason, the knowledge that they were around before I became known counts for a lot. She's still S.P.J. today, but I've lost the knack of getting her giggling – sad, that.

I respected Miss Robinson, our English teacher, and really wanted to learn from her, but it wasn't to be, for she kept her lofty distance, frightening me with her haughtiness. She was a stickler for correct spelling, but she never looked beneath it. Which was a shame, for beneath my inability to spell was some kind of need, trying desperately hard to be heard and released from its paralysis.

Without S.P.J. to turn to for cheating or giggling, inevitably I began to rebel again and again.

Miss Hildebrandt, a German, taught German. *'Der Zug kommt. Ich kaufe mein Fahrkarten auf dem Bahnhof.'* This is the only German I learnt in almost two years. German is a very saliva-ish language, and she made me sit in the front row, to keep an eye on me. This forced me to scrunch up my eyes in order to make as small a target as possible against continual spittle penetration. Finally I was given no choice but to bring my umbrella into class with me for protection.

'Vat's dat?' she asked.

'A raised umbrella.' The class snorted.

'Sarah Miles, stay behind, I vant to talk to you.'

Miss Gilmore took maths and Latin. She was a robust potato-faced Scot, lodging all her discontentment behind an excessively long upper lip. She disliked me intensely. I was an inciter, so she said, anyway, but I never knew what it meant.

'Since you cannot find the ability to try yourself, you do your best to stop the rest from having a go, and that's wicked.'

One day in maths, after she'd made an exhibition of my incompetence in front of the whole class she asked me to clean the blackboard. When I'd finished, I put the wooden wiper out of the window. It was very near the ground, easy enough to bend out of the window and pick up. But I went and sat down, like a good girl. Miss Gilmore approached the window herself, and leant out. The sight of her half out of the window was a temptation I couldn't resist. I persuaded myself it was kinder to assist her all the way out on to the grass, rather than witness her struggling up again. To see her petticoats fluttering, suspenders flashing as she disappeared was a treat I've savoured – the vanishing Gilmore.

The prefects kept a black book. Each time you were lazy, disobedient, rude or downright wicked, you received these black marks. Up to four a week and you were punished with extra work. More than four and it was off to Mrs Baines, who would decide your future. The black book was kept in a drawer in the hall, I made a special point of noting its whereabouts . . . just in case. I never thought beyond 'just in case'.

CHAPTER TWENTY-SEVEN

URING ONE Christmas holidays, my father and I
had our first real sparking match. He was growing tense, observing Mummy in her Christmas
dither, climbing to the top of the Polly Tree.

'Why don't you get a divorce?' I asked him, while we
were alone in the drawing room. He looked at me like he'd
never looked before. 'And what's that supposed to mean?'

'Well,' I replied, shrugging cockily, 'all the best girls at
school come from broken homes.'

His face went white. 'And what's that supposed to mean?'
he repeated, colder now.

'What I mean is, if you and Mummy got a divorce, then I
would have two homes to choose from, not just the same
boring old Barn Mead.'

'Boring here, is it, madam?'

I went blithely on. 'Well, nobody is anybody until they're
well and truly divorced – and four parents means double sets
of presents.'

Daddy had taken more than he could stomach: so mad
was he that he threw me across the drawing room. Fortunately my journey was interrupted – CRASH – when I fell right
over his world (he had a very large and expensive antique
globe of the Earth, set up on a beautiful stand). 'Now look!
See what you've done! You've smashed up my world.' He
bent down to examine his broken globe. 'I never want to hear

you speaking that way again! You're growing into a little bitch – like all the other spoilt little bitches at that hoity-toity school of yours.'

How dare he blame me for my school! 'If I'd gone to a local school all this would never have happened!'

Still examining his broken world, 'Get out of my sight,' he said, waving me away as if I was contaminating the air.

Luckily his world was only dented, but it never smoothed out again. I felt bad about it, really bad, and asked for his forgiveness later over table-tennis. Fortunately for me he was winning 16–12 in the final game, so his anger was smoothing away nicely. After all, I was only testing his love for Mummy. His response had made me feel secure and happy.

Towards the end of those same holidays I was out with Margery, the local cowhand's daughter. We had grown close over the years: she owned Kipper and we rode out together. That day, though, we were going exploring to a derelict stately home nearby called Toby Priory, a real romantic's dream. It sat in the middle of nowhere, with six huge ancient pillars holding up the remains of a Gothic conservatory – pure Gothic – and now steeped in loneliness. Poor Toby Priory. I loved it so, its faded grandeur mirrored in the lake; crowning this melancholic ruin were several massive cedars of Lebanon, leaning forlornly over a history of grand balls, banquets and lovers' trysts, all gone for ever. I could still smell the times they must have had there in the stillness of the air. A skeleton of a chapel overlooking the occasional crumbling grotto or folly scattered along the pathway, once so lovingly paved, leading down to an overgrown secret garden. Margery saw a ghost there once, but I never did. I didn't believe in all that rubbish, then. Many girls at Crofton Grange had seen the famous ghost, the Grey Lady at the top of the stairs, but I never saw her either.

On our way home, I went behind a tree for a pee, and discovered that my pants were bloody. I couldn't believe it, I just stared at the blood, stunned. I felt too embarrassed to confide in Margery. As I straightened to pull my trousers up, Margery said, 'Quick – there's Tom, the ploughman.' She saw my face. 'What's up, Pusscat? Seen a ghost, or something?' She looked down and saw the blood.

'I don't know what's wrong. Maybe I've got cancer like Grandma . . . I suppose I must get to a doctor.'

She stood there for a moment or two, waiting for Tom to get out of earshot. Then, almost bending herself in two, she began to snort incredulously which upset me because I believed it was at my expense. 'Marge – stop! What's so funny about it?'

She looked at me as if I were the village idiot. 'You're having me on.'

I wasn't sure who was having whom on, or indeed what was going on. 'What do you mean?'

Marge put her hands on her hips. 'Are you seriously trying to tell me you don't know what that is? How old are you, Pusscat?'

'I'm thirteen. Why?'

She'd turned all serious, shaking her head in the direction of my house. 'What goes on up there, then?'

'What d'you mean, Marge?' trying to hide my growing confusion.

'Here, you'd better take this.' She gave me a rather dirty hanky to put in my pants. It was getting cold, so we walked on. 'You have what all we women get. It's called a period.'

I was stunned, yet it all rang true. I began recollecting little tell-tale signs from the last few terms at school. Certain girls would be off games, and when I asked them what was wrong, they just laughed at me. It really showed up my backward, incurious nature when it came to certain aspects of life.

'It's nothing to worry about, it's a fact of life. The rest you can learn from that strange mother of yours.'

'Why is she strange?'

She put her arm around me protectively. 'You tell her to come down and live on the farm for a while.'

I was truly grateful at that moment to have the earthy strength of Marge's arm around me. I'd seen blood coming out of cows and sheep when they were giving birth, but I never connected them with us. I'd seen kittens being born, but I'd never dreamed that we were all the same.

Mysterious feelings were growing shoots inside me – perhaps the very beginnings of sexual passion?

The seed had undoubtedly been planted when Olivier cried, 'Cathy! Cathy!' in the Brighton cinema that day. Later, gypsy Ted nudged me into an awareness of its existence a second time, warming it and giving it light at the Ingatestone fair. From then on, Olivier gave it mulch and water. Little did I know then that this 'thing' that was growing inside of me would eventually become a veritable Jack's beanstalk of lust. From his photograph's tender care it grew so unexpectedly rampant that I found myself continually getting caught on its prickly questions and secret hankerings.

*

Back at school, we were sitting in class waiting for Miss Robinson to arrive. All the girls were talking about their holidays.

'He nearly managed to rape me on the sofa!'

'You mean you didn't surrender?'

'I don't want to lose my virginity – yet – thank you!'

'Nor get pregnant – thanks a ton!'

'Imagine actually having a baby – euckh! Foul!'

I kept my head well bent in my exercise book.

'Have you ever gone with a boy, Smilo?'

Someone butted in. 'Hard for poor old Smiles with her radar scanners!'

I was so used to being teased, it hardly had any effect any more.

'Where do babies come from – big ears?' someone said.

In for a penny in for a pound. I flapped my ears. 'Lucky baby to have such big ears to climb out of!'

This was heartily appreciated, then everyone dissolved into a thoughtful silence. I was glad of this, for I still wasn't sure whether babies came out of the titties (mine were both taking their time) or the tummy button. Angela, a real blonde bombshell who had beautiful breasts already, broke the silence. 'Imagine climbing out from such a tiny weeny hole, it's so hard to believe.' Addressing the whole class, she went blithely on, 'When you wash, d'you actually wash in it, or just around it? When I'm washing down there, I can't even get my little finger in, so just imagine a whole baby crawling out.' Silence.

'Yeah,' said someone. 'I think it's imposs—'

In came Miss Robinson. 'Nothing's impossible, that's lesson number one,' she said.

I was left devastated, utterly dumbfounded! I couldn't think about Byron and Shelley. How positively disgusting it all was! How obscene – to think of babies coming out of the same place where I did a pee, the same place where all that blood had started coming from. Well, I was going to have no part of it – no part whatsoever – and that most definitely was that!

One day having changed for games, I closed my locker door (where Laurence Olivier was displayed on the inside) and bumped into a guilty cluster of girls huddled in the corner of the yard. Everyone was meant to be playing games. 'What's up then?' I asked nosily.

'Nothing. Have you ever drunk any alcohol?'

'Of course,' I replied confidently, lying my head off.

'Have you ever tried vodka?'

'Of course,' I said, bending over to tie up the lace of my gym shoe.

'I'll give you seven and six if you can drink this down,' said one of the girls, nudging her friend.

Seven and six was a great deal of money in those days. 'So, where's the bottle?' I asked with indifference.

I took the half-sized bottle and gulped it down without coming up for air. When I finished, I gave a little bow and turned around. As I made my way back to the classrooms, I began to feel the urgent need of a fire extinguisher. But I wasn't going to give that lot the satisfaction of seeing me keel over.

Safely out of sight, I keeled over all right – I was burning up inside. I rolled all over the corridor in scalding agony. Fortunately – or unfortunately – one of the kitchen staff found me, and took me up to Matron. I had no choice but to gasp out the truth, more or less, except –

'Where did you get this vodka from?'

'It's my own bottle, Matron, I smuggled it into school.'

She put me to bed, which was much worse. Nauseating dizziness burned my windpipe. A frightening despair overcame me as the room spun relentlessly for what seemed like a week. Mother was informed. She was scolded by Mrs Baines for allowing me to bring alcohol to school in the first place. She was very puzzled about this. I'd never shown the slightest interest in drink, not even asked to have a sip of theirs.

The good part is that the experience left its mark. I've hardly touched drink since, let alone ever been drunk. I sipped socially in the early days, so that I wouldn't be considered a goody-goody, but I never enjoyed it. The very smell of the stuff nowadays turns me off, probably taking me back to that week of hell.

The bad part is – I never received my seven and six.

I only attempted one exam in my life. Mock O Level: scripture. I grabbed a nice warm seat by the radiator and sat down. It was all very quiet, the girls were bowing their heads ritualistically into the question paper with the appropriate reverence. I wrote my name and the date on the top of my exam paper, put my pen down to contemplate which question to tackle first, put my right hand down the back of the radiator to warm it up – Bingo! It had got itself completely wedged. I put up my other hand.

'Be quiet, the exam has started, put your hand down!'

'But my hand—' I said.

'Quiet, please!'

'But my hand is wedged behind the—'

'Either keep quiet, or leave the room!'

'Please!'

'Shoosh!' said a chorus of grumpy girls.

'But—'

'Shoosh!'

Sad, really, because I knew a few of the answers. So I just sat there thinking about Jesus, and the more I thought about him, the more I was convinced that Christianity was a whole lot of codswallop and that I was well out of it.

When the bell rang, only 'Sarah Miles' was written on the empty white page – oh, and the date too. The teacher came over and inspected my stuck hand. She shook her head, called another girl over, and between them my hand was finally pulled free. The girl said, 'Shame on you, Smilo, you do go to bizarre lengths.'

This staggered me, because I'd certainly not stuffed my fingers down there on purpose . . . or had I? Had I also stuck my fingers in the pipe at the Chase swimming pool on purpose? My motives for the latter seem a trifle oblique – unless I wanted to kill myself, of course. I don't remember feeling that bad about life. If it were true and I had done either on purpose, even accidentally on purpose, my conscious brain wasn't aware of it at all.

*

Every Sunday after church, we were allowed to sit in Mrs Baines's study and listen to *Family Favourites* while we knitted compulsory baby garments for charity. I knitted vests (or paid someone to knit something for me). Although I could never get off on knitting myself, I loved its wholesome rhythm, especially in that study with the fire burning in the grate. It was all so homey and safe. And the good news was, I discovered, that there was an easy way to get in there more often: get yourself confirmed.

Mrs Baines took her confirmation classes in there every Sunday afternoon, so I committed myself to going through with it. After all, just listening to Mrs Baines's voice reading the Bible seemed a harmless enough way to gratify my fervent need to lap up the kindly, sunny atmosphere of her study.

I know my motives weren't totally pure, and that during the scripture exam I'd decided that most of the Bible was a load of old codswallop, but I was sure Jesus would have agreed with me. I didn't for one instant believe that He was codswallop – good heavens, no! He, I'm sure, was a real smasher and performed miracles. Why not, pray? So many can. But it's a tricky business saving mankind, especially when it's always left to others to distort what you really stood for. The poor chap has been abysmally ill served, for the most part, and I'm sure He would have enjoyed the warmth of Mrs Baines's study – or at least forgiven me, especially if He, too, suffered from the cold. Besides, with Mrs Baines reading the Bible to me, perhaps my problems with the codswallop were about to be solved. I might even receive some enlightenment.

One afternoon, having tea, crumpets and biscuits by the fire, listening to Mrs Baines's voice droning on, orchestrated by crackling logs, knitting needles and the crunch of ginger snaps, one of the girls passed me a book that was doing the rounds. I was never at all keen on reading – it was such a struggle – but this particular book came via Min Musker, who nudged me, her eyes enhanced by the firelight, an amber urgency. She pointed to where she'd turned down the page. Min Musker disliked reading as much as I did, so I began lazily to glance at it.

Suddenly some of the words came jumping out at me, almost as blinding as a lightning flash. The book stated clearly and categorically that Ee-Ees wasn't wicked at all, and that there was no need to heed the old wives' tales because Ee-Ees caused you no harm whatsoever. It didn't send you blind, nor did your hair fall out! After the news hit me, it began to caress me – a blessing from heaven!

I *knew* I was meant to be in Mrs Baines's study. I knew I was meant to be confirmed, for this was my own personal confirmation. I *knew* Jesus wasn't angry with me for not believing all His Bible, for merely wanting to be in the warmth. For here He was giving me a concrete sign that I could go on safely doing Ee-Ees knowing that people all over the world were doing it too, and that none of us should get punished, for there was no sin to punish. Thank you, Jesus.

Perhaps it would be prudent to assure you that I was no Olympic wanker. No, just every now and then to release rampant energy. (I loathe the word 'masturbation'. It sounds almost as alienating as 'meditation'. But I fear both will become more and more necessary for releasing dense dark energies as the chaos on Earth thickens.)

Decades later I went on a crusade for Ee-Eees, because of my deliverance that day. It was a time when sex was on the point of becoming the norm in movies but, as yet, no one had ventured into Ee-Ees territory. The film was an adaptation of Mishima's beautiful novel *The Sailor Who Fell From Grace With the Sea* in which a young pubescent boy removes a notch of wood, and peeks at his mother while she discreetly performs Ee-Ees at her dressing-table mirror. She is husbandless at the time.

When I first read the novel, I got goose-bumps, for the scene reminded me so much of that day I spied on Mummy's secret moments at her dressing-table mirror. This made me doubly determined to re-create Mishima's lyrical, penetrating passages with as much integrity as I could muster. I wanted to do him proud, not just because of his poetic prose, but because I salute him for dying the death of his philosophy. Self-delusion is so common that it's a joy to find someone practising what they preach. He believed we should die at our peak, before we start wasting food and air belonging to others. When his mind and body were at their moment of ripeness, he committed hara-kiri. I'm no advocate of this philosophy.

I felt a great weight of responsibility descending on to my shoulders as I attempted to perform my most private Ee-Ees ballet in front of a whole crew of men. The director, bless his heart, couldn't direct 'woman performing women's private ways'. Even his wife's way wouldn't be my way. So I was completely alone. I have to admit, I hadn't foreseen the lonely pit of despair I'd dug for myself. So great was my *fear* that day – it came at me from beneath, lapping swiftly up between the floorboards, sticking out its tongue at me, polluting my courage, coarsening my vulnerability, lashing feelings of doubt all over my Ee-Ees mission. The director, Lou John Carlino, said sympathetically, 'Right, action, Sarah.'

I so wanted my mission to prove worth while. I so needed to make the scene lonely yet real, elegantly erotic, gentle and kindly all at once.

Looking at rushes the next night I felt I might have done both Mishima and the film a little justice, but the editing I had no control over. The film speaks for itself.

Personally, I'm glad to have tried my best to put some of the old wives' tales to rest at a time when they were still rife, and to have done my humble bit towards removing the stigma attached to one of the most harmless, humane, free – and Aids-free celebrations. Separate or together.

Alas, the reactions from the press here in England showed that perhaps my mission was premature, for I found myself a trifle out of favour. Never mind, being burnt at the stake isn't so terrible, once you get the knack.

More important – was my mission accomplished? And would Jesus forgive me for putting confirmation classes to such strange use?

CHAPTER TWENTY-EIGHT

THE FOLLOWING Easter holiday I met the first young man who showed any interest in me. We were in Austria, staying beside a lake whose name I have forgotten. The hotel nestled close to the lake's edge, with hills graduating into picturesque mountains towering up the other side of the lake road. I was playing with Pooker on the steep hill opposite the hotel. From high up she started to run down towards the road. The lake road was a busy one, and I saw Pooker gaining speed as she began to outrun herself, her little legs going too fast for her to be able to fall, or to slow down. I had to act fast. I ran with all my might to block her off from the road.

She crashed into me with enormous force, sending us both rolling down for quite a distance, ending up a few yards from the road. I was severely winded, but really chuffed. That's why the incident remains so vivid. Doing something constructive gave me a jolly nice feeling, squeezed in between the chaos.

When we told Mummy of our adventure, she said, 'It's all your fault, Pusscat, taking her up that steep hill in the first place.' As usual she was right.

Standing beside her was a rather sensitive-looking young man. 'Darling, this is Michael. He's kindly offered to take you out on his boat.'

Though it was only a simple little sailboat, he turned out

not to be simple at all. He wanted desperately not to be who he was. From what I could make out, being the eldest son of an archduke seemed more of a burden than a privilege, especially since he was a Habsburg, as they were now pretty well penniless.

He took me to meet his mother on his motor-bike. They lived in a very modest holiday villa. Wearing bright pink plastic gloves, the Grand Duchess was washing up as we came in. I really liked them, probably because they'd lost everything and dropped pretension into the bin. Now, so much lighter of heart, they reminded me of my gypsy friends, Ted and Ethel.

I wasn't sure why he'd taken an interest in me, still being flat-chested (in contrast to my ears). Nevertheless I found his attention comforting, flattering – and why not? He was gentle and reserved, and I'd taken a liking to him before I knew who he was. I decided to give the inverted snob in me a rest for once.

Michael and I got on so well we arranged a secret evening assignation. He told me to meet him at his motor-bike at nine thirty the following evening, after Mummy and Daddy had seen me into bed.

As I lay there waiting for half past nine, I began to wonder what this dating lark was all about. Here was I, on the verge of my first date with a young man I hardly knew. I didn't really think beyond the fact that I wasn't so much excited by Michael as by the secrecy, though inwardly I felt Jack's beanstalk growing steadily, poking me with its prickly curiosity and tickling me with the same old mysterious hankerings.

Out I crept. There was Michael standing by his bike. I was

a little nervous, never having deceived my parents in such a manner before. Having ridden on the back of his motor-bike already, I knew that Michael, like me out hunting, had an appetite for speed. He gave me a sweet peck on my neck, which I remember liking a lot – more the unexpectedness of it than anything seriously sexual but it did give me a tiny thrill.

'Hop on the back, we'll go to a club a few miles up the road.'

Off we shot at full speed. Those winding lake roads were fun. Sometimes there were sheer drops to one side of the sharp bends. Each time we came to one of these corners, I shut my eyes tight. Just like at the fair – I *love* fairs! (I miss Battersea Fun Fair like hell, America for all serious roller coasters – they take me back to the good old banister days.) The roads were a little slippery and my excitement was just beginning to feel the chill of insecurity. I clutched Michael a little more firmly.

'That's it, hold on tight,' he said confidently. 'Enjoying it?'

'I was,' I said, as politely as possible.

'Ha! You're afraid!'

I didn't like being accused of cowardice. 'I just think the roads are too slippery, that's all.'

I could hear my toffee-nosed attitude ricochet off the valley below. Help! I shouldn't have looked down. That was foolish.

That was all. Michael came shooting up behind a huge lorry, failed to judge its speed, couldn't overtake, slapped on his brakes, failed to steer into the skid, and sent us into an irreversible spin. We shot off the side of the road, where, thank God, the bike turned over. If it hadn't we would have been half-way down the mountain, receiving my toffee-nosed echoes.

The bike fell on top of me, ripping my knee to bits. 'Are you all right?' I asked.

'Yes, and you?'

It was fairly dark and I didn't want to make a fuss. 'I'm fine, Michael. I just want to go back now, please.'

'I'm very sorry, I feel so ashamed,' he mumbled.

The bike wasn't too damaged so we were able to drive back – slowly. He tried to kiss me goodnight but I wasn't in the mood. I wanted to make for home, fast. Like a cat, creep into my nest of healing silence.

Once inside I began to cry, for I was badly hurt and frightened. I looked at the blood spurting out of my knee; it reminded me so much of Mickey. I went to put it under the tap. I couldn't remember which one to use: the cold was freezing but it stopped the flow better. I remained bent over the basin for ages, the wretched thing wouldn't stop bleeding. Finally I wrapped a pillow case around the throbbing mass, and got into bed.

'Open this door, Pusscat, the chambermaid wants to clean.'

I must have drifted off. 'My room's perfectly clean, I'm not feeling well, I want to sleep—'

'Open this door immediately!'

I opened the door and leapt back into bed again. In glided Mummy, her usual elegant self. She felt my head. 'You have no temperature. Now get up and go and eat breakfast, before it all gets—'

She'd seen some blood on my arm, I must have missed it.

'What's all this?'

There was nothing for it, I took a deep breath and confessed.

'That'll teach you,' she said, giving me a wry look. 'I keep telling you, Pusscat, you won't see twenty-one, and I'm right.'

Mummy was a strange woman. I never knew which way she was going to jump. When she actually saw my knee she became very business-like. First she called a doctor then began to bathe it herself with great concentration, even choosing to overlook my night-time antics. If he had been gypsy Ted rather than the Archduke's eldest son, might things have been different?

My knee took ages to heal and I was bandaged up for the rest of the hols. Oddly enough Daddy was more cross than Mummy. 'You'll get yourself mugged, raped or murdered, Pusscat, mark my words.'

But I suppose I did learn a lesson: act faster when hit by that first chill of insecurity. Michael was full of remorse. He wrote to me many times, but I stopped answering after a while . . . I was no letter writer.

CHAPTER TWENTY-NINE

I WAS BACK at school, and hating it. The hot summer term, which I spent avoiding exams (actually avoiding everything I possibly could) dragged on. Mummy and Daddy came to my confirmation, and I deeply regretted the whole affair. Having betrayed myself with Jesus, my conscience rankled. I was a charlatan, a cheat and a fraud.

I managed to wash myself clean of some of my guilt afterwards, when we discovered the local Royston swimming pool. What a pleasant surprise it turned out to be, close to school with excellent diving boards chock-a-block with teddy boys!

We had a stage at school, not too grand, but big enough to have some grand old times. One of the prefects was head of drama. She was called Marianne Lawther, known as Chubby because of her size, which never marred her acting ability. We all felt sure that Chubby's time would come, when she was about forty. Then she would become a great star, for she had an uncanny resemblance to Margaret Rutherford, with a touch of Edith Evans thrown in. Her timing was superlative, her delivery commanding, her overall ability unquestionable. I learnt a great deal from Chubby. She had vision as well as an understanding of me and my problems. She literally yanked out of me a wizard Shylock. I revelled in that part and, thanks to Chubby, gave, I think, one of my better performances.

I didn't only learn about acting from Chubby either. No, I learnt about coping with physical problems without complaining or feeling hard done by. Chubby's plumpness was a real stumbling block for her, yet her outlook was always so sunny, so utterly devoid of malice or bitchery. The whole school held her in the deepest regard. Sadly, her time did not come as we'd hoped it would. Many years later, she, S. P. J. and I rekindled our old friendship. Chubby had never married. She worked as a speech therapist with handicapped children. Tragically she died of cancer last year. As she fought the disease, she came occasionally to stay with me in the country. An incandescence shone out of her towards the end. So seductive was it that all who knew her were greedy to bask in its warmth and light while there was still the chance.

As the term ground on, I decided I'd had enough. Enough of my own sublime incompetence and total lack of ability to mould myself into a pack animal, enough black marks, enough detention, enough snobbery, enough classroom hierarchy and enough of bloody school itself.

I planned an afternoon out. I would set off on Sunday as soon as lunch was over. I had over three shillings saved for my tuck. I stole some Elastoplast from Matron's medical cabinet to stick back my ears. I put on make-up, my tightest skirt and my highest heels. I checked myself out in the long mirror. Fairly chuffed at what I saw, I grabbed my unbecoming swim-suit and made a run for it.

I stood on the verge hoping to thumb a lift. Within no

time a man drew up and rolled down his window. 'Where do you want to go?'

'Only to Royston.'

'OK, jump in.'

I gave him a very seductive smile, full of self-assurance. After all, my ears were now streamlined and utterly irresistible, surely? I was brimming over, nostrils twitching with the scent of adventure.

He hardly gave me a glance. It was quite a posh car with a wireless and all. I wasn't going to let on that I hadn't seen one before.

'Playing hooky, then?'

I nearly choked myself. 'No, why?'

He laughed. He knew.

'Does your wireless play pop music?' I was getting into Johnny Ray, Harry Belafonte, Ray Charles at that time.

'Radio, not wireless.'

'Oh.' We drove along in silence. He was a strange chap, couldn't put my finger on him.

'What time d'you have to be back?'

I told him.

'OK, I'll be outside the swimming baths at six.'

'Thanks,' I said, not believing my luck. I gave him a little come-on, to guarantee he kept his word. 'Promise?'

He laughed at my attempts at temptress. 'I promise.' And off he shot, down the High Street.

I didn't have a great time at the side of the pool that afternoon. There was too much competition in the beauty stakes, and I couldn't dive in case I lost my sticking plasters. Feeling more lonely and lost as the afternoon wore on, I decided radar scanners be damned! Once I began to show off my different dives, the teddy boys' attention shifted. They dunked me, chased me, tripped me, in fact it all became quite a merry dance until one of them started pointing at me and nudging his friend, who then nudged another, until they all fell about laughing, and promptly departed.

I took my things and went into the changing rooms. There, staring at me, was the reason. My ears had had their way as usual. Wretched stubborn things, they looked quite ludicrous with plaster hanging off them! Grotesque, with my eyes all red and black from make-up and chlorine. It was nearly six o'clock, however, so I thought it best to go and wait outside the baths for my chauffeur.

I waited and waited but he never showed up. Why was I ever stupid enough to think that he would? I started to walk. For some reason, no one stopped on the way back to school. Perhaps it was because of my ears, or that I'd lost that perky confidence I'd started out with. Whatever the reason, I was late for prayers.

So there I was in the headmistress's study again, just like at Roedean. Mrs Baines's two Border terriers came up to me and gave me a lick. She never approved of them liking me, let alone licking me with such gusto.

'I've turned a blind eye to your midnight feasts, your black marks, your subversive behaviour, your complete lack of any kind of discipline, because I believed you had something, somewhere, to offer. Obviously I was wrong, and I'm left no alternative but to expel you.'

'Do I leave right away?' I tried to keep the excitement out of my voice, but I think I must have failed again.

'No, you'll stay for the last ten days of term.' I turned to leave. 'Sarah?'

I turned to face her. 'Yes, Mrs Baines?'

'Miss Clap says your tennis is good. Why don't you at least take that more seriously?'

For some mysterious reason I did a little curtsey. 'Yes, Mrs Baines, I will.'

Ten days left of school, then I'd be free!

It turned into a strangely empty victory. I tried to discover what caused the emptiness. I managed to whittle it down to a feeling of unfulfilled potential in Miss Robinson's English classes. During those hours of English, something very important had slipped me by. Those memories of lost potential didn't fade as I expected them to, but grew into something quite painful. Miss Robinson had been the best teacher there, unquestionably. But I was too afraid of her to get anywhere with her or with English. I couldn't untie the knot of regret, for I felt strongly that English and I could have been friends. The fact that Miss Robinson was too arrogant to see past the end of her intellectual nose left me with an enormous amount of stifled fury (so what else is new?), which was all tied up with my total frustration at failing to conquer my brain blindness problem caused by dyslexia.

About two years later I took a party of friends back to Crofton Grange one night to wreak my revenge. We set off in two vans. It was all meant to be a harmless St Trinians prank. The mission was to let off the fire extinguishers, to tear up the horrid black book, and to tie up Miss Robinson – gently, of course! I wore a woolly hat and we all wore masks over our eyes in case someone recognized us.

I found the black book, where it always was, in the middle drawer of the dresser in the hall. Tearing it up, I remember feeling a bit of an idiot. No, demolishing the black book wasn't anywhere near as wizard as letting off the fire extinguishers. But Miss Robinson, with her academic superiority, probably smelt a rat, for she was nowhere to be found.

Still, you can't win 'em all. 'Dash my wig and bees!' as Daddy used to say.

I had every intention of omitting this tale, so ashamed of it am I. But then I thought it would not be correct.

CHAPTER THIRTY

MUMMY AND DADDY were in despair.

'What do you want to do, then, Pusscat?' said Daddy at his wits' end. I shrugged arrogantly, not wanting to tell him about being a film star in case he laughed, so I played safe. Anyway, I didn't actually *want* to be in the movies, it was just that something that day back there in the rose garden told me I was going to be.

'I want to be a groom—'

'Don't be stupid, darling,' said Mummy. 'Grooms don't get anywhere in life – that's a mug's job.'

I shrugged again. 'Then I'd like to join the circus – you told me I had the ears for it.'

They both laughed.

'You have to be born to the circus, Pusscat,' said Daddy.

'What about tennis?' said I, half-heartedly.

'God, no!' said Mummy. 'There's no future in that!'

'Besides, you haven't the temperament,' said Guess Who.

I had begun show jumping in earnest because the previous year Mummy had kept her Palomino Promise – golden chestnut with a white mane and tail, like Trigger – up to a point. It turned out to be an albino promise, pure white horse with pink skin and blue eyes. Sadly, palominos were too expensive.

Prince Charming was his name. Although he wasn't a natural jumper, he was, none the less, eager to clear them. Over a two-year period we gradually made our way up the amateur junior show jumping circuit. All my sweat and hard work culminated at the Essex County Show, the biggest horse show I'd ever been to. As soon as we arrived I began regretting my foolhardy determination to scale the higher rungs of the snotty (in those days) show jumping ladder – so many stunning competitors littered about the show grounds. We cantered around the collecting ring, trying to put aside all comparison. Daddy's words began to echo in my throbbing pinned-back ears, 'You have everything going for you except temperament, Pusscat.' I knew deep down he was right. We waited nervously for our number to be called out, my knees were wobbling against my saddle flaps. I say we, but it was I who was sweating with fear, not Charming. But that's it, the very heart of my temperament problem: *fear*. 'Number twelve, Sarah Miles on Prince Charming,' boomed the loudspeaker (his name before I got him).

Prince Charming had the devil in him that day. He did something he'd never done before – a show-jumper's nightmare. He refused three times at the first fence, which happened to be a brush. On his final refusal I found myself more than half off, trying with all my might and his mane to stay on board. All this would have been hugely humiliating if it hadn't been for the welcoming roar of laughter from the crowd (echoes of Roedean chapel, laughter, best sound in the world). When I dragged myself back on, I realized it wasn't me who was the clown, but Prince Charming. Having failed to jump it, he thought he'd eat it instead. I had to sit there while he munched away at the brush.

'Number twelve eliminated. Jolly bad luck, number twelve.'

No doubt about it, I'd sent a destructive negative force straight through my wobbling knees to poor Charming's tummy. He picked up every feeble, egotistical emotion – and the fear as well. Not only was he called upon to carry me, but all my neurotic baggage too. But I, coward perhaps, took that as a sign that I wasn't cut out to climb the gold-plated rungs of the upper-class show-jumping ladder. I can't blame the upper classes, it's me. Why am I so frightened in a crowd?

That Essex show shook me up a lot. I'm pretty well fearless whatever life throws at me, and I choose to cope with things alone. There's *almost* nothing I wouldn't do as a bet or a dare, but give me a crowd and I turn to jelly. I think I've finally overcome the fear of death, but give me humanity and off go the knees again. Perhaps in another lifetime I was trampled to death. Or perhaps that's what's in store for me in this one.

But my pride was soothed beautifully by endless rides with Pooker, who had really got the riding bug at last. Prince Charming and Mizzer were as thick as thieves as we roared along the bridle-paths all summer long. A few days later while out exercising Prince Charming, I saw our neighbour Anthony Blond, Reba Marsham's son, slide by me in his silky Rolls-Royce. He stopped and asked me if I'd like to go for a drive? He looked so clean and handsome in his grey flannel suit and red and white spotted tie that I found myself feeling most flattered.

'When?'

'Sunday morning at twelve,' he said, shooting off at high speed.

That Sunday noon the storm clouds gathered outside, keeping pace with Daddy's anger. He didn't want me to go at all. Perhaps he felt threatened because I wasn't his little Pusscat any more.

Oddly enough I found Mummy defending me. 'Oh, come on, John, we've known him since she was this high,' she said pointing to her knees.

'You be back here by one o'clock sharp – d'you hear me?'

Dead on high noon Anthony slipped up our drive in his Rolls, looking dashing in a roguish, Etonian kind of way. He leapt out and opened the door for me, promising Daddy I'd be back in an hour, and off we went. He took the corners of our narrow country lanes at full pelt. I was determined to keep smiling, for although half of me was frightened that his skill may not be equal to his speed, the other half was relishing the danger.

'Don't you go doing too much riding,' he warned with foxy slyness.

'Why not?'

'You might lose your virginity,' he said, lighting a cigarette as we zoomed over Mill Green Common. I wasn't sure what he was on about, so I kept my eyes on the wet slippery road ahead – still smiling, of course.

As we approached Church Hill, famous for its hairpin bend at the bottom of the hill, I hoped he couldn't see my knuckles clenched tightly on the soft leather strap beside me.

Just as I thought, Anthony failed to make the turn, and we ended up in a notorious and muddy ditch. He tried to reverse, but the wheels merely skimmed round and round.

Calmly he scratched his head, deep in thought. 'I read

somewhere to put a rug or a blanket under the back wheel to give it something to grip on to.' He began to search for some such material. There was nothing in the car that would serve, and the rain was bucketing down.

'I know!' He jumped out of the car, taking off his jacket. He stuffed it under the back wheel, and leapt into the car again.

I stood in the rain watching his smart Savile Row jacket get chewed to bits, and spat out again from under the wheel. He leant out of the window. 'Stuff it under.'

'There's nothing to stuff, your jacket's in ribbons.'

Thoughtfully he scrutinized his ruined jacket, then proceeded to take off his trousers and stuff them, more vigorously this time, under the other back tyre. 'This time it'll do the trick,' he said confidently.

He started the engine, and exactly the same thing happened again. The delightful thing was that Anthony didn't seem a bit perturbed by the ruined suit, only by the failure of this tip that he had read in a book somewhere. 'I must have got it muddled,' he said, taking off his shirt and waistcoat. 'I'll give it one last try. If this fails we'll have to walk.' He looked at his watch. 'Or rather, run, it's ten past one. Blast!'

And that's how Daddy found us, standing at the bottom of Church Hill in the pouring rain with Anthony in nothing but vest and pants. Looking as we did, so idiotic and utterly unromantic, I think even Daddy could see that no mischief had occurred, and by the look of our po-faces there wasn't going to be any either. .

The incident prodded me into thinking it was time to drive a car. What with the few accidents I'd had so far, it might be that there were more tucked away on the horizon. If this was so, I thought it wisest to be in the driving seat when I died – besides, *all* film stars drove.

I'd been tinkering a lot lately with the film-star thing. It would be simpler, certainly, than being a theatre actor and having to take on all those crowds. I was having doubts about the circus too – crowds again. Falling off the top wire from nerves didn't make sense.

Once, at Bertram Mills' Circus, the human bullet was shot across the marquee to a crescendo of drums into a deadly silence. Daddy broke it after giving Mother a nervous look. 'Let's leave before the crowd.'

We left to whispers of 'What happened to him, where is he?'

No, I didn't fancy any of that clown business. Shame, because I'd put such a lot of hard work into my horse acts and my trapeze. My handstand was getting strong (I was walking nowadays) – but crowds.

I'd always assumed that I was Fearless Fred. It turned out I was Feeble Fanny.

It came down to two possible alternatives: either a humble groom, just quietly getting on with my day with no hassle, or go for this film-star lark.

That summer hols, after I left Crofton Grange, I really got cracking. I started stealing Mummy's Austin Seven, HOH 22, for jaunts around the country lanes. I was only fourteen, but I felt fairly secure behind the wheel. Mummy was a brick on these occasions. Although I never had permission, she turned a blind eye. I think she knew that (a) driving might be the only way to get me out of her hair, and (b) I was as likely to meet the police in our country lanes in those days as I was the Yeti.

The Mileses' social life was hotting up, and we found ourselves being swirled up in it a fraction. We went to see Julian Slade's musical *Salad Days*. It mirrored the arousal of mid-fifties hope, which began to creep into the toes of our shoes. Slade's songs seemed so full of sunshine and innocence, as if all was well with the British Empire and Britannia still ruled the waves. Another family outing was *Pieces of Eight* with Kenneth Williams. Chuzzer and I laughed and laughed. I'd never experienced anything quite like it before. Not even S.P.J. could have competed with us that outing. As we left I remember looking at my seat rather guiltily, for it was a trifle damp – but how could I help it?

I don't remember laughing so hard with Chuzzer ever again. Kenneth did something to Chuzzer and me, much worse than the Chase swimming pool. We got hooked on him. My husband turned out to be a close friend of Kenneth's, so I got to know him and introduced Chuzzer to him. Kenneth always reminded me of one of the little people, a woodland elf, perhaps. He certainly wasn't of this world, which is why he felt so alien. He found living devilish hard. No wonder, it takes a great deal of pain to allow an audience to free themselves with laughter in that way (in my case all over my seat). For comedians it truly is the agony and the ecstasy. They give us the ecstasy and pummel themselves at times to death with the agony.

Mummy made a huge effort to get me to socialize with the county that summer, as if, at the tender age of fourteen, she might find me a classy beau, and get me off her hands.

She must have been desperate – poor Mummy! She especially wanted me to become friendly with a family who lived near Shenfield. One day Piers, the eldest boy, asked me out to the local flicks. Mummy astonished me by not only being all for it, but offering to take us in!

Pierse was certainly better than the rest of the local talent, though I found him a trifle spoilt, as I did most of the privileged people I met living in Essex at that time. They lacked chutzpah, the courage to 'go for it'. But Piers was sweet and kind. We went out together quite a few times. He held my hand, put his arm around me, and I think would have liked our innocent courtship to continue, but Jukes wanted me up in Norwich for the show he was putting on, which severed our prospects somewhat.

Was I ever wrong about Piers. I need to brush up on my first impressions. His surname was Courage and he grew into his name, becoming a fearless and internationally renowned racing driver, quite brilliant. He died in an horrific accident as we were all watching him on television. Which just goes to show I shouldn't make snap judgements.

Although I'd never mentioned becoming a film star to Jukes, it seemed as if he already knew, intuitively, where I was headed, and decided to give me some practice. It was most strange. He pulled and I followed, always with mixed feelings, but always there none the less. He hauled me into two hilarious TV commercials he had cooked up years before they were ever a TV reality.

Jukes was deeply involved with his *Begmilian Show*. The name 'Begmilian' derived from joining his name, Miles, with that of his best friend from Winchester, Nigel Begbie. The show was a kind of review, like the *Footlights*. Everyone was most enthusiastic about it, me included. He had kindly asked me to dance in a bikini as Noël Coward's 'Nina from Argentina'. Jukes was to be Noël Coward, dancing around on stage behind me (typical creator-writer-director-producer modesty!). I went up for three days of rehearsal and one performance in Norwich, and stayed at the home of Nigel Begbie. Nigel, though too upper class for my taste, was irresistibly Byronic with an effete aquiline, aristocratic air – quite the opposite of my dashing gypsy Ted. Yet I grew rather partial to Nigel, and was thrilled to be staying in his house, away from home. I felt very grown-up indeed.

Rehearsals went well, so did the show. Everyone said I was jolly good, I didn't believe them a hundred per cent since I had to stuff my bras, and stick back my ears beneath my fuzzy hair. Jukes and Nigel got a lot of praise, deservedly, for it was a most ambitious evening. Mummy and Daddy laughed a lot, and seemed genuinely proud of Jukes. A good time was had by all.

The last night at Nigel's, with hindsight, was predictable. What with the potent odour of success charging the air, we inevitably ended up going to bed together. I'm not sure who initiated it. All I can remember, hovering somewhere in the shadowy recesses, is a sweetly innocent affair, generous cuddles and a few clumsy yet harmless fumblings. Harmless it certainly was. We played around, neither of us truly committed. Two little babes trespassing on the edge of virgin woods, not sure whether to go in. To give Nigel credit, he was very gentle and patient with me, for I believe I was being what is called a cock-teaser. Next morning we faced

The Chantry Hall, Norwich

In aid of the R.S.P.C.A.

NIGEL BEGBIE with CHRISTOPHER MILES

presents

THE
BEGMILIAN SHOW

"It's naughty, but it's nice"

FRIDAY and SATURDAY
6th—7th SEPTEMBER

Performances at 2.30 and 6 p.m.

For the third year in succession this young cast produces, presents and performs a real delightful, delicious, decolete performance

Alice Ashworth

Rosemary Begbie

Stephen Boardman

Elizabeth Buxton

Lesley Chittock

Colin Coleman

Peter Coleman

Cynthia Goodchild

Anne Hammond

Anthony Hammond

Sarah Miles

Ann Richardson

Nicholas Richardson

Susan Richardson

Michael Watson

Vanessa Watson

Tickets 2/- obtainable either at the door, or in advance from

Mrs. Fletcher Watson, Wicklewood Grove, Wymondham, Norfolk

Please send S.A.E. Any donations for the Society in connection with this show will be most gratefully received

REFRESHMENTS WILL BE SERVED AT EACH PERFORMANCE

DENNY BROS., Printers, Bury St. Edmunds.

everything sideways, all very oblique, not confronting each other or our previous night's escapade full frontal.

My Jack's beanstalk had surreptitiously grown so lusty, that its branches had conveniently blocked out death fears. So for the next two decades lust would be my main focus of energy. I hadn't forgotten I was going to die before I was twenty-one, but I'd tucked those horrors safely away under self-delusion, denial and a mind-blowingly juicy randiness!

'Now, stop! I won't have you wasting your life as a blasted groom.'

'It's my life I'd be wasting, not yours!'

'Well, it's too late now, and since they were prepared to accept you sight unseen, I quickly paid the first term's fees just to be on the safe side.'

I was horror struck.

'You mean I'm going to the Arts Educational, willy-nilly?'

'Yes, young lady, you're going to the Arts Educational – willy-nilly. And if you get expelled from there, then—'

'Then I can be a groom after all.'

'You are impossible!'

We were driving into Bloomsbury, ready for a stay in the University College Hospital to have my ears remade. I was in two minds about having it done, wheras Mother's mind was singularly made up. My future was clearly focused in her sight line and I wasn't allowed to take a peek. This future was to be acting, like the Sarah Bernhardt she had named me after. Only now do I see it all as clearly as she obviously did then.

'At the moment, darling, you can't see the wood for the trees. But once you have ordinary ears like the rest of us, you'll see that I'm doing what's best for you.'

'My riding hat will fit better with flat ears, that's for sure.'

'Now do stop!' Mummy was stuck in traffic, dangerously near her Polly Tree. 'Besides, to ride professionally one needs hoards of cash.'

'Like Mauzie had in her attic?'

University College Hospital was huge and gloomy, inside and out. Finally the surgeon came to visit us on the ward. Surgeons, I've noted, have three times the ego of actors. Why is that? This one was typical, but he seemed to know his job, though procedures in the mid fifties were somewhat more primitive than they are today. It wasn't just a job of pinning my ears back, they had to be remade, reshaped into man-made, perfectly flat little pink shells.

He peered at my ears. 'I hope you have plenty of patience.'

'Why?' I asked.

'You have to wear the bandages around your head for two weeks.' He patted my hair, and collected his notes. 'It'll all be worth it, surely, to have beautiful little ears like everyone else?'

Mummy left soon after the surgeon. She gave me a kiss. 'I'll be up again tomorrow or the next day. Be brave now, and know that I love you.'

Next morning they gave me a pre-med, which made me feel omnipotent. As I lay there waiting to be wheeled down,

I meandered over the plan Mummy had cannily mapped out for me. Would I be a movie star after all? Or did I lack the bottle, just like at tennis, just like at everything else? I was going to live in London, staying with Mummy's old friend, doctor and gynaecologist, Mary Adams, in one of the Nash terraces, Kent Terrace in Regent's Park. I was going to the school for dance and drama, the Arts Educational in Berkeley Street near Marble Arch, just up the road. So, the first steps were already taken. 'What's done cannot be undone,' as Lady Macbeth so wisely put it. I had clearly made a botch of my life so far.

But it's never too late to start again. Mother was forever willing – if impatiently on occasion – to open new doors for me, as fast as I ungratefully slammed them in her face. She kept giving me fresh opportunities to put some of my past to rights. Maybe I'd be like Dick Whittington – come to old London Town and find the streets paved with golden Crunchie bars. A pair of sparkling new ears might work wonders. All things are possible. 'Mind over matter, Pusscat!'

Is it any wonder Dick Whittington found the London streets paved with gold? He was, after all, travelling with a great black cat for good luck. Do you suppose he had any contacts in London's gold business before he arrived? I doubt it, and nor did I. I knew no one in showbiz, not a sausage – and no black cat either. How could I possibly be lucky without black Mizzer – or even brown Chan for company? Although I found that no gold Crunchie bars shimmered off the pavements for me, I did notice a melancholy, yellowish hue hanging over everything and everybody. Condensed petrol fumes permeating the freshly aroused senses of a country bumpkin, intermingled with the whiff of uncharted adventures to be lived to the hilt, were heady stuff, putting a new edge on life.

Hope, youth and luck were all I believed in, in those early days. I wasn't lucky with Daddy's ideas about inherited wealth either. He had every intention of making each one of us earn our own living, so he gave out mingy allowances that hardly covered our basic needs. He fervently believed that those who expected money to come their way lay back and waited for the monthly cheque to roll in, never realizing real potential and worth.

I'd have taken money over potential any day – then.

Mary Adams's house, 9 Kent Terrace, Regent's Park, sounds posh, I know, but it was cold and unwelcoming. My bedroom was bleak, but I was very lucky to have a bedroom at all. Although I knew this, I also knew I had to get away as soon as possible. My claustrophobia conflicted strangely with that spacious draughty old house, with its impersonal waiting rooms, and the once gloriously proportioned drawing room insulted into a cold and foreboding surgery, full of ugly torture equipment – stirrups, high beds and white sheets. I dreaded to think of her peering up some poor woman's fanny. The whole place gave me the creeps. I've always had doubts about women reeking of perfume and houses reeking of disinfectant, for what are they trying hide, I wonder. I could see that Mary worked too hard; she was always so abrupt, in her white overalls, with bags under her tired eyes and a black stethoscope hanging gloomily around her neck.

I was determined to tap into that inner potential that Daddy was always on about; also I wanted to test his 'mind over matter' theory. Mummy was right, I had to learn to act.

I supposed you had to know something about it if you were going to be a movie star.

So I wrote out my list of dreams which were going to have to come true pretty quickly, because I didn't fancy living as part of somebody else's life for too long. It went something like this: I'd become a famous movie star, marry my Knight of Wisdom, buy myself a country house older than my mother's, with rooms painted all colours of the rainbow. My children's wellies would be strewn about the hall. The atmosphere would be an easy, Bohemian, elegantly organized chaos, with crackling fires filling every room with rosy warmth. At last I'd get my white Pyrenean Mountain Dog, just like God. He'd need a kennel which would mean a large conservatory. I'd want a big homey kitchen-cum-dining room, the womb of the house, a kindly cook, maid, groom, gardener and a chauffeur for my Rolls-Royce convertible. With my new singing voice equal to Edith Piaf's, I'd have enough money to afford an efficiently run stud farm on the same property for breeding quality palominos, a well-equipped stable yard, a Land-rover and trailer. I took this dream of home straight out of my subconscious, or wherever this vision lurked, the vision I'd had that day when I saw HOME in my wrinkled palm, the old house by an ancient church, with a river running through woodlands surrounding this little paradise on earth. Although I still felt leaving school at fourteen was great news, something within me knew I'd have to catch up on all the stuff I didn't know – which was everything. So I planned a short cut to this enormous void of no knowledge by marrying this Knight of Wisdom, someone I could revere for his brains as well as his . . . I knew I had to move fast if I was ever going to tick off any of these items.

I saw *And God Created Woman*, and I had to have straight hair too, swinging around my breasts like Brigitte Bardot's. But to achieve this B.B. look with breasts still a murmur and a mass of fuzz wasn't easy. I went to a hairdresser at Marble Arch and asked if he could straighten it. He said they could, but that the whole process was the reverse of perming, and might ruin the quality.

'But my hair has no quality,' I said.

'Exactly,' he replied. 'Therefore it may break off at the root.'

I didn't like the sound of that so I either had to iron the damn stuff on Mary Adams's ironing board when she wasn't looking, or place big flat silver clips right down to the bottom of each section, using as many as fifty silver clips on my head at one time. The result resembled a judge's periwig or an ancient Egyptian – no Queen of the Nile, alas. These clips hurt my still vulnerable ears as I throbbed gently to sleep.

(My ears still hurt at night, leaving me no choice but to carry an extra soft pillow wherever I go, which is rather embarrassing as I don't see myself as a fussy type. The reason for this is because the surgeon forced them too flat to my head. The operation took place while muscles and sinews were still growing, so I have to pay the price every morning with a few seconds of excruciating pain – well worth it in those early days, but I'm not so sure now . . .)

I wore yellow lipstick, green rouge and purple eyes. I decided to dye my dull brown locks black – a grave error of judgement. My skirts were quite a bit shorter than the average shop assistant's, and I wore blue, green and yellow wooden beads in three long rows that reached down below my skirt hem. Although I tripped over them from time to time (a subconscious need to return to my bow-tails perhaps) the effect was stupendous. I thought I was the bee's knees as my own knees buzzed with the clank of the beads. I'd actually done it! After a great deal of hard work, even I had one poor fellow bumping into a lamp-post. Was I aware, I wonder, that it wasn't out of admiration but shock? How lucky I was to be living at a time when shocking people was relatively easy, rather than now, when striding up Hyde Park naked with a feather up your arse would hardly warrant a second glance.

Although the Arts Educational was a bit mimsy and tame, I was fortunate to meet up with a real goer. She was very sophisticated for her fourteen years – she had, after all, been a child star in the television series *The Railway Children*. She had finished her bout of luck for the time being, and wanted to be a movie star like me. Unlike me she was absolutely stunning. Her colouring alone made one gawp. Straight silky hair framing an almost olive skin, and huge doe-like glistening black eyes. Her bone structure closely resembled that of Audrey Hepburn, in fact she could have been her double except, of course, Anneka Willis was blonde. Anneka regularly came down to Barn Mead for weekends. Jukes took advantage of her star status and shoved her in one of his home movies *All That Glitters Isn't Champagne*. Anneka was the beautiful heroine and naturally I was the villain. I thought I'd camp it up to high heaven. It worked! I thought I stole the show, until Pooker, who played the maid, got the best close up, right at the end. She was brilliant, lying there playing dead on the drawing room carpet covered in tomato ketchup.

So there we were, me with my new black hair hanging in stiff curtains all over my face, both of us in our daring purple, black and olive green get-ups, covered in make-up of similar hue, swinging our long beads, posing and puffing, me through my long black cigarette holder. What were we doing? Looking for date rape if you ask me . . .

Daddy had been told by Mary that I went everywhere in a taxi, so my allowance was cut. All problems solved. Anneka and I got bikes and rode our way barefoot around all our favourite haunts. (I still bike round London today, it's the only way). I took a part-time job in a coffee bar. It was fun, having a real job, even though it was rather short-lived. It was a tatty place off Baker Street, and the food was much better and cheaper further up, on the left-hand side near the cinema. My boss overheard me suggesting this other café to a customer one afternoon and I had to leave. Which was a bore because it meant back to tap-dancing class which I hated. I'm no tap dancer, too much counting, too many 'lefts' and 'rights'.

King's Road was a regular haunt. Why it held such fascination for me was a complete mystery. There was no sign of the coming sixties, but there was something hovering around Markham Square. Precious packages of promise pierced the air, getting me punch drunk on things to come. Suna Portman reigned supreme. What a rare Bohemian beauty she was, resembling a finely chiselled upper-crust version of B.B. I used to sit and stare at her stillness, or was it just that she seemed still in comparison to the many eligible bees buzzing around her, vying for the attention of their queen? She never noticed me, for I was invisible, tucked away in the corner of the Markham Arms pub.

I didn't like Regent's Park, it was too prim and proper. I much preferred the very heart of town or Chelsea. My favourite places were Soho and Shepherd's Market. I found

both so potent, villagy and homey, the exotic smells reminding me of Ted and Ethel. I liked the tarts on the streets, too;
they were friendly. If all else failed, I thought that being a tart
would suit me fine, but I was at this point still a virgin –
unless Anthony Blond was right (his remark still echoed in
my newly streamlined ears). Perhaps I had lost my virginity
by too much riding . . . and so what? I was never sure what
it was that a virgin lost, anyway. I was too scared to go
venturing for the answer myself – and anyway what would I
be searching for? It seemed to me to be Much Ado About
Nothing and, besides, I could think of worse things in life
than losing my virginity to Prince Charming.

Anneka and I couldn't afford to eat out, so we pedalled
home. Home for me was still with Mary Adams in Kent
Terrace. It was in total contrast to Anneka's mellow, ram-
shackle house in Hampstead, where she dossed with the
Craxton family, notorious for their eccentricity, a wonderfully
mad Bohemian bunch if ever there was one. John Craxton
was an artist. He was very fond of Anneka, but I don't think
there was any hanky-panky going on between them. I hadn't
asked Anneka if she was a virgin, one didn't ask that sort of
thing, it just wasn't done. Thank God!

I loved going to pick her up in Hampstead, because Mrs
Craxton was so refined, so vague on the surface, but, like Mrs
Baines, sharp as a whippet underneath. Their home was also
my idea of organized chaos that I only saw in my dreams.
Animals, flowers, tasteful messes scattered all over beautifully proportioned crumbling rooms. The drawing-room windows opened on to an overgrown secret wilderness. I'd have
given anything to have been staying there.

'Hmm,' said Mary Adams, taking out some forgotten food

from the oven and placing it in front of me. 'You wouldn't last at the Craxtons' for more than ten minutes.'

Mary had been around our family always. Having brought us all into the world, and been a regular weekend guest over the years, she was part of a continuity that was precious to me. But although I was fond of her, she wasn't so fond of me. She referred to me as the rotten apple of the bunch, which really helped my confidence no end. It was probably due to the fact that I was never around to listen to her, having absolutely no capacity for gossip on the one hand, nor any great thirst to digest her medical gynaecological jargon on the other. What fourteen-year-old wants to hear intricate details about some poor woman's collapsing womb, infected ovaries or endless miscarried fetuses? Sometimes Mary frightened me, too, with her severe black bun scraped back off her sharp features and a jutting chin fit to fry an egg upon. I told Mummy one weekend that I thought Mary was after me. 'She came into the bathroom and looked at me most strangely,' I said mischievously.

'So what?' Mummy immediately sprang to Mary's defence.

'Perhaps, Mummy, if someone is continually looking up other women it gets to be a bit of a habit?'

'I should have sent you to Châtelard after all.'

I had been threatened with this snobby nonsense of a Swiss finishing school before. As the end of term was drawing dangerously close something drastic had to be done. I had a brainwave. I knew a girl who had gone there, so I told Mummy I was looking forward to Châtelard because I thought I had lesbian tendencies which would be well catered for.

'What?' said Mummy, appalled.

I went on. 'I heard from Fiona that it's reached epidemic proportions. But don't worry, Mummy, I can cope, in fact I'll have a ball.'

Poor Mummy: the horror of lesbianism saved my bacon twice. My place at Châtelard was cancelled, and Mummy came to London in a flash searching for cheap and cheerful bedsits to save me from the Mary Adams 'problem'. I knew my leaving would make Mary happy. Never having had any children herself, she found me an enormous responsibility, so we all got what we wanted. We found a little basement room on Haverstock Hill, where Mummy lied about my age to the landlady.

CHAPTER THIRTY-ONE

S EX WAS ABOUT to crash into my life. With my avid sense of curiosity it couldn't be put off much longer. Jukes and I were off on a skiing holiday together with a group of teenagers roughly our age. I was a little younger than the rest, but I'd promised Mummy I would behave myself. Neither of us had skied before so all kinds of adventures beckoned. We puffed our way across Europe towards a picturesque Austrian village called Brandt, sparklingly neat and nooky, the snow right at our door. I absolutely loved the whole atmosphere of the place.

I loved skiing too, and thought I'd made a pretty good job of it until I got home and saw Jukes's wretched family movies. I couldn't believe my eyes. I wasn't at all the Nijinsky of the slopes that I had imagined – far from it. I closely resembled Danny the drake, wings flapping up the pond in one of his panics, all tense and hunched. Catching the truth can be cruel. It's always the same when I see myself on film and reality sends me crashing down to earth where I suffer hellish bruises. There were other bruises in store for me that holiday.

In the evening we would all dance to a wonderful gay (as in gaiety) band. I loved to dance with Jukes. Like Daddy he was a nifty dancer, elegant, too, rarely treading on my feet which made a nice change. Unfortunately his neat dancing feet were removed from me by a girl called Sleepy. Not too sleepy either when it came to Jukes. They got married (still are).

How I loved to dance. (Maybe it was lucky Jukes hadn't his camera with him on the dance floor too.) I can't remember the band leader's name, but he was very sexy. He could pick up chairs and tables in his teeth, a party trick which was guaranteed to get every stupid girl in the room (me) weak at the knees. But he couldn't carry a table in his teeth and sing at the same time. I asked him to try, and he failed. He rather liked me I think. Whenever I appeared, dressed to kill, down the central staircase (perfect banisters for sliding down) attempting to ooze my way as erotically as possible, slipping my arm panther-like along the banisters, wiggling my bottom, the band leader would start serenading me with a song specially for me. How flattered I was! 'Buona sera, signorina, buona sera!' It lifted my heart, but how low it sank when Jukes informed me, ten days later as we were chuffing home again that, *Buona sera* didn't mean 'Good Sarah' in Italian, but 'Good evening'.

One night, sitting with my legs crossed provocatively on my bar-stool, another man caught my eye. I'd spied him last night too, and the night before. He was older than our group, and he resembled a demonic, foreign-looking Leslie Howard. I found him very sexy indeed, much more so than the younger men. I'd noticed the way he danced. He was the only man there who really knew how to hold a woman, how to envelop her without stifling her space for movement. I wanted to be in his arms, so when he turned towards me, I licked my lips and recrossed my legs on my high bar-stool, turning my back on him to order another drink.

He came over to me, bowing slightly. 'May I have the honour of a little dance with you?'

Being in his arms was better than I had anticipated, as I'd dreamt dancing with your lover should be. I almost sent Jukes upstairs for his movie camera, to have proof of this harmonious togetherness. Oddly enough, I cannot remember his name but, then, what's in a name when two hearts are beating as one?

After our dancing – more like smooching by then – became too much for us to stand up for any longer, 'Would you care to come with me? I have something up in my room that I'd like you to have.'

Without a second thought I followed him. At the bottom of the stairs he let me go first. Going up the stairs I wiggled my hips as best I could, but it probably wasn't too effective from his angle, not having anything really juicy to wiggle. I felt so grown up, so wickedly voluptuous as we entered his bedroom, his male territory, his private space.

'Sit down and I'll pour you a drink.' I obeyed. The bed was quite a bit harder than mine. But it was nothing like as hard as the great ramrod he produced, like a rabbit out of a hat, and waved in front of me. I have to say it was absolutely huge, or maybe that was because it was the first one I'd ever seen properly up and about. Christ, he was strong! Without a fumble, as if it was something he did every day, he pulled up my skirt. Quick as a flash, he collected saliva from his mouth and rubbed it all over the top of his 'thing', which repelled me no end. He aimed it at my thighs, violently poking his way into my plain petrified pants. Even if I was willing there was no way that I could have received that great German dragon tail into my cold, horrorstruck den.

How fast it all happened! Fear spewed up, spilling over into panic as he slapped a hand over my mouth to stifle my screams. Yet even through it all, I was able to observe how ludicrous he looked, fully dressed with his naked monster bulging all purple with bloated promises and saliva. With dangerous ease he managed to pry open my knees with his knee. He was utterly preoccupied with what he was doing, forcing my skinny thighs further and further apart, thighs hardly any bigger than his 'thing', which was leaving behind it a trail of saliva . . . like a snail lane. It was all so new, so ugly, so grotesque.

I knew he was proud of the size comparison. He gave me a truly evil look, as he placed 'it' alongside my thigh as if to say, 'Just look at that.' Then snapping back my head so I could no longer see, he pinned me down with an iron vice of a grip. I screamed, 'No!'

Wider and wider he prised me open, simultaneously stuffing his fat tongue down my throat to stifle my screams. Malcolm came whizzing into my consciousness, Malcolm's face looking up at my slit from the grass, so eager and wild to open me up further.

I caught a glimpse of his sweaty face and icy eyes glaring, fierce as a demon. But I was fierce too, fiercely protecting myself with all my strength and with all my might. I screamed again, but he merely stuffed my mouth with his garlic tongue.

At last I managed a kind of stifled scream, at which point I found myself flipped over as lightly as a pancake, my head stuffed into the pillows. I felt my pants being slid down and off. As he stroked his hand back up to my softer parts, I heard the filthy grunts of pleasure that my bare bum framed in a white suspender belt was obviously giving him. I could do nothing, not even scream any more.

Suddenly a memory of the Chase swimming pool rushed into my head, how on two occasions I had managed, due to my lung capacity, to stay alive. With his great plonker finally about to plonk itself into some hole or other, I used all the strength I possessed. With an almighty wrench I managed to wriggle myself loose. As I leapt sideways, I screamed and screamed.

Those who know my lung capacity would understand how my screams shuddered the foundations of the hotel, stopping even the biggest German liver sausage in its tracks. I opened the door and ran. He didn't follow me.

I was profoundly shocked by the ghoulish horror of it all, and I wasn't myself for days, yet I could share my nightmare with no one, for I felt so ashamed. I remember saying something about it to Jukes, but I was too scared, much too raw still, to go into detail. But the German liver sausage was to be seen no more in those parts.

A serious lesson was learnt that holiday. Cock-teasing is a very dangerous game. Men and women are different and I had to learn to revere that difference because within it lies the magic.

CHAPTER THIRTY-TWO

THE ARTS EDUCATIONAL was barely fulfilling my acting needs, let alone extending my abilities. In fact I was still unsure that I had any to start with. I had two drama lessons a week, only one of which was with a teacher I respected, Anthony Sharp. I recited a poem for him once, 'No coward soul is mine' by Emily Brontë and came top of the class. It's a poem that clearly displays such a knowing of God that anyone learning it off by heart couldn't fail but come top of the class.

My dancing, worse luck, was pathetic. It was the same old problem of not knowing my left from my right. No teacher had the patience to help me catch up, because the rest of the class, including Anneka, had been dancing since they could walk. Though I wanted to dance as much as I wanted to sing, I was, yet again, the dunce.

I soon worked out that the school aspired to produce dancers, not actors. Having no fervent ambitions to be part of the chorus myself, I stayed away as much as I dared. When Mummy got wind of me missing classes she'd give me hell. Daddy had simply washed his hands of me, still convinced that I could have made it as a tennis player had I had the temperament.

*

Poor Mummy. Nothing had really changed since I was a toddler, for there she was pulling her hair out with the worry of wanting to get me out of her hair. My dyed black hair was not a success. I couldn't tolerate the short frizzy bits at the front, because they wouldn't iron, nor would they stay in the silver clips. Then I happened to read in a magazine somewhere that Laurence Olivier had done something rather interesting when he started in movies. His hair grew rather low on his forehead, so he'd had almost an inch ripped off his hairline at the front. So I had a quarter of an inch of hairline ripped off my forehead. It hurt a bit, more than a bit if I was honest, and the after effects were somewhat grim, leaving me with an unnecessary harshness. My mother despaired. 'I'm sure English Japanese geisha girls are in great demand – just what they're looking for at RADA.'

Yes, RADA, Mummy's next step for me was looming. Although I was still only just fifteen, Mummy had already lied to get me my bedsit, so was quite happy to lie again to get me into RADA. I was sent the bumf on RADA's auditions and rules; only two audition pieces were required, one classical compulsory piece, and one of your own choice, modern or otherwise. I chose Viola's, 'Make me a willow cabin at thy gate', from *Twelfth Night* and Celia's speech from Oscar Wilde's, *The Ideal Husband*, 'Tommy has proposed to me again, Tommy does nothing but propose to me.'

Mummy got increasingly nervous as the audition got closer. I wasn't too perturbed. It was Mummy's idea, after all, Mummy who wanted me at RADA so she could tell all her cronies. I knew no one to tell, except for Anneka, Mr Sharp and a few of the Shepherd's Market tarts.

When I saw the intimidating bunch of boys and girls –

some of them stunningly pretty – queuing up to be auditioned I knew I had to do something special to make them sit up and notice for my talent alone was hardly sufficient. 'Next one, please,' said a man in uniform. In I went to pitch blackness. I couldn't even see the stalls.

'Good afternoon,' said a female voice from the void.

Help.

Through the nausea of nervousness, Viola's 'Make me a willow cabin at thy gate' was feeble, and, through nerves, lacked any daring. I felt I'd blown it. How was I going to put it all to rights?

I took advantage of the silence to clear my dry throat, then squinting into the black void I said, 'For this next piece from *The Ideal Husband* I'll need three extra chairs, please.'

'But you have two up on stage already,' said a peremptory female voice.

'Yes, ma'am, I'm fully aware of these two chairs, but I need three more.'

After quite a time and a clatter, three more chairs were brought on stage from the wings. 'Thank you very much,' I said, and placed four chairs downstage facing me while I sat frozen with fear on the fifth. Taking a deep breath, off I went. 'Tommy has proposed to me again, Tommy does nothing but propose to me . . .'

When I'd finished I realized I had completely forgotten to integrate my imaginary characters into my speech: they had remained ignored and overlooked, ghosts at the feast sitting on three extra chairs that had been hunted for with precious time and great difficulty.

'Thank you so much, you may go now,' said the same impersonal voice. This time I knew I'd blown it, for I heard lots of whispering going on. If I were to apologize, I thought, it would have made it all much worse, so I got up, did an automatic little curtsey, 'Thank you, ma'am,' and left with my head held high.

Out on the street, Mummy said, 'Where's your handbag?'

'Oh, God!' I ran back to the wings. Fortunately my handbag was in a patch of light. 'Sorry, my handbag.' I grabbed it. 'Can I put the chairs back where they came from?'

'Thank you, but they've already been taken back.'

I couldn't see a damn thing, so I tucked in one last little bob and left.

Mummy became really nervous awaiting the news of my audition. We both knew I hadn't done well, we both knew the chances of my being accepted were slim.

One evening I overheard her talking to Daddy. 'If she fails RADA I don't know what on earth we are going to do with her.'

'I don't know either, Wren, I don't know I'm sure.'

I entered darkly. 'I heard all that. I'm sorry I'm stupid, I'm sorry I'm a failure, I'm sorry for ever being bloody well born in the first place, and that's your fault – not mine!'

I ran up to my room and sobbed and sobbed. No one but no one understood my awful feeling of alienation. There was something wrong with me, as if I viewed life from a blind and lonely angle, an angle without shape or logic. All I could see was a jarring nothingness where everything I did always ended up wrong. My continual catastrophic *faux pas* were the only coherent thing about me. Yes, in that respect I was as reliable and solid as a rock.

CHAPTER THIRTY-THREE

A s SOON AS the letter arrived with the good news about RADA, Mother's attitude towards me changed overnight. She kissed me, really kissed me, stood back and looked at me as if she'd never seen me before, then hugged me, a real hug that came from her heart. I felt as if I'd been waiting for that hug for a hundred years.

Daddy was pleased that Mummy was pleased, but he wasn't whole-heartedly behind this acting lark. 'It's all infested with second-raters. Actors have no real depth.'

So over the moon was Mummy that she decided to give me a treat by taking the pair of us on a cruise to a place called Tenerife in the Canary Islands. 'Just you and me together, darling, it'll be such fun.'

Mummy had been simply longing for another cruise ever since Daddy took her first class to New York on the *Queen Mary*, where she obviously had the time of her life. 'I went to the lavatory one evening, and there was Lady Docker having a pee with the door wide open. She looked up at me as if nothing was wrong. 'Don't mind me,' she said. When she was all done, she stood up trailing a forlorn mink stole. 'Blast! I've dunked my tail again, it's too damn long.' She swished her wet mink in circles all around the ladies' room to dry it off.' They became quite friendly after that. 'You would have liked her, Pusscat, she had an earthy outrageousness.'

There's no escape on a cruise, you simply cannot get

away from the mob. Mummy had tiresomely won the affections of the captain and thus we found ourselves once too often at his tedious table. The whole ship was chock-a-block with man-made fibres, perms and varicose veins – even Mummy realized she'd made a huge mistake. We remained hidden in our cabin for most of the trip – I hate both boats and reading. The good thing was that Mummy and I became a little closer, and, although still far from what I hoped we'd become one day, her childlike joy at my going to RADA spread all over the decks. It was rather touching, really, to see her telling all and sundry.

Our hotel on Tenerife was just as ghastly. Bob Monkhouse was there with his red-headed wife Elizabeth; both liked Mummy a lot. So now I'd met three famous people: Robert Beatty, Tarzan and Bob Monkhouse. Things were on the up.

We were told the sun was ruthless, and to keep out of it as much as possible. For me the place was hellish gloomy, not only because of the black sand but because of a thick bank of immovable cloud dangling over the sea, determined to darken the whole area and the holiday as well. I really was a terrible snob in those days. Since there were no cowhand's daughters, apple farmers or gypsies to commiserate with, I took out my pent-up frustration on Mummy.

On the fourth day of thick cloud, I went off on an early morning hike into the mountains to try to get a smell of the Canary Islanders themselves. Although the mountains were nothing special, rather arid and brown, there was something very special about being free from tourists for a while. I stopped at a primitive café and had a drink of strange-tasting lemonade. The Islanders weren't the most beautiful-looking people, but they had a kind of wary warmth, and they seemed to accept me, the damned tourist, with a shrug of necessity. I remember a skinny dog who came to me eagerly wagging his tail, but when I went to stroke him, his master gave him an almighty kick. He yelped and I left.

Higher and higher I climbed. Looking down towards the bay I decided this was a forgotten land, black, brown and harsh. All this way to the Canary Islands and not a single tree to be seen, let alone a canary. They must have fled as soon as they heard that British tourists were coming. My head began to throb. I was naked, except for a halter-necked sun smock, but the clouds were impenetrable, so why were my shoulders burning like billyo? It was now about mid morning, and I decided I'd better not go up any higher. I was already two and a half hours from the coast and our horrid hotel.

By the time I got back I was feeling nauseous and dizzy, rather similar to the day I drank the vodka.

'Where were you? I've been worried sick! Look, your back's scarlet, I told you.'

'But it's thick cloud out there.'

The doctor arrived, gave me some gigantic horse pills and ointment, and said I was to remain in bed till my temperature subsided. I had severe sunstroke, my head had been uncovered for almost five hours. Mummy was at her wits' end, where her Polly Tree grows. Apparently the cloudy weather was more dangerous than the sunshine – but how was I to know? The aching reminded me of polio in a way. I had to remain in bed for a week, Mummy said it ruined her holiday, but I wasn't sure what she meant since the holiday was a wash-out from the word go. We flew home, thank God.

CHAPTER THIRTY-FOUR

O N MY FIRST DAY at RADA I looked around the room at the fifty hopefuls to see if there was anyone who I thought had something extra, someone (besides myself, of course!) who would definitely make the big time. And there he was. I got a tingling feeling inside me. It wasn't a particularly handsome face, but it had real charm and character. He saw me looking at him, and gave me a lovely smile, displaying a fair number of crooked teeth. Nevertheless, bad teeth or not, I wasn't about to change my bet.

On the first day of voice class we all sat in a circle, taking it in turns to say a little ditty. So simple that even *I* could avoid making a fool of myself, perhaps. 'Gold. Gold. Gold. Bright and yellow, hard and cold.' What could be more simple than that?

The boy I had previously recognized as someone who was going to make the big time was called Tom Courtenay. He was from Hull, so his, 'Goold. Goold. Goold . . .' had a very northern twang to it, but that could soon be remedied, I thought. In fact, as we went round saying the ditty, it was fascinating to observe that hardly anyone spoke what I considered standard English.

RADA, so Mother kept telling me, was a place where lots of débutantes went to be finished off. Well, RADA must have finished them off, because within this group I couldn't hear a

266

single upper-class vowel sound. Still, it would soon be my turn, and then they'd all know what correct English sounded like. On and on they went; some, 'Gould', others, 'Guld', others still, 'Goold' and even 'Gawled'.

At last it was my turn. Full of confidence for perhaps the first time in my life, I cleared my throat. 'Geld. Geld. Geld Bright and yelleh, hard and celd.'

The whole class went into a chorus of guffaws! At first I didn't know why they had found my correct English so comical. Then at the end of the period, all together they said, 'Come on, Saaraah, let's gah to raahaarhsaal.'

So the die was cast. I was the odd one out. I was the only posh voice in my class, and frequently found myself hauled over the coals (kells) for it. The late fifties was the era of the 'kitchen sink'. Working-class heroes and heroines were in vogue and there was nothing I could do about it. Typically I had missed the boat, born out of my time, with the Tom Courtenays of this world being in and me being out. Nothing for it but to talk common. If you can't beat 'em, join 'em!

So I did. Our gang consisted of Tom Courtenay, Mike Blackham, John Thaw and me. Jennifer Hilary was a late comer. She was beautiful and she must have been a brilliant actress for she won the gold medal. John Thaw has grown consistently younger through the years. He was as old as Methuselah at RADA. Mike Blackham is the only one who hasn't made the big time yet, but he's a most colourful character, so I'm sure his day will come.

Tom Courtenay, who gave the appearance of an enchanting little boy lost was as shrewd as a lorry load of monkeys. With his grant money he found a light, spacious flat in Finsbury Park where we all dossed down when it suited us. I also dossed down on the Belsize Park floor of a beautiful ethereal-looking boy called Anthony Gardener, who was so romantically mysterious and softly spoken that I got quite a crush on him. I never felt threatened by him, in fact he made me feel safe.

I spent most nights at someone else's place, a kind of a stray dog, sleeping on anyone's floor (not making love) who would have me. I didn't like being alone – then.

I can't remember much about acting at RADA. One teacher I appreciated was Peter Barkworth with his acting technique classes. Even with Mr Barkworth (who wasn't well known then) I wondered why if he was so damn good he wasn't earning his living at acting rather than teaching it? Peter Barkworth interested me, and sometimes I'd follow him home to his ground-floor flat in Hampstead, near my basement bedsit. I'd watch him enter, and then reappear in his sitting room; most days he'd conveniently forget to draw his curtains, so I could play Peeping Tom. He never did much. Poured himself a drink, read the paper, made a few phone calls and then read a book. Maybe I was plucking up sufficient courage to ask him if I could spend a few nights on his floor too.

Learning to act didn't interest me nearly as much as life itself. People's lives were fascinating to me always. Not to hear them gossiping, or indeed being gossiped about, but to watch, or sneak a peek through open curtains at dusk. I find people's private moments to be a short-cut in attempting to understand human nature. It's not usually what people say that I learn from, but how they behave, what they do. To sit in a roadside café watching the people go by – my idea of heaven.

Nigel Stock was another good teacher. What I
learnt from him was that I shouldn't altogether give up
That same message came across to me with most w
enthusiasm from Milos Sperber, a passionate and n
Italian Jew, who believed that, chaotic though I was,
something to offer.

Gradually, after the first few terms, RADA began to
its appeal for me. Apart from my acting, which wasn't up
much, there were so many beautiful girls, the place v
swarming with them. I was never going to make it. My pai
showed itself in that same old behaviour pattern: rebellion.
pretended not to care, and that's when my habit of missin
class began.

I did learn one thing from Edith Evans – all I really
needed to know. She gave a lecture alone on stage with no
microphone or chair. She stood there, haughty and proud,
with a very strange hat perched on her hair, somehow apart
from her head. At the start of her lecture she looked drawn,
old, irritable and plain as a pike-staff. Her theme that
afternoon was her experiencing of the process of becoming
Cleopatra. She knew she was not the type to be indulging
herself portraying great beauties. No one more ill-suited to
playing the Queen of the Nile. She told us about her pear-
shaped body, her generous hips – 'Not exactly the type to
launch a thousand ships!' She perked up and said innocently, 'However, I do possess one quality,' raising her leg a
little and proudly pointing a shiny brown court shoe,
'extremely pretty feet.' We couldn't see her feet from the
auditorium. Realizing, she let her pointed toe hang, sad and
forgotten. One student got up to have a look, others followed. So chuffed was Edith she went all coy. 'Don't get up,

ny child . . . sit, gels and boys, sit . . . how sweet, how
weet . . .'

Gathering up both girth and thoughts, she went on. 'Just
before curtain up, I made the error of catching sight of myself
in the mirror. Perhaps not so much an error – a catastrophic
mistake! I prayed Cleopatra couldn't see.' She went on to
explain how she reapplied her make-up, making it look
much worse. She told us wittily of the panic setting in. She
had started talking to herself: how could she possibly escape
from both theatre and mistake? Walking downstage, her
magic story began, turning all careless *cannots* into the cosy
comfort of *can*. Using the auditorium (us) as a mirror she
began to talk to her image. 'You're beautiful, Edith, just get
out there and show them all!'

She stepped further downstage, as if scrutinizing her
profoundly inadequate Cleopatra. She continued talking to
herself – stamping her feet. 'You're beautiful, Edith – don't
shift those eyes sideways while I'm talking to you! You're
beautiful – you *are*!'

She stood still in the midst of silence, took a few deep
breaths, then relaxed her shoulders. Pause. 'YOU ARE BEAUTI-
FUL, you know . . .'

As she said it that time she changed. Both her face and
body seemed slowly to acquire regal stature, yet her hat was
still perched firmly, yet strangely high on her head. 'You're
beautiful! Cleopatra! Can you hear me? It's true! That's me –
not you! *I am beautiful!*' Before our eyes she became Cleopatra. Her whole countenance shone with supreme confidence,
and sultry femininity. She was beautiful, there was no doubt
about it. 'I AM BEAUTIFUL!!' (She truly was.)

Quick as a skunk she was back into her old self, and with

a merry glint she said, 'And do you know, boys and gels, by the time I finally got out on stage I was really rather pretty? So this is my lecture for today. Where there is sufficient will, one can always find a way!' (*Exit Edith*.)

It was the 'doubtlessness' that said it all for me. I sat there, grateful. I tried chasing back that special moment. How beautiful it was, her final triumphant transformation into the Queen of the Nile. Illusion is powerful stuff. I could have sworn after her transformation that she wasn't wearing a hat. After that day, I stopped whingeing and whining to myself over my shortcomings and decided to be beautiful. If the old bat in the hat could do it, so could I!

CHAPTER THIRTY-FIVE

Even though it wasn't my favourite end of town, Haverstock Hill was good in one way because it was within easy walking distance of the Everyman Cinema in Hampstead. I loved going there. It became my temple. I'd go alone, or with Tom Courtenay and Co. to drink in all the latest foreign offerings.

Those late fifties/early sixties movies of Bergmans, Buñuels, Renoirs, Truffauts, Godards, Kurosawa lifted me up to other realms. For one so poorly educated it was mind-blowing stuff. I regularly thought in that cinema that my brain would blow. Films like *The Seventh Seal* and *Wild Strawberries* made me look at life and the living of it in a completely different light. *Hiroshima Mon Amour* gave me sleepless nights. And when I did manage to nod off there they were, those new-wave films, trespassing into my dreams and pushing at the walls of my subconscious.

My money was always running out, so I had to move into a disgustingly sordid bedsit – well, that's how I made it seem after being in it for a few days. I never stayed there, though. I was still spending my nights on some kindly soul's floor (poor soul!) saving my pennies for important things like the Everyman and Pinet high-heeled winkle-pickers.

Mummy found out about this. Before the beginning of the spring term, we looked at a flat near Shepherd's Market that I could share with an American girl from RADA called Gail

Gladstone. 'That way,' said Mummy, 'I can keep my eye on you through Gail.' I was as pleased as punch!

It was an enchantingly wonky flat on the top floor of a battered Georgian house in Half Moon Street. The landlady was called Miss Hocking. We got on well since she turned a conveniently blind eye to my dubious carryings on. What bliss it was to have one little dream come true; to be actually living six doors down from my favourite haunt, Shepherd's Market! Life was taking off at last. Gail was very pleasant-looking, in a classical way, always smart and together with straight strawberry blonde hair and freckles. We were never to be best friends, but we suffered each other gladly.

I celebrated this Milestone by changing my name to Mummy's maiden name, Baskerville. In a dream I saw this name up in the lights. It was a damned shame I hadn't hit upon Sarah Baskerville before I'd started at RADA.

'Look out! It's the Hound of the Baskervilles!'

'Aaah! Is the Hind of the Baahskaarvilles coming to raahaarsaal?'

Literally hounded back to Miles, I was.

I remember much more of the canteen than I ever remember of lessons or rehearsals. I suppose that's normal, the canteen being the relaxing centre. Everyone was up there between classes, a great buzz of chatter filling the nicotined-fry-ups-and-coffee-saturated air. There was one fellow in the year above me who was very interesting-looking, almost resembling a ghost with his pale skin and thick ash-blond hair. He was always by the phone waiting for it to ring or talking into it. He gave the impression of being someone of importance, or so it seemed to me at the time. His name was Edward Fox and, unlike me, wasn't mocked for his posh voice. Perhaps it suited him better. Of course, it might have been because his father was a top theatrical agent as well as an impresario, putting on plays jointly in the West End with Robert Morley.

Tracy Reed (with legs way up past Kingdom Come like Mummy's) introduced us one day, and Eddie was much less formidable than he'd seemed from a distance. The following week he and Tracy were going to some smart party, and he invited me to be his younger brother Willy's date. This younger brother, Eddie told me with a twinkle, wouldn't do me any harm. He was an officer in the Coldstream Guards and knew how to treat a lady.

Willy Fox (now known as James) was perfect. The absolute answer to any young maiden's prayers. Tall, pale and handsome, he had such a way with him, such natural grace and inborn elegance, that I was immediately transported to seventh heaven. He also danced like a dream. I'll always remember that first night with him. I'd fallen in love. I'd fallen in love with a stranger, in a crowded room. And, as luck would have it, with someone who had perhaps fallen in love with me a little bit, too. Or maybe I'd fallen in love with the idea of falling in love, or possibly it was even more complicated still. Perhaps it was to justify the fact that I knew one day soon we'd end up in bed together, and falling in love first was the only proper thing to do. Maybe I'd simply fallen in lust, and cloaked it in love . . . but I don't think so.

How excellent life had suddenly become! I occasionally got a whiff of Dick Whittington's luck in the Half Moon Street air, Willy's busby, my silky black cat. Half Moon Street was next to St James's Park, so Willy would sometimes sneak across while he was still meant to be on duty, guarding the

Queen Mother at Clarence House, and appear at my front door in full scarlet and gold. He'd gently remove my hand from stroking his, 'so silky, your busby . . .'

'Bear-skin,' he corrected me, then kissed my hand to get one step closer to my lips. And there we'd stand until the pain of parting overcame all – even Jack's lusty beanstalk. Knowing he couldn't stay, I'd watch him march back again. What a sight he was – my man! I had to go and lie on my bed and calm Jack's beanstalk.

Sometimes, in the evenings I'd go to the Palace gates, and creep behind into the great barracks, my entrance noted by the frisky pirouette of a horse breathing out cones of warm whinnying air. A masterful voice would bellow into the crisp night, 'Who goes there, friend or foe?'

This was certain to send a shiver down my spine. 'Friend,' I'd say, as Willy had taught me. There'd be a great stamping, clicking of guns and changing of position, followed by the heavy rhythm of marching feet crunching through the gravel; at last there he'd be, my Guards officer, tall and handsome, lifting me up into the clear night's stars.

(I hope England doesn't cut off her royal nose to spite her ever plainer face, because she might regret it – besides one needs a good nose for business.)

Willy was chosen to hold the flag at the Trooping the Colour. It's still a thrilling sight, but then, for a young girl in her mid-teens, that wondrously flamboyant uniform and within it my love, shimmering scarlet and gold, was enough to melt an already racing heart. I got myself into a ball of yearning. My heart was racing, my pulse a continual pitter-patter, my Jack's beanstalk bursting with ripeness. None the less I wouldn't allow curiosity to prevent me drawing out the courting process, because it gave me such a high. I was caught in a trance very close to Paradise, and I had no intention of breaking the spell. Willy didn't push himself on me, for he, too, wanted the magic of our mating game to take its natural course. After a while, though, this voluptuous sensual aching slowly began pulling my insides apart. My beautiful aching beanstalk was getting too heavy to carry around – it might burst through the top of my head.

Though nothing was said we both knew the time had come. Willy bought me a record of Ella Fitzgerald singing Cole Porter. And one evening, when Gail was out, I turned the lights down low, Willy arrived, we put on *Love For Sale*. Perfect. Taking me to him, embalmed in gentleness, I felt a weighty mass shift around inside me as I tried to make sense of everything. Those dearly treasured erotic, yet innocent fantasies of Laurence Olivier and King George VI were gradually demystifying. The once jagged edges of Jack's lusty beanstalk were slowly smoothing out, not into anything tangible but into a new and terrible hunger.

'If you want the thrill of love, I've been through the mill of love . . .'

I took all the time in the world with my surrendering. How succulent it is, the slow surrender. All those years of practising the Three Deadly Ps and finally succeeding with Ee-Ees were about to pay off. All that I had been waiting for – posing in cafés with Anneka, licking my lips, exposing my thighs, wiggling my bum in silk stockings and sexy suspenders – all those blind naïve blunders that had been my love life up till that moment were about to find reason.

'If you want to try my wares, follow me and climb the stairs, love for sale!'

As we made love, all the feminine part of me, the unformed sexy thoughts, the lusty leaves of curiosity that made up Jack's beanstalk began melting within an inner sunshine. Gradually, through every sweet new experience of our rhythmic sacred togetherness, all yearnings crashed into clarity, culminating in an abundant feeling of womanliness.

'Let the poets write of love, in their childish way—
I know every type of love better far than they.'

CHAPTER THIRTY-SIX

S OON AFTER our first night together, I met his father, Robin Fox. What a handsome creature he was! No one dresses like that any more, such a shame. From top to toe he smelt of gentleman, from his exquisite Savile Row suits, tie-pins, cuff-links, hand-made shoes, up to his forever fresh carnation. In the beginning, through all the obvious charm, I sensed a tiny chink of chilliness, as if a lump of ice was tucked neatly away, never melting beneath the collar of his exquisitely finished-off hand-made shirts.

Weekends were fun. Either Willy would come down to Barn Mead, or I would go down to the Foxes' cottage in Cuckfield, Sussex. At Barn Mead Willy had a fairly rough time proving himself, because the Mileses, described as the 'Miles Mafia', were a pretty tightly knit group. At first Daddy was left-footed by Willy's angelic countenance. Taking me aside and pointing ferociously to his forehead, he said, 'But has he got it up here?' Willy's stunning looks were finally eclipsed by some pretty nifty tennis. He gave Daddy a real run for his money during an exciting needle match. His table-tennis and croquet were well up to scratch, too. 'He's an excellent chap, Pusscat, but no left-hander, alas.'

Mummy had taken a real liking to him. Perhaps she thought she should have spawned this pure golden type of offspring, rather than the fuzzy, wizened Celtic bunch she had produced. They got on like a house on fire, and

Mummy's rather latent nurturing nature came blossoming forth. All in all, as beaux went, the general consensus of opinion was that I certainly hadn't let the side down.

At last I began noticing that I didn't miss the animals so much, probably because I was turning into one myself. Although I still longed for weekends with Chan, Mizzer, Prince Charming, my legs were opening just as willingly to my other charming prince. Pooker, who was still at Benenden (surrounded by massive trees!) lost enthusiasm for riding, so Mizzer began a very élitist early retirement, giving rides to children at the Hurlingham Club in London. I went to visit him many times, and he always whinnied with recognition, but boy, oh, boy was he spoilt! All that wickedness ending up in horsy heaven – where's the justice?

The Foxes' Cuckfield Cottage was enchanting. It sat plumb in the middle of that Sussex village. I was given just as good a run for my money down there as Willy at Barn Mead. There were three Fox brothers, all dishy, all blond. The youngest was still on his tricycle, but would later follow in his father's footsteps and become Robert Fox, the impresario. Their mother Angela Fox, from whom they all got their striking golden looks, was a pretty powerful lady and strong as a pit pony. Because I never underestimated her intelligence we got on well, I wouldn't have liked to be in Angela's bad books.

Robin's father was still alive, in his nineties he was then, and he would honour us occasionally with his Edwardian presence at weekends and I'll never forget that old rogue. So dapper, so sexy, so rakish in his immaculate attire. It was easy to see where Robin got his elegance – all of them, come to that. I've always had a penchant for the old – men and women. I think it has a lot to do with my dyslexia, the need to learn from oral wisdom and ancient ways rather than from books. (Daddy, of course, was no spring chicken.)

Another glorious old timer was eighty-year-old Captain Buckmaster. Willy and I used to eat regularly at his exclusive Buck's Club, next to Robin's flat in Old Burlington Street. It was terrific to be able to take such exotic leaps back in time, and to know I was always welcome when hunger struck. He'd open his arms to me, giving me my favourite asparagus or fresh salmon, flirting like an old Cock Robin. The very best of what used to be the best of England.

Robin Fox and Robert Morley worked with a woman called Ros Chatto who later joined Robin as an agent, when Robin joined forces with Leslie Grade's organization. Ros was very generous-spirited, not only with her own family but also with all of us too. Her house has remained unchanged decade after decade, with its unpretentious welcoming simplicity. She was a wonderful cook. Great smells wafted up the street from her Chelsea home, sending starving taste buds haywire. Even at sixteen, it baffled me how one woman could hold down a full-time job, be a fabulous cook, feed a family as well as in-laws, and always keep a warm hearth and open heart for all late comers: 24 Christ Church Street became a second home to so many of us so-called actors/artists. She was very patient with me, spent many an evening trying to teach me the fundamentals of cooking, but ended up defeated.

Because my private life had picked up dramatically, RADA began to pale by comparison. I was getting bored with the endless talk about acting; I so wanted to get up and do it – and get paid for doing it. I was complaining about this lack of real experience at Ros's house one night. Willy and I were round as usual, sponging off her incredible generosity, gobbling down a delicious dinner, when Robin said, 'How would you like a real job?' I was naturally stunned at this, since I was still a student.

'I don't think students are allowed to work professionally, worse luck.'

'I wouldn't bet on that. If it was allowed, and I got you a real job, would you take it?'

'Need you ask? Like a shot.'

CHAPTER THIRTY-SEVEN

S O IT WAS that simultaneously I got my first professional engagement and on to the client list of one of the most prestigious agents in town.

'Now listen carefully, Sarah,' said Robin patiently, at another evening at Ros's. 'It's only a walk-on part, but it'll give you some experience. All you have to do is walk sexily across a Roman street, whereupon Warren Beatty glances through the barber's shop window, giving you a horny look as you wiggle by.'

I simply couldn't believe my luck. I was actually going to be in a film – and I wasn't too bad at wiggling. Robin Fox was obviously a man of influence; he'd squared it with Mr Fernald, the RADA principal, so it was all above board, I wasn't skipping class.

The film was called, *The Roman Spring of Mrs Stone*. It starred Vivien Leigh, Lotte Lenya and a new American boy called Warren Beatty. Here was I, just turned sixteen, about to play my first professional part – albeit only a walk-on – in a real movie!

When I arrived at Elstree Studios I couldn't help stifling a great gulp of disappointment, the place looked like the Marconi's factory we passed in the car going home to Essex on the London Road, impersonal, grey and ugly. I found Stage B, as instructed. The porter, who was expecting me, gave me my key. 'Good morning, Miss Miles, dressing room

45. Up the flight of stairs on the right, first floor, dressing room around to the right.'

Up I went, and there was dressing room 45 exactly where it should be. About to put the key into the lock, I saw the name Lotie Lenya above the door in capital letters. Funny, I thought, could there be some mistake? No, there couldn't be. I'd followed the porter's instructions to the letter. I double-checked my key, it said 45, I double-checked the flight of stairs, only one, like the porter said. I went down the other end of the corridor, where the numbers read 50 upwards. With my confidence returned I went back to 45, and assumed that Lotte Lenya didn't mind sharing dressing rooms with walk-ons. For a second time I aimed the key in the lock.

At that moment, I felt a rather harsh tap on my shoulder. I turned. I had to look down to meet the hot, vividly intent green eyes of a rather small woman in a rather large state. 'You can't go in there,' she said, breathing fast.

'Why not?' I enquired, fairly fearlessly.

'You can't go in there,' she repeated, 'that's Lotte Lenya's dressing room.'

I rode the waves of her formidable storm pretty calmly, I thought. 'But the porter has just given me this key.' I showed her.

'You can't go in there!' Snapping this time. 'There's some mistake, I tell you!'

Trying not to rise up in fear, I said, cool as I could, 'But my key fits the lock – look!'

I demonstrated the perfect fit, and turned the key, which prompted her to start shouting at me. 'Go down and check again with the porter. There is obviously some mistake.'

She looked uncannily like Mummy up the Polly Tree – or

perhaps even royalty. Her whole overbearing attitude finally pierced my cool façade. 'Why don't you go down and check it out for yourself?' I entered the dressing room. I didn't slam the door but closed it gently – I always try to be as well mannered as possible without licking arse.

That fearsome confrontation on the first day of my professional career began a pattern that has lasted all my life. I just manage to get my foot in the door when I get bullied by an old lady (she wasn't all that old, but I was young enough to see anyone over forty as old). If the truth be known, I felt more frightened that day than I had in Miss Horrobin's house at Roedean. Was I going to be expelled before I'd even started? Even more bewildering were those fever-hot eyes of hers – uncannily like Mummy's. It was Vivien Leigh.

I looked around the dressing room. It did look as if Miss Leigh had a point. It was full of personal knick-knacks, lots of photographs of Lotte, with various members of her family probably, scattered here and there. I remember a huge cut-glass face-powder jar, with an equally enormous swansdown puff lying by its side. It, too, reminded me of Mummy and her dressing table. I sat down nervously, as if I were indeed an intruder. Perhaps I had made a mistake . . . perhaps I should have gone back downstairs and double-checked?

Just as I was about to make a call to Robin Fox, to enquire about the mix-up, the door opened, and in came Vivien, scarlet as fuck and hungry as a street cat before a territorial confrontation. She thrust a piece of paper at me. 'Here's a list of colours you can't wear.' The door slammed. What an exit! Fiddle-de-dee!

Sitting down again, really terrified now, I began to read the long list of colours Vivien Leigh had forbidden me to wear. My mind drifted off to my late (before Willy) romantic hero Laurence Olivier, and I was filled with a great feeling of compassion for the man. Did he have to put up with that day and night? But hadn't I read somewhere that they were no longer man and wife? Or was it again merely gossip? Perhaps Vivien was like Mummy emotionally, too. After all, both had been radiant beauties in their day, and Mummy was fine, it seemed, as long as she wasn't around me for too long. Perhaps I brought out in Vivien what I brought out in Mummy – the very worst!

I couldn't believe what I was reading so I read it again. It was true, the only colour not on Vivien's list was black. I went down the list a third time, for surely I'd made a mistake. No, black it was.

After what seemed an eternity, I heard a careful knock on the door. In came an old lady who reminded me of Kate Camps, the sweet-shop lady on Mill Green Common. She had a quiet vagueness, which I automatically found relaxing. She was called Bumble Dawson. 'Well, I suppose you'd better come along with me to Wardrobe, and we'll get you fixed up,' she said, as if really it was the last thing she wanted to do.

Wardrobe was full of every garment, every fabric, every colour known to man. Never had I seen so many beautiful dresses in one space before.

'Now, young lady, what colour would you like to wear?'

Should I come clean immediately, or should I somehow withhold the Vivien List for a while? I remained silent.

'Speak up, no need to be shy,' she said. 'The director tells me you're to look as sexy as possible, and in my experience, one can't look sexy if one isn't feeling sexy, don't you agree?'

I cleared my throat. 'Yes.'

She went over to a rail of stunning little items, and pulled out a very sexy pink number. 'How about this? It'll set off your black hair beautifully. Put it on.'

I climbed self consciously, guiltily too, into the divine little pink dress. It didn't look half bad, showing off my better points. 'Let me see,' she said, turning me round to face her. 'Yes, that does the trick very nicely – oh, – wait, there's this little blue one too. Try this on for me would you?'

The blue dress was tighter and therefore sexier, but I still preferred the pink one, and after some deliberation, so did Bumble. 'The pink one wins, don't you think?'

Again I cleared my guilty throat. 'No, I'm afraid—' I interrupted myself and nervously handed her the scrumpled list.

'What's this?' said Bumble, taking it from me. I heard her whisper something to herself. 'So, young lady, black it will have to be, I'm afraid.'

I felt a million dollars as I walked down to find the stage. Bumble Dawson felt sorry for me, I suppose, so she put me into a supple black leather suit. In those days soft sensual leather was still very rare. She wouldn't let me raise up the skirt too much, but we both reached a compromise. I wished Willy could have seen me that day, all dressed up like a high-class hooker! Funny business, sexuality. Because I never saw it in the mirror, I was naïvely out of touch with my sexual power. This got me into endless hassles.

As I entered that vast expanse of space – a film stage – for the first time, I sensed a dark, heavy atmosphere. Obviously things weren't going too well. However thick I might have been intellectually, I could instantly pick up trouble in the air. I saw Miss Leigh punctuate my arrival, just as the director came over to welcome me. He apologized that there was still one more shot before mine, so an assistant brought me a chair. I thanked him. Although it was interesting to watch the Roman street being sprayed, touched up and the extras being given direction, there was something more intriguing going on elsewhere. It was the interplay between Vivien Leigh and some chap I didn't know, sitting in a chair similar to hers, on the other side of the Roman street. They were playing glancing games with each other, and through it all I got the feeling that Miss Leigh was as sad and vulnerable as could be. I wished fervently that we hadn't had a row already because I would have loved to have gone over to her, sat and talked and maybe even asked her questions about her life and her love – Olivier. But even if I hadn't already blown it, she wouldn't have deigned to climb down from her highly strung, highly bred but oh so dangerously brittle high horse to talk to the likes of me.

Out of the blue the chap across the street got up, put a magazine cover in front of his face and began walking towards me. It was a rather surreal effect, having a magazine coming at you across a Roman street in the middle of suburbia. When it came into close-up, under my very nose, it was whipped away to reveal the same man, but in the flesh this time. I wasn't sure how I was meant to react to this, so I kept still.

'Hi,' he said shaking my hand with hearty sincerity. 'My name's Warren Beatty.' He didn't have a squint exactly, more of an eye that strayed a little. 'What's your name?'

As I said, 'Sarah Miles,' I caught Miss Leigh taking all this in, and Warren doing the same. I rose and went for a breath of fresh air down the Roman street.

Finally, we shot the scene. I did my best, it only took a matter of seconds and the director seemed pleased with me. All that hassle, hierarchy and game-playing for a few seconds – was this typical of the film business, I wondered. I sincerely hoped not.

Back in Lotte's dressing room, I phoned Robin Fox. 'Lotte told me you could use it, I didn't want you down with the extras. Start as you mean to go on.'

I wrote a note of thanks by Lotte's swansdown puff, grabbed my belongings and bumped into Bumble Dawson who kindly gave me the leather suit for keeps (I'm wearing it on the cover). 'I'm sorry about everything,' she said with a shrug.

About three years or so after this incident, I was at a garden party at Robert Morley's home in Wargrave near Henley. I was sitting alone, drinking in the atmosphere with tea and lemon, when I noted a deal of commotion surrounding a newcomer's arrival. I saw a small lady dressed in black, with a tall, handsome matinée idol-ish man, who rarely let his eyes stray far from her. I learnt later he was the actor Jack Merrivale.

After a while she wafted down the lawn in my direction. 'Hello,' she said.

'Hello.'

'What a lovely afternoon.'

'Isn't it.' Heavy silence, but I was at a loss as to how to smooth it over.

She did finally. 'I'm so sorry about that day on the *Roman Spring*. I wasn't quite myself.'

'That's perfectly all right,' I said.

'It isn't though, is it?'

Her question went deep into my eyes, and I, like the rest of mankind, I suppose, found myself being pulled into her seductive charisma. Or was it the magnetism of madness enhancing her beauty, brightening up her vixen gaze? Any answer would have been quite redundant. I lowered my lids because I had to draw myself back from her dazzling chaos. I was profoundly moved by her remembering the incident at all, but I wasn't going to let on.

'Black suits you,' I found myself saying. And that was it. We sat in another silence, but this one was different, because this time all had been said.

CHAPTER THIRTY-EIGHT

LIFE TURNED into one continuous whirl. I was having a ball in London during the week and in the country at weekends. I knew I was lucky. I even felt the luck dancing around my bed at night though I never took it for granted. Was my black cat Willy's black busby?

In the late fifties the Royal Court buzzed with activity and exciting new talent. I remember seeing Diane Cilento in *Orpheus Descending* by Tennessee Williams. She lit up the stage for me. At that time I found most theatre actresses full of style and technique, yet sadly lacking in animal magnetism, so to find such a potently sexual performance tightly controlled with integrity and great style filled me with gratitude.

I'd sometimes wait for her at the stage door, and follow her along King's Road to Alexandra's restaurant, where she'd often have dinner. Once I followed her in and had dinner on my own, just to watch her. She reminded me of a Greek goddess – or maybe a blonde Red Indian Chief, with her fine beak of a nose.

The other performance which mesmerized me with its electric energy was Peter O'Toole's in *The Long and the Short and the Tall*. It still remains on my list of magic moments. But great globules of Miss Hildebrandt memories came hurtling at me in the stalls. I regretted not bringing my umbrella. Spittle aside, I revered his daring. At that time there was nothing remotely resembling his anarchic rebellious fury.

Alas, both he and Diane chopped off a fine beak of a nose, removing their uniqueness with it.

The actor who displays the tricks of his trade with style isn't as interesting to me as the actor forgetting his tricks. I'm on the edge of my seat for her or him. Difficult, though, for his tricks (personal technique) are his safety net. There's great danger in just 'being', and having the courage to surrender nakedly. The best examples I know of this are Ralph Richardson and Wilfred Lawson.

> The Musician's robes – some glorious instrument,
> The Writer's robes – paper and pen,
> The Artist's robes – paint, brush 'n' canvas,
> The Actor's robes – nakedness again and again.

Echoes of RADA classes with the girls sitting around the walls watching the fascinating process of the *actor* finding the capacity within him to meet the demands of *his* part. Us wallflowers were lucky enough to get a part at all. It was my realization of the shortage of women's roles that awakened me to the existence of the feminist movement. (I'd been too busy trying to grow into a woman to look any further.) But sitting there in class watching only a small number of girls allowed an opportunity of displaying their talent (some of them never) really got me thinking. What else could an aspiring actress do but shrink at the lack of any depth, breadth, significance – vision, even – in most of the female roles written? Since I hadn't the wherewithal to put actresses' injustices to rights by penning Woman some worthy words of my own – only putting pen to paper for the occasional thank-you letter – I was left no alternative but to start skipping class in earnest.

Willy and I would use the Royal Court Theatre Club late at night. It was run by Clement Freud who always gave us a lugubriously colourful welcome. Paradise comes in all shapes and sizes and for me, on that Royal Court dance-floor, it was the size of a postage stamp. I remember those dancing days so warmly for they were my only ones. None of my other lovers danced, or only danced disco. Such a shame, I think learning to dance cheek to cheek should be made compulsory.

One day Robin Fox asked me if I would like to go to Paris to see Edith Piaf perform. Willy wasn't in London that week, he was away on a manoeuvre somewhere – bang, bang! (You know, men's work.)

Although it was my first time in Paris, my passion for Piaf was a long-standing affair. That anguished cry of hers, 'je ne regrette rien', mingled quaintly with Coward's 'Mad Dogs and Englishmen' all through my childhood. How could I not be excited about the trip? I had passed through Paris fleetingly three years back, but now that Jukes was starting a two-year course on directing at the prestigious film school EDEC, perhaps I'd be coming over more often.

It was dark when we arrived. I felt so sophisticated with the immaculate Robin Fox. He hailed a taxi, 'The Ritz Bar, s'il vous plaît.' I'd heard of the Ritz Bar through Mummy and Daddy, but I was expecting something much Ritzier. The lighting had that tasteful mellowness that borders on the dingy. But perhaps the dinginess was in comparison to the bright glow of Piaf Expectations. I was interested to know why he had brought me to Paris – after all, Paris was made for lovers, so I was led to believe. 'Purely business,' Robin said, kissing my hand and jokingly giving me a pillowy wink. Apart from that moment he never flirted again, which was shrewd of him for I was in love with his son. 'I know what she means to you, and I believe every artist, every aspiring actress, even, should see Edith Piaf perform, for she won't be with us much longer. But it's our secret, I don't want any flak when I get home, OK?' I never had any problem with people's secrets – in fact I pride myself on the ability to keep them.

Sitting in that packed theatre waiting for the lights to dim was enthralling. All my life I'd known her as my 'noise'. Any minute now, I was about to hear her in the flesh. What if I were disappointed? Perhaps I should have left my noise as it was, a magical noise of childhood? Perhaps I would be let down seeing the owner of my noise in beholding the art?

Robin's voice broke into my doubts. 'Watch her carefully, study her.'

The curtain went up slowly, the lighting was dim, the stage empty. After about thirty seconds, a minute figure appeared at the back. The lights came up, harsh street lights on this tiny person, the music struck up. She walked very slowly downstage, wearing what seemed like the white mask of a clown. Her thinning clumpy hair looked forgotten and doll-like, as if lately rescued from an old chest in the attic. Her little arms protruded so frail, so transparent from a simple black dress. She was in pain, her hands were all stiff and bent. I was about to turn to Robin to share with him my growing fears of her ability to last more than a minute or two, when her mouth – an immense vermilion vent – poured that familiar sound all over us, smothering the auditorium.

The only instrument not tampered with by man is the Aborigines' didgeridoo. It is made by the termites who eat away at the inside of a tree or branch, leaving it hollow. Those familiar with the sound of the didgeridoo will know what I mean when I say that the sound emanating from it hits you in the solar plexus with such mesmeric force that you are left with no choice but to sink into a reverent trance.

That night Edith Piaf was a didgeridoo, for it was as if the pain of her life had eaten her hollow too. From her sacred echo chamber of hollow rawness, her pain came billowing up and was transformed into an overwhelming love, shaking the foundations of the theatre, along with all who witnessed it. Deep pain enlarges the boundaries of our wholeness, often blessing us with more potential. So, too, Edith's magnificent pain soared forth from her blood-red gash of a mouth, reverberating down those beloved streets of her Parisian past.

Sitting there silently recovering, I felt a wave pass over us, sending a final shiver through me before there was nothing left to share except a silence of passion spent. I welled up with gratitude, for my noise was indeed an art.

'Come on, let's make a move, I'll take you round to meet her, if you like.'

I panicked. What if she wasn't *up* to her 'noise'? What if she wasn't equal to her art? What if . . .? What if . . .? What if . . .?

Inside the stage door, Robin gave his name, and after a few moments – it could have been an hour, I wouldn't have known the difference – we were shown to her dressing-room door. I was in a kind of a trance, had been since I arrived. Robin knocked. '*Entrez*,' a voice said. It was hard for me to open the door, as if there was something in the way. Robin pushed it open the rest of the way and, as he did so, I got such a blast of warmth, a sweetness, smelling of honeysuckle.

Perhaps the reason she'd spent her nights on the streets of Paris, sleeping with anyone she could drag out of the night, wasn't loose morals, or loneliness even, but a need to share what she had in abundance – unconditional love. She looked up into my eyes as Robin introduced us and I was spellbound. Never before had I been able to penetrate black eyes. (But then hers seemed to be more purple.) I found myself being lulled by a benevolence way down in their velvet inky depths, in such contrast to the brittle green of Vivien Leigh's eyes from which I'd tried to retreat. When I'd managed to haul myself out from their purple power, I noticed a beautiful young man beside her, who doubtless was her mate.

I met her again in London, outside the Royal Court theatre one night. She was still with her beautiful man. Her hands were a lot worse. Her teeth, too, were hurting her that night, for she'd raise her bent claw of a hand to her mouth to prevent the cold wind whistling into the pain. It was grotesque just to witness such brilliance withering away inch by aching inch, so what must it be like for the woman herself? But her purple eyes were laughing, probably laughing at what those years on the streets had finally brought her to. She was so paralysed with arthritis by then that she could hardly hold the roses she was carrying. She made a joke about it and handed them over to her man. Rumour had it that he didn't really love her, but hung in there for the money, fame and glory. Bollocks to that, I say. Her body might have been deteriorating bit by bit, but the love between them was clear and even stronger than before.

For me to have found at such an early age an example of someone who surpassed their art was, with hindsight, not a good thing. I have been searching for another example of this all my life – alas, in vain.

CHAPTER THIRTY-NINE

WE WERE ALL down in Cornwall at our family holiday house, called Shag Rock, for the summer. It was a delightful spot, real *Rebecca* country, two miles down a mud track. An overgrown garden path ultimately led to a rope-ladder, the only access to our own tiny private beach amid the mass of craggy Cornish seascape. The little island of Shag Rock was a fair swim out, and a good place to be alone – that is if you didn't mind the boisterous belligerence of shags (large gulls).

Daddy was grumpy. He had promised me a car if I passed my driving test first time. Knowing I hadn't passed anything in my life, except the RADA audition, he thought he was on to a safe wicket. So my triumphant pass wasn't being digested too well. 'I'm damned if I'm going to buy you a car. You can have Jukes's old one, I suppose,' he conceded grudgingly.

'Just because I'm the third and a girl, I have to make do with all their cast-offs.'

'I'd hold your tongue, young lady.'

'Why are you being so beastly today?' Silence, as we both sat with the inevitable coast wind whipping up the anti.

'What's up, Daddy?'

'Speak to your mother about it.' He got up to find a calmer spot to light his pipe, quite a distance from me. He could

296

have been in Timbuktu, I'd still have felt his anger through his stubborn little back.

I went into the kitchen, and Mummy was just as moody. I hoped Willy would hurry up and arrive, he always brought the sunshine with him.

'Sit down, Sarah, I want a word with you. I had a letter from the RADA principal—'

'Who, John Fernald?' I was stunned.

'He has decided it isn't worth your while returning next term. He says you hardly ever attend, and there's a mass of hungry talent out there who'd give their eye-teeth to step into your shoes.'

'But—'

'No "buts", some things never change, and you're one of them.'

'Mummy, there's some mistake, John Fernald thinks I'm—'

'Shut up, you silly, spoilt . . .' She couldn't think of the word she wanted, so she wagged her favourite threat at me. 'I tell you, you won't live to see your twenty-first birthday, you little witch, you mark my words!' As Mummy left the kitchen, she didn't let me see her face. I think she was crying.

Why did Mummy always keep calling me a witch? Why did she keep threatening me with an early death? Surely it's the good that die young? I slumped in my chair. It seemed I'd really gone and done it this time.

I went up to her room. 'Mummy. I'll go and see John Fernald, he likes me really—'

'It's not a matter of liking you – believing in you, even – it's a matter of turning up.'

'But I'm not learning anything there, I want to go to rep, I want to act, not sit around talking about it.'

'You just don't give a damn, you never have, and I don't suppose you ever will.'

Mummy wouldn't let me sort it out with Mr Fernald. Instead, she got herself all dressed up like a dog's dinner (a pedigree dog, that is) and went to see him herself.

'I went down on my knees on your behalf, madam, and I don't want ever to have to stoop so low again.' I didn't believe her for a second. Mummy on her knees?

Anyway, I found myself reinstated. Actually it had been Milos Sperber and Nigel Stock who stood up for me, and promised Fernald I would do well in their productions at the Vanbrugh. It was their belief in me that did the trick.

A few weeks later, fear made me do something really wicked. I was driving back to London from Barn Mead one Sunday evening in Jukes's secondhand-to-start-with, cast-off Mini-Minor, when I was caught speeding. I panicked and told the police my mother had been taken to hospital. 'Which hospital?' said one of them, quick as a flash, so quick, in fact, that I couldn't think of a single hospital. 'Which hospital?' He was getting stroppy.

Then I remembered my ears. 'University College Hospital – she's having an emergency operation, I must hurry.'

They were most kind, most sympathetic, and ended up offering me a police escort – as if they had nothing better to do. That mournful guilt-ridden drive from Stratford East, the gloomiest part of the East End, through London, was a real bummer. I kept checking to see if I could lose them accidentally on purpose, but all I could think was what the hell was I going to do when we reached the damned place?

As soon as I saw the main entrance, I parked my Mini (a lot easier in those days), waved to them in their police car, and on the run said, 'Thanks so much, I really appreciate your kindness – must dash!'

As I scampered up the main steps, I saw a man in a white coat pressing the lift button. I squeezed inside the closing doors, as he said. 'This lift is for staff only.'

'I'll be staff, then, I'll be anything you like, but please, please, take me up!' He could see I was hysterical, and allowed me to explain my deception. He laughed, and offered to go back down in a few minutes to see if they'd gone.

The police remained hanging about the entrance for quite a time, and my dear little doctor friend went down twice to check. He was a lovely fellow, he gave me many cups of coffee, and we talked about life – his life in the hospital. He said the police had searched for my name in the register so they knew I was having them on. 'They'll leave in time, when they receive another emergency,' he said, offering me a biscuit, before going to check again. He was right. They finally gave up, almost an hour later. Think of all the real crimes they could've prevented in all that time.

About two months after that episode I had a call from Mummy. Would I come into University College Hospital the following day, and not say a word to anyone? When I arrived at her bedside, I was really taken aback by her frailty, though she wasn't feeling in the least bit sorry for herself. She delivered her bombshell as if it were the weekly grocery list. 'There's nothing to be alarmed about, Pusscat, but I have to have my breast removed for cancer tomorrow. I'm telling you this in case of emergencies, but I don't want the rest of the family to know. Is that perfectly clear?'

I was horrified. 'Yes, M-M-Mummy, that's perfectly clear.' Was she going to die, I wondered.

'Don't worry. All will be fine. Once the cancer has been removed, I'll be as good as new.' Those beautiful breasts – I couldn't take it in.

'But don't tell a living soul, do you promise?'

'Does Daddy know?'

'Of course, but no one else. Is that clear? Say, I promise.'

'I promise.'

In bed that night my whole world fell in. Two months earlier I had told the police that my mother was in the very same hospital having an emergency operation. The lie to save my own neck had become a grotesque reality. It was my lies that had brought about Mummy's cancer. I became convinced that I had instigated this tragedy. The brutal thing was, they told us later after they'd butchered her, that it hadn't been necessary to remove the whole breast at all. Those were the days when breast surgery, in fact all surgery, was much more barbaric.

What a proud woman she was! She went about her business, her 'busyness', in just the same manner as before, head held high, with no trace of self-pity, not a smidgen's worth of regret for the stunningly perfect part of her beauty that had been mindlessly destroyed for what turned out to be no reason. I found it strange that Mummy chose to share that highly intimate piece of information with me above all other family members. After all, I was the one she cared for least – so it seemed to me anyway. I took great pride in the secret I'd been honoured with, for it was my first sign, my first little grain of hope, that one day Mummy and I could indeed become the friends I'd always thought we could be.

CHAPTER FORTY

WILLY WAS BEING sent to Kenya for a year as part of his National Service. We spoke of marriage like lovers do – but a year, hell's bells! I couldn't swear fidelity for that long.

'Just try,' he said.

'Will you?' I asked.

'Of course.' I think he was probably telling the truth. But I wasn't about to make any promises.

I was amazed how this news affected me. I went into a kind of mourning. Everything had been so perfect between us. What depressed me as much as the parting was the fact that Willy liked the army, and was thinking of making a career out of it. Having been a success at the Central School of Speech and Drama, and having been a child star, with his wondrous good looks the army seemed a bit of a quaint choice. Nothing like as quaint as the thought of me as an army officer's wife.

Gail Gladstone had left Half Moon Street to return to America. I told Mummy not to worry because I had been lucky enough to meet a very nice girl who was willing to share the rent. What I didn't tell anyone was that she was a tart.

Coming home from RADA I'd go through Shepherd's Market to see the tarts walking their beat, all dressed up, mostly mutton dressed as lamb, but always colourful and spicy. I was certainly drawn to them, though I wasn't sure why at the time, but I suppose it was for the same reason that I was drawn to Ethel and Ted the gypsies. Something about them struck a note, a reassuring echo slicing through all the social bullshit, enabling me to recapture some part of the earth I'd lost. Perhaps it was also because I was getting closer – thanks to Willy and the posh people I'd met through his family's generosity – to a real whiff of the corrupting stench of the Establishment. So false and unstable was it that the closer I got, the more I yearned for the return of my days in the stable yard, and since they were long gone, the next best thing was my nightly breath of simple fresh air from the whores of Half Moon Street and Shepherd's Market.

One particular tart intrigued me. She wasn't like the rest; never before, in my short experience, had I seen a tart without make-up, or sporting twin-set and pearls, court shoes and talking the Queen's English. She was called Sylvia. Her hair was naturally dark blonde. I can't remember the colour of her eyes because of the sadness in them. I was in a bad way too. I was being regularly engulfed in foul waves of nausea and I hadn't had the curse for too long. Willy had been gone nearly three months, and I had a frightening feeling that our last nights of love were about to bring forth fruit. What was I going to do?

I thought of Mary Adams in that cold bleak surgery with those high beds and gruesome-looking stirrups, her eyes probing into my private torture. 'Oh, ducky, ducky, what will Wren say about this?' No, I couldn't turn to Mary, I just couldn't do it.

I really missed Pooker at that moment. Pooker would have helped me through, I know she would. But since she had just gone to Benenden, I went to talk it through with Mizzer at the Hurlingham Club (and have a quick game of croquet – I'd happily die on a croquet lawn). Mizzer welcomed me with his usual whinny followed by a coughing fit. He told me he wasn't too well versed in matters of abortion, but kindly let me bury myself in his familiar, oh so huggable smell.

But who could I turn to? I thought of Sylvia. Surely she would be familiar with the problem, and could give me some advice. I plucked up my dwindling courage and went to Shepherd's Market to find her. She'd been crying. 'What's up Sylvia?'

'Nothing,' she said walking away.

'Come on,' I said, 'let's have a cup of coffee.'

Her pimp had chucked her out. She wouldn't come forward with the reason, except to say that he worked her too hard for too little, so she decided to stick up for herself, and got her suitcase chucked out of the window for her trouble. She had nowhere to go.

After I'd shared my woes with her, she seemed to stop feeling so sad. 'It might be a bit late to use the gin and hot water routine, but we'll go and give it a try.' I hated gin. My worries had worked wonders on hers.

It all turned out perfect timing, Gail having left. We planned it carefully. Mummy and Mrs Hocking, the landlady, would be told that Sylvia Drummond was an old friend from school. Mrs Hocking wouldn't be a problem because she wasn't at all nosy, thank God. Otherwise Willy wouldn't have got past the front door.

I had mixed feelings lying there with Sylvia alternating between pouring gin down my gullet, more boiling water from the kettle into the bath, and continually punching my tummy with her fist. 'We have to loosen its hold on you.'

Babies never entered my brain while being transported by Willy to those far-off feathery realms. I somehow believed babies were so important that I'd only conceive when *I* wanted to. If life is so precious how come it can be dumped in with a couple of seconds 'Humma – Humma'? How come this God of ours hadn't invented a more inspired and mutually worthy way for two people to conceive a baby? No brains are needed, no athletics, stamina, commitment, artistry, love, spiritual awareness, nothing but a quick in and out. I knew neither of us wanted a baby yet, we weren't ready for the commitment. I knew that lust was no bed to lay a baby on, even though I was sure I was in love at the time. Willy didn't even know I was pregnant, and I had no intention of telling him. It was my fault I got pregnant, and what could he possibly do about it anyway, out in Kenya, busy on manoeuvres? Bang bang! (You know, men's work.)

After roughly two hours in the bath, familiar waves of nausea welled up, swirling me back to Crofton Grange and that vile vodka vomit. I couldn't stay in the bath a moment longer – I'd rather go to Mary Adams, and make my shame public. 'No more, Sylvia, sorry, it seems I'm a bit of a wet.'

Three days later there we were, trundling along on a double-decker bus through unfamiliar parts of London to a woman, a friend to all prostitutes, who Sylvia knew in Kennington. I guessed Sylvia had been in my shoes herself. She rang the bell of a tall, neglected house, recently patched over with a dark pink wash. A fat elderly woman opened the door. 'Hello. Please come through,' she said, with a northern accent.

I noticed the place stank of Dettol or some such stuff to

hide the murder underneath. 'You'll have to pay now, I'm afraid, before you go in to see Dr Murphy.' I got out the twenty-five pounds and handed it over. That was a great deal of money in those days, being roughly two months' living expenses. I'd just had my next month's allowance put into my bank account. What with that and Sylvia beside me to hold my hand I felt pretty lucky.

I denied myself a real look at the horrors ahead, by concentrating on the sparse décor of the so-called waiting room with its high ceilings, two broken chairs and no papers or magazines to read. Back came the elderly woman and pointed to Sylvia. 'You wait here, she won't be a moment.' She led me through a large black door.

I didn't like what I saw next. It made Mary Adams's surgery look the cosiest place on earth. I turned towards the door and started to make a run for it. Obviously my reaction was common, for Sister was there, a thick fat wall before me. 'It's all going to be fine, you don't have to remove your clothes, just take your skirt and pants off, and we'll get you ready for Dr Murphy.' I noticed the yellow and gloomy lighting as she took my pants from me, and led me over to the equipment. 'Up we get,' she said, as she helped me on to the high table. Who is this 'we' that nurses always talk about? 'Now relax, otherwise we can't get your feet through these stirrups, can we?' As she forced open my thighs while hitching me up to the stirrups, she peered and prodded between my legs, as if she were checking the freshness of the cod in the local market. She produced a razor out of thin air and began to shave me without a 'do you mind?'

I was outraged. 'How dare you do that? What on earth do you need to do that for?'

'We're not relaxing, are we, young lady?' she gently warned, as she stretched my thighs till I thought they'd split. 'Dr Murphy insists we to do this, it's regular procedure. Now keep still.'

'But surely the doctor doesn't do the abortion out there?' I said indicating the soft fluff in my groin.

'It's all got to come off,' she said, grateful to me for pointing out a bit she'd missed.

I tried to close my eyes and think of England but I was too frightened. Funny . . . as I saw my skinny legs thus, my feet thrust into the stirrups, I can remember thinking that I'd have to sell Prince Charming one of these days, because I hadn't been riding him nearly enough lately.

'I think you'll grow to like it all smooth, they often tell me the men really like it.' She said this as she washed the now tender skin. This was the last straw.

'I'm no prostitute!'

She looked at her finished work with pride. 'I never said you were, did I?'

Then, as she began pushing my stomach, the door opened and in came a very small grey-haired man with specs, and a quiet underhand manner. 'Hello. This won't take a moment,' he said. He put on some plastic gloves, while prying me even further apart. 'You're three months' pregnant, is that correct?'

'Roughly,' I grunted, as he pushed his filthy plastic fingers into my most private world.

I saw something glint, brutal and silver, before Sister came and pushed my head flat again, while removing an under pillow, so that I could no longer strain my neck upward to see.

'Lie back, dear, just relax.'

The pain that then followed was as if all the angry Gods up there had decided to rip me open with sharp cold kitchen utensils, cheese graters and serrated knives. Even if I could, I hadn't the strength to lift up to see what equipment was being stuffed up me, for I thought that I was going to pass out. I began to think this man had it in for women. He was so brisk, so lacking in compassion in his handling of my embarrassment, my shame. Finally a wave of pain began pulling down on me; so excruciating was it that I thought my innards were going to drop out, and I let out a cry.

'I've had to fix a stretching device on to the neck of your womb.'

'I don't understand.'

'Unfortunately you are built too small for me to be able to bring on the abortion. But with this stretching device in place within twenty-four hours all will be well.' He took off his gloves, and went over to the sink. 'I'll want you back here tomorrow at the same time, please.'

'Right,' said Sister. 'We'll get you dressed now, shall we?'

Would the stretching device hurt, I wondered, for I always find I can be braver if I'm prepared for it. But I forgot to ask, because Sister said I'd have to pay another fifteen pounds. I hadn't got fifteen pounds, nor did I know anyone who would give me fifteen pounds with no questions asked. It was good when Sylvia put her arm around me as we left.

The journey back to Half Moon Street on the hard seat of a bumpy double-decker was no joy ride, what with the newly exposed skin all raw and tickling me, and the strange foreign instrument of torture prodding at me, deeper and deeper, pulling the pain inwards. As I was walking back into Half

Moon Street, it began trespassing into the very source of my newly acquired feelings of womanhood. I blacked out.

I kept hearing Daddy's voice telling me to pull myself together. Typical of Daddy not to understand that these relentless waves invading private places prevented me from feeling on tip-top form. 'Mind over matter, Pusscat.' I tried – Goddamn it, I tried.

Sylvia helped to undress me. 'I like your pubes all naked, don't you?' she said, as if trying to cheer me up.

'No, I don't,' I replied angrily.

Back in bed at last, Sylvia said, 'Come on, who can we get the money from? You must know someone.'

'I know no one,' I said rolling into a different position as a buffer to the next attack.

'Of course!' said Sylvia. 'Keep it in the family. What about your Willy's Dad?'

Would Robin Fox lend me the money? After all, it was his son's baby? I'd never asked anyone for money in my life, and, oddly enough, I never would again, because I felt truly awful having to beg from dear Robin, who had shown me nothing but kindness. I had to steel myself to ring his office.

'Robin, I must see you, it's rather urgent.'

'I can't talk now, meet me at the flat at ten thirty.'

Even though I put on a good show for Robin, he could see I was desperate. I bade him not to ask what I wanted the money for and promsied I'd pay it back with my first job. It was the longest and the worst night of my life so far. Why did nothing ever happen for me like it did for other people? Why was my womb neck so small? Isn't an abortion enough punishment without having a deformed womb neck on top of it all?

I lay there thinking Mummy was wrong, because here I

was dying four years too early. But did it really matter that much? That night nothing mattered except its length, for it was longer than those two weeks in Ilford. Death seemed a most comforting alternative.

The next day I was back in the saddle again, my exhausted legs wide open in their familiar stirrups and Dr Murphy peering and prodding. 'Now take three deep breaths and then relax, there's a good girl.' I can't remember anything after that because the body has its own automatic switch-off mechanism, so when the pain is too much for us to bear, we supply our own anaesthetic. Thank God.

'There now,' said Sister, as I came round in that bleak waiting room. 'You must get into bed double quick, because you haven't aborted yet.'

I was astounded at this extra piece of good news, and lost my temper. 'What was all that about then, for Christ's sake?'

'Dr Murphy only releases the foetus. You will abort within a few hours, so take it easy now and get to bed quick, and it's essential to rest for a few days.'

Sylvia splashed out on a taxi to get us home. Robin had been very generous and given us two pounds extra, and I was still alive, so things could have been worse.

They were, round about midnight. I never expected the brazen brutality that a mere speck of life can deliver in its need to survive. As the flood gates opened, I felt this was the culmination of every loss of every woman who had ever given birth. As the loss ripped through me, it left a raging rawness lining a new gaping chasm. None of it was good, all of it was bad, really bad, as I lay there in a bed full of blood and afterbirth, Sylvia wouldn't let me see the foetus, and I wasn't in the mood for arguing with her that night.

When all was calm again, when the agony had seeped away leaving merely soreness and bruising, I had time to reflect on what I'd done. I came to the conclusion that what my heart, my intuition, had been telling me through the experience was that I was by no means ready to bring a baby into the world. Surely readiness was the least I could offer? I had committed murder in my bed of blood in Half Moon Street that night. Was the overwhelming loss and regret at my own carelessness sufficient for me to heed the lessons and gain some wisdom from the experience? After a couple of weeks things began to get back to normal, although I was unsure that I ever wanted to make love again. (Whatever else time is it's a great healer.)

On some occasions I became Sylvia's madam. I'd open the door, take the client's coat and lead him through to her bedroom, always asking if he wanted a cuppa tea and a biscuit first. Sylvia said I made an excellent madam, 'But, poppet,' she said, 'perhaps leave out the tea and biscuit routine, because I have to hang about while they drink it – and time's money.'

One day Sylvia volunteered to show me the tricks of her trade. 'You hide in that cupboard', she said, 'and I'll shift the bed up a little. That way you can see.'

I went into the cupboard, but couldn't see a damn thing. 'No silly,' she said, 'you must leave the door slightly ajar.'

'But then he's sure to see.'

'Nonsense.' Sylvia scented herself up with Chanel No. 5 all ready for her next trick. 'By the time the candles are lit, with my red silk over the bulb and my expertise on the high trapeze, he'll never see anything!'

I have to admit I found the prospect of playing Peeping Tom once again rather exciting. Is that wrong, I wonder. When does naughty get out of hand and become bad? Sylvia wanted to show me one specific client, which meant I had to be patient.

'Why do I have to wait so long?'

'Because I want you to have your money's worth,' said Sylvia, while darning one day.

At RADA I was about to play the stepdaughter in Pirandello's, *Six Characters in Search of an Author*. Since she was rather a seedy character who became a prostitute, my lark with Sylvia fitted in rather well. I could put the whole experience down to research. John Fernald had given me one last chance to prove myself totally dedicated to my craft, and here it was. No more messing about.

On the appointed day I couldn't play madam *and* be in the cupboard, so as soon as the bell rang, I crept into my hiding place, leaving the door slightly ajar. They were both out of sight for the undressing part – shame, I would have liked to have seen that bit. Never mind, you can't win 'em all. Sylvia guided him down – smack right in the middle of my view. They were both naked, the candles were lit, and the red glow from her whore's lighting made the whole effect soft and rosy. My wretched heart was ricocheting around the cupboard, I only hoped the sound wasn't as earth-shattering out there.

He wanted her bum up in the air. Sylvia had a nice little body, I was pleasantly surprised. A wee bit short in the leg perhaps, but all shortcomings paled beside her wonderfully ample breasts. I still had a thing about breasts and Sylvia's were just the ticket. Large and firm with round, perfect nipples, neither too pale nor too beige, too big or too small. As he got her up on all fours, I could see them wobbling about beneath her torso, a pair of luscious jellyfish swinging around as he smacked her on her largish bum. Even through the rosy glow I could tell both his face and Sylvia's buttocks were well past rosy and into the realms of puce. As her bum quivered with kisses and smacks, I kept thinking of her upper-class voice, and giggled – almost as silently as S.P.J.

He pointed to the cupboard. Help! Had he heard me? What was I going to do? As I shrank into the furthest corner, Sylvia put her hand in and poked around until she found a buckle. Returning to her client, she handed over a long leather belt. He then placed her back on all fours and proceeded to thrash her with it. It bewildered me how he could refrain from grabbing hold of those great danglers – how could he resist their voluptuous existence? I found my excitement deflating somewhat with this thrashing business. To each his own, I suppose, but it didn't turn me on.

What would Mummy think of me now? I blushed.. Peeking at her private moments in her bedroom that day came flooding back. What an extraordinary business it is growing up. Having made it so far was mainly due to my rampant curiosity. As the thrashing and the rhythmic squeak of the bed continued, my mind wandered back to Ee-Ees, the crab game, grown-up Ee-Ees, and then on to the same squeak in the school dorm. Do we manage to make it through, solving at least part of the mystery that links the sexes, merely to be thrashed like poor Sylvia?

Alternating bum kisses with bum thrashes he whipped himself up into such a massive frenzy, that he finally threw away the belt and thrust himself underneath her. He pulled Sylvia's lips on to him and she began licking as if it were honey from a Crunchie Bar. He was much more vocal than she, sounding uncommonly like Charlie used to, slopping and grunting at his trough. What acrobatics! I was certainly being given a few hot tips here. And in those days they were the only ones I was likely to get without furtively rummaging through a seedy Soho bookshop. What food for thought – good old Sylv!

But *why* wasn't he tempted by those juicy beauties so close to his hands? He must have read my thoughts. Better late than never, he got hold of them. Squelching two large handfuls of breast, he pulled them towards him and began rubbing his face in them. Then he rubbed his face between her spread legs, then buried himself again in her blubbery bundles – back and forth, back and forth he went, burying himself in their mutual wetnesses.

I have to admit, as he played with her breasts that did it for me. I was able to – look, no hands! Perfect it was, from my angle, anyway! I felt really dirty, really low. Look at me, I remember thinking, just look at this grimy little mouse rattling away in its cupboard! When he was finally on top, doing the usual stuff, I lost interest, rather hoping it'd end before it actually did. I have to confess I find that part can get rather monotonous.

As Sylvia escorted him from view, I remember giving quite a sigh of relief that it was all over. I fell out of the cupboard all hot and sweaty, in need of a bath. But I had to wait for Sylvia who naturally wanted to go first to wash away all alien traces. I'd noticed how obsessionally clean she was – she had to be, I suppose.

'Come here,' she said, opening the bathroom door. 'Look at my bum.' She turned around so I could see the welts that had risen up like car tyres all over it.

'Does it hurt?' I asked, trying not to sound too shocked.

'No, it stings a little. I would love you to stroke it for me, poppet, as a favour. First I'll run the bath.' As she bent over to turn on the tap, I got a good view of her bum. What a mess. Why had she let him do that to her? I found it all most odd. She turned to me with a matter-of-factness that I found most endearing. 'Was he worth the wait, poppet? He's the best of a pretty bad lot, I'm afraid.' I got undressed, longing for the soothing warm water. 'Answer me – was it worth it?'

I looked as nonchalant as I could and shrugged. 'Beggars can't be choosers, I suppose.' Underneath I was yearning to know what else two people can get up to together. 'He hadn't much hair, had he?' was all I could think of to say.

Sylvia then told me that you very rarely see a man with a thick head of hair in a strip joint. 'For some reason, nine times out of ten they're balding. So are most of my clients, come to think . . .'

'D'you mean bald is sexy?' I asked nervously, thinking of Willy's great blond mop.

'I don't know what conclusion to draw from it, I'm just telling you my observations,' Sylvia went on, while picking up my clothes from where I'd left them all over the bathroom floor. 'You can also pretty well judge the shape of a man's penis by the shape of his middle finger. If it has a tapering end, or a great blunt knob, his penis will be the same.'

'So if a man's got thick long fingers, his cock'll be the same?' I asked, emphasizing 'cock' because of my revulsion for the word penis.

'No, poppet,' said Sylvia patiently. 'I said the shape not the size.'

She took my hand to her breast, knowing full well what she was doing. 'What bit turned you on the most?'

I turned to climb into the bath. 'Let's not talk about it.' I've never discussed love-making with anyone, not even with my lovers. It's all too sacred, too private. If I did, I feel it would somehow foul up the mystery for me.

Once I was in the bath, she turned her bottom towards me, and began to demonstrate what she wanted. 'Like that,' she said.

Sitting there in the bath stroking a whore's bum gave me a strange sensation. I remember asking myself, What on earth am I doing? Whatever it was, I couldn't find it in me to feel too terrible. I certainly remember thinking that what I was doing ought to make me feel bad, but it didn't.

'Hey! You're getting me horny!' I thought this strange. After all, she'd just been at it hammer and tongs. 'You should be exhausted,' I heard myself saying rather prudishly.

She laughed. 'I never come with my clients, that would be the day!' She laughed again, and as she laughed she spilled backwards into the bath; and splashing water everywhere, she opened her legs perhaps just a little too wide, for it was then that I realized Sylvia had the hots for me.

That first evening it was fun – to be honest, more than fun. It was exhilarating exploring and playing with a woman's body in the luxury of warm water. There I was actually holding those breasts for the very first time. I'd never held breasts before, I'd wanted to, so often. Sylvia's breasts certainly didn't let me down. Her nipples were up, and sticking right out, I could have done a handstand on them. Everything was like that moment in springtime when quite suddenly, or so it seems, every tree, every flower bursts out with a simultaneous quiver, reaching for the sun. As Sylvia reached, she suddenly, joyously, came. I didn't know how I knew for certain, except she gave such a grateful grunt of fulfilment, and her smile became softer and easier, as she rested her cheek on my knee. Then laughing, rather triumphantly, I thought, she turned to put some more hot water on to our already steamy skin.

Slowly she leant forward and began playing with me. She got the flannel and stroked it through my legs, back and forth, back and forth, just as I used to do as little girl. It turned me on no end. 'See how quickly it all grew back. Would you like me to shave it smooth again?'

'No, thank you.' I was sure about that if nothing else, for the weeks of itchy moments had finally ceased. She moved over me with such style, playing with my breasts, my mouth, my tongue, my thighs, everywhere. 'No, Sylvia! Please, not my ears!'

'What's wrong with kissing your ears, poppet?'

I gently managed to direct her tongue away. 'Nothing, except they're not mine to kiss.' Her puzzled look soon evaporated, as she got drawn into more serious matters. Preparing the sponge with more soap, she said, 'Stand up.'

I obeyed. As her soapy hands and fingers wrapped their way around my hidden nooks and crannies, I felt weak at the knees. Should I be so excited by this? I felt every part of me filling up with curiosity. I became her slithering, slathering pet snake.

Then, out of nowhere, came great flashes of Daddy, Mummy, washing me and the boys in the bath, powerfully vivid images from God knows where, pictures of Malcolm, Alison, the date rape, my Willy – I'd betrayed my Willy. A dreadful darkness fell. What right had any such darkness to hijack my harmless snake dance? I made a huge effort to regain the far-off paradise from whence I had slipped so suddenly. It was no good. I felt ashamed, and wanted to get out of the bath as quickly as possible.

'Guilt kills everything almost every time,' said Sylvia raising her still scarlet striped bum, and bending it towards me as she climbed rather primly out of the warm water.

'How d'you mean?' I asked, stunned at the way she'd hit the nail on the head.

'You were completely surrendering just now, until something ruined it. Am I right?'

'Yes, you're right.' I just sat there.

'Don't look so guilty about your guilt, for Christ's sake – it happens to all of us!' She finished drying herself. 'Cuppa cocoa?' She asked in that rather quaint upper-class drawl of hers.

Perfect I thought. 'Thanks.'

In time, Sylvia began to need me, and sadly I couldn't take it. This was a pattern that was inclined to repeat itself often as time went by. I find needing an unattractive quality because it gives the spirit nowhere new to go except down, drowning the love.

'Do you love me?' is a doomed question. Love is love and

need is need. In needing to ask the question in the first place, one's not in love, but in need. Or in need of specs, because it's easy to see if you're loved or not. Having it verbally affirmed is an insult to that love. For there's no love, which is, after all, a selfless state, in such a loveless question.

Although I didn't love Sylvia, I was very grateful to her for getting me through that abortion. I don't know what I'd have done without her . . . Well, I suppose, I would have simply gone a different route. To have had an abortion without any drugs was quite an experience. I wouldn't care to repeat it, but I nevertheless feel that I was part of some ancient primitive rite – barbaric times long gone.

Sylvia went as softly out of my life as she'd come in. She not only showed me the ropes, but loaned me those stupendous breasts. She was called back to Leicester to take care of her ailing mother.

'Who is Sylvia, what is she, that all our swains commend her?'

CHAPTER FORTY-ONE

MY EXOTIC Half Moon Street days were coming to a close. The house was being sold up for demolition. This news followed like a treble blow in my solar plexus: no more Willy, no more Sylvia, no more Half Moon Street. I loved those times, and I love them still, those golden days of 'firsts', of experimenting with love. Twenty-one Half Moon Street isn't there any more, nor are the whores.

With Sylvia, I had the feeling I'd been unfaithful to Willy – in a harmless kind of way. I wouldn't describe this feeling as guilt, more horniness. I liked the power of lust, and the power it gave me, a damn sight more than letterwriting. I also found the idea of a whore (high class) much more engaging than being an officer's wife. Willy's letters were always warm and loving, but he wanted me to go out to him. The thought of staying among those army types gave me the Kenya shivers. I shivered at night, too. The draughty gap in my romantic life, was more than unfortunate, it was a bloody nuisance. I wanted to find the strength to wait for Willy, because I still loved him dearly, but I didn't like the cold draught one bit. RADA was getting a bit heavy. I was having to prove to both Mummy and Daddy that I wasn't fooling around all the time. My performance in Wycherley's Restoration comedy *The Gentleman Dancing Master* was apparently worthy of a final term student. I certainly love playing

Restoration more than anything else, but it's always hard to know, when you're up there. Robin Fox came to see me, with his associate Kenneth Harper. They were partners, and although Kenneth became officially my agent, to prevent it all becoming too incestuous, it was Robin who cracked the whip.

Then came the stepdaughter in Pirandello's *Six Characters*. Perhaps, because of all that research with Sylvia, perhaps because, as Milos Sperber said, I was sprouting into my sexual power, whatever it was, I knew that I was being true up there. I knew Milos Sperber was pleased with my work, I knew that Robin Fox was so impressed that he got some of the heavyweights along to see me. I didn't know at the time that they were out front, or even that they were impressed, all I know is that I got signed up for a three-year contract with the impresario Binkie Beaumont of H.M. Tennants.

Mummy and Daddy came to see me. Mummy was thrilled, tossing her mink stole around her with pride, congratulating everyone while lapping up the praise for her daughter like the cat that had stolen the cream. Daddy didn't say much. He didn't even say whether he liked or disliked my performance. He never really approved of me going on the stage in the first place, though he never said it to my face. He didn't need to, his body language said it all: bending to kiss me, he pecked at thin air around my forehead instead. As if trying to sniff out his old Pusscat, the tennis partner, the horsewoman, his goose-girl, the spirit of the stable yard after his long sweat at the office.

I wasn't blind, I could see the loss in his eyes, for his loss was my loss, too. Sad, really, because we couldn't find each other that night. As he sat there lighting up his dwindling pipe, I think he saw my life as dwindling too, into a rather false and peripheral shallowness. Here was his Pusscat meta-morphosing into a creature he didn't feel at home with. All his fault for sending me away from home in the first place, ripping me away from the very life he now wanted back for me.

But it was all too late, my new life was under starter's orders and I was off. I felt my lucky star was shining directly above me, or perhaps it wasn't a lucky star at all, but Dick Whittington's black cat brushing past me? Whatever, I passed through two years of RADA without being expelled. I got my diploma at last, and I even won some special award, but I've lost it – not that it matters much since I can't even remember what I won it for.

Tom Courtenay was already making a name for himself in Chekhov's *The Seagull* at the National Theatre, so my predictions were coming true. Then, bingo! I galloped right out of RADA and into a posh job being directed by John Gielgud – I'd even heard of him! Straight into the West End production of a new play by John Perry and Molly Keane called *Dazzling Prospect*. Margaret Rutherford was to play the leading part. The play was about horse racing in Ireland. It also starred Joyce Carey, Richard Leach and Brook Williams (Emlyn's son). My part was that of an upper-class beatnik called Aroon Fox Collier. From then on, whenever we met or worked together, John Gielgud would call me Aroon. I played her rather like Sylvia, actually, a square peg in a secretive and saucy round hole.

I had a great deal of time for John Gielgud – such dapper style and inborn good manners. Genuine humility, too, so rare among directors. But he did have a penchant for chang-ing all our moves daily. Each morning he'd come into rehearsal at the Globe Theatre, Shaftesbury Avenue, and say, 'Good morning, everyone, you're all going to have to be very patient with me today, I'm afraid, because I want to start again from scratch, I'm so terribly terribly sorry.'

Finally after about a month I received my one and only note. I remember it well.

'Aroon, come down here a minute.' I eagerly went down-stage to him. 'Hold your head up higher, and it's not pronounced "jools" but "jewels".' I personally thought my character would say 'jools' but I wasn't going to argue the toss with my one and only note in the production so far. 'Come on, Aroon, jewels, jewels, jewels.'

I almost said, 'You mean "jewels" as in this play?' But I didn't dare, I parroted him immaculately, 'Jewels. Jewels. Jewels.'

'Excellent, thank you.' As I turned away he called me back with a quiet twinkle in his voice. When I was close enough he whispered, 'Did you know you have a bottom just like a boy? Two poached eggs in a handkerchief.' Then aloud to everyone, 'Now let's take it from the top.'

I wasn't sure whether this was a compliment or not. But gradually, through the tour, my respect grew for this delight-fully elegant man. He was always intent on being caring and considerate. He had to be because he was forever battling with a natural tendency towards acute vagueness which caught him in many a faux pas.

In no time at all we were off to the Olympia Theatre in Dublin, for the première. Where else would one go to open an Irish play about Irish horse-racing folk? But the Dubliners weren't taken by the play, and the reviews were cold.

Margaret Rutherford and her husband Stringer Davies

were a perfect couple. So much in love with each other. They'd have to be because Stringer had the habit of reading poems out loud all the time, his own poems, naturally, and Stringer, bless his heart, was no poet:

Poor little Robin Redbreast had a terrible cold.
'But robins don't get colds, not ever so I'm told.'
'We do get colds, we do, we do!' I hear a robin cry,
'Eagles and lions get colds too, the same as you or I.'

He often had a cold too. As he read to us from the day's harvest, he'd sometimes have to wipe his nose, at which point Margaret would nudge me and wink. Love, compassion, patience and, above all, humour sparkled in that wink.

I was also given the honour of being Margaret's swimming partner. She would insist on swimming every day, come hell or high weather and, believe me, it was damn near freezing on that tour. After Dublin, we toured all around England, and wherever we happened to be it was my job to look up the local swimming pool and get Margaret there in the morning, all togged up ready to dive in. She wore a black utility swimsuit with little legs. Oddly enough, she wasn't as fat in the altogether as she seemed on stage.

I can see her now, the furious wobble of her turkey bits as they hung beneath her clenched and stubborn jaw. How she'd grind her teeth and roll her eyes, around and around they went as she plucked up courage for the plunge! Some people are never old, even though their bodies seem to be telling another story. Margaret's spirit on those early-morning swims filled me with sprightliness that I didn't think I had any more – and I was sweet seventeen.

One night – Hull, I think it was – during a performance I

heard from my dressing room an unfamiliar ominous silence coming from the Tannoy, a silence prior to Margaret's entrance in the second act. I ran into her dressing room, to find her fast asleep in her chair. I gently woke her up. Poor Margaret.

'Oh, God, whatever next?' She reluctantly grasped hold of me, tearing herself away from the luxury of dreamland. 'Have I been missed, d'you suppose?' We scuttled to the wings. She made a fine and hilarious entrance. What a great dame of the theatre she was! I don't give a tinker's fart whether she was actually a dame or not – and I'm sure God doesn't either! From then on I was given the responsible nightly task of seeing that it never happened again and, of course, it never did, nor would it even if I hadn't been there to play policeman, because Margaret was much too professional for that.

Things got steadily worse. *Dazzling Prospect* was turning decidedly dim, yet Mum was the word. For it seems to be the done thing, when one is touring a new play round the provinces, never to utter home truths. One just keeps on saying how great everything is, even if the truth is that the play one is lugging around is an absolute crock of shit. Everyone managed to grasp a slice of the truth one day, when Binkie Beaumont came up to Liverpool to inspect the sinking ship. The atmosphere got fearfully tense, and gossip began to whirl round the wings. Apparently John Perry, the writer, turned out to be both John Gielgud's and Binkie Beaumont's bosom buddy – not necessarily the ideal chemistry for clear artistic vision.

We all trundled our way like mindless cattle to the Globe Theatre, Shaftesbury Avenue, slaughterhouse. I'd asked

Mummy and Daddy not to come but they disobeyed my wishes. It wasn't that I was ashamed of Aroon, for I'd got some good reviews on tour – so I should, the part was small but showy. No, I smelt coming doom in the air, and wanted them to wait at least until the play had come off.

By the interval my heart was in my boots. Why was the audience so uncannily quiet? I quickly went into Margaret's room, to take up my duty as policeman to her dreams. No chance of her falling asleep that night, though – she was up and roaring, powdering not only her nose, but everything in sight. 'Margaret,' as I brushed off flying powder, 'why is everything so strange out there?'

She gave me one of her amazing jaw-wobbling, eye-twizzling looks. 'If you think this is strange just wait for the curtain call.'

When the curtain call arrived, as it's bound to do, alas, I was placed right next to Margaret. The curtains opened with the great wild beast bellowing, 'Boo! Boo! Boo!' I was astonished at the fury emanating from everywhere. As the booing rose to a peak as something almost hit Margaret on the head, then something else, I could see the prompt corner nervously whispering, 'Shall I bring the curtain down?'

'No,' said Margaret with great gobbles of pride wobbling her turkey bits. 'We'll stay here till they run out of ammunition.' Fortunately for us, there wasn't – ammunition, that is.

Only later did that first night animosity become clear. The play before ours was still happily enjoying a successful run, even accumulating a kind of cult following, before we chucked it out in the cold. It was called *A Man For All Seasons*, by a chap called Robert Bolt. I'd never seen the play, and I'd never heard of Robert Bolt, but because Binkie had chosen to take off this hugely successful play before its time, theatregoers up there in the gods were demanding blood. I think it was the last time vegetables were thrown from the gods, but even if it was only the odd tomato or two, it was still a baptism of fire.

We only lasted two weeks at the Globe. We heard the news that we were coming off from Margaret's *Evening Standard*. I think she deserved better than that.

CHAPTER FORTY-TWO

I WONDER WHY I've had so many catastrophes in and around water?

Anthony Blond's younger brother Peter asked Anthony and myself on a jaunt to Deauville, to christen his new motor yacht as well as a new girl friend. Virginia was a corker. The cliché of the Engish rose type of top model. Everything about her was golden perfection. Some women, like Mummy, don't have to do a damn thing except keep crossing their long daffodil stalks and the whole world drools. So it was with Virginia.

Nautical types drooled with equal relish at Peter's new boat. I can't remember whether it was a motor boat or a yacht because I'm confused about all things nautical. Sailing types use a completely separate language, which is tricky for someone who has difficulty mastering plain English – let alone lefts and rights. Although she was a compact little ship, she slept the four of us with no problem. I can't remember from which harbour we finally motored out (set sail) but I do recall Peter getting to grips with the role of captain and the nautical jargon with a great deal of panache and expertise, impressing us no end. The weather as we left was fair to good. Virginia, having done the catering, sat there looking luscious, legs crossed languidly *à la* Margaret Leighton, straight out of *Separate Tables*. She looked pretty nautical, I thought, dead chic, right at the height of fashion. I wasn't. In fact I was dressed all wrong, never having been on a boat before. So there we two girls were – Virginia, the *Vogue* model, Sarah the vague muddle. Anthony was sporting a roguish air. It was his first time on a boat, too, looking not unlike Aly Khan, a brightly coloured monkey with immaculately crisp togs.

Out of nowhere mid-Channel the sea whipped up with furious gusto. Virginia had to uncross her legs and grab the china and cutlery. Peter gripped the driving wheel (helm) and began shouting nautical gobble-de-gook at Anthony and myself. We knew he was within his rights to shout, that's what captains do, but Anthony and I simply weren't prepared, we had no storm dictionary, and had never practised storm drill.

'Hold on tight to the mainsail!' shouted our captain, as Anthony and I slipped and sloshed around the floor (deck), gripping on to anything we could find to stop us shooting overboard. If we ever took a breather, our captain yelled, 'For Christ's sake – the foresheet – it's come loose! No! The other side! I said port not starboard – fool!'

At the front of the yacht there was an inconvenient hole (hatch) smack in the middle of the deck. I can't imagine what it was doing there. Anthony and I took it in turns to fall down it, landing with a vicious thump outside the main bedroom (cabin), and each time one of us disappeared Peter would continue to scream. We did our best, leaping frantically around like blue-arsed flies, alternately colliding into each other or plunging down that damn hole.

As the seas got angrier, so did I. I never felt inadequate on a horse, bike or playing field, but on that wretched boat I felt an utter nincompoop. Gradually, getting more and more drenched, I caught a glimpse of Virginia through the raging waves; she reminded me that I'd forgotten to bring a change of clothes. She'd brought a change of clothes, all right, that was clear to see. She'd exchanged her slightly damp pre-storm gear for something appropriately chic for mid-storm. She reminded me of an advert for Fairy Liquid, smiling, completely calm and in control of her territory, the kitchen (galley).

How that storm came in from left field and whipped up the Channel with such speed I just don't know. What power! Things get out of control so fast – so fast! I certainly got a taste of the sea's lack of mercy that night.

There were moments during the crossing when we all wondered if we'd make it. Thanks to Virginia's beautiful head being firmly glued to her luscious body, and Peter keeping his captain's hat firmly on, we eventually arrived at Deauville battered, shattered, but in one piece. Both Anthony and I had failed to do anything constructive the whole trip. We managed, however, to find immediate café chairs, and both slumped simultaneously with loud squelches. Virginia, however, swung off the boat last (having washed up and put away all the coffee mugs from her last round of playing Florence Nightingale) looking absolutely spot on with her *après* storm gear. She was so calm and well organized throughout. It wasn't merely her fashion that was a step ahead, but her brain, too. What a beautiful brick she turned out to be – I was really surprised.

In those days my first impressions were judged too much by outward appearance. I used to assess women by their clothes, legs, breasts, shoes, hair texture and labels. Now I see all of those things, but I attempt to return to my childhood intuition – no labels and an honest smile. The storm was a good test of Virginia's true grit. She must have passed with flying colours because Peter married her and they're still married today.

Alas, I couldn't fly home like I had with Mummy from Tenerife. I almost plucked up the courage to ask, but they might have thought I was frightened and it wasn't that at all. In fact the storm was the only good thing about the trip. I'm just not – and never was – a boat girl.

I was miserably wet on the trip home across the sea, which was flat as a pancake. 'Here, Miles, you have a go.' The last thing I expected from Peter, always the captain at the bridge, alert in his captain's hat. 'Come on, it's your turn.'

'I've never driven a boat be—'

'Not "driven", steered.'

With some trepidation I took hold of the wheel.

'Just keep your eye fixed on that point,' he said, pointing to a jutting piece of coastline in the far distance.

'Where's that?' I asked.

'That's called the Eye of the Needle, off the Isle of Wight.'

He patiently demonstrated how simple it was to keep a boat on course with modern technology, taking great pride in showing me all his swish gadgets. I stood there mesmerized, just watching his mouth move. 'No, Miles, don't take it *through* the Needle's Eye, just stay on course until I get back – just going to get some coffee from Virginia.' And he was gone.

I saw the straight line I had to keep (any moron could) and I sank into watery reminiscences.

Life was just one big Chase swimming pool. Shallow

parts, deep ends, belly-flops, swallow dives. Without Willy I could easily have found myself drowning in the·deep end, but decided to use as much energy as is required, to hold my breath as it were, and move on, keep moving on, counting imaginary widths underwater, with or without fidelity, until his return. Was that wicked, I wondered. I'd known Peter and Anthony most of my life, Anthony Naughty, Peter Nice, as Mummy called them. Anthony knew how much I missed Willy. He had been a good companion to me in his absence. Willy and Anthony had known each other for a long time because of family connections. Robin Fox had many dealings with Anthony's father, Neville Blond, who owned the Royal Court Theatre.

I was tickled pink with Anthony's debonair Bohemian life-style in Chester Row. Never a dull moment, and I appreciated that. Although my dream, my romantic ideal was of ending up in an ancient home surrounded by organized chaos, Anthony's chaos was often too disorganized. Beautifully romantic though Chester Row was, I always felt I was in danger of too much excess toppling me off balance. He spoilt me rotten, taking me out on the town in his Rolls, always there if I needed a shoulder to cry on, never demanding or suffocating. He told Mummy he had an old girl friend with a spare room in her flat at Clare Court, St Pancras. It perfectly suited both their needs. Mummy was relieved to have me living with a girl, not alone, and, Hatty, as she was known, could keep her beady eye on me and report back to both Mummy and Anthony if I misbehaved. If Willy represented the angel-choir part of my nature, then Anthony represented my nest of demons – after all, every young lady has to have a bit of contrast in her life.

SCRAPE! SHUDDER! SCRAPE! Perhaps Virginia had crashed, I thought hopefully, or fallen over and spilt the coffee . . .

'What the hell's going on?' said Peter, coming up from behind me and frightening me half to death. He snatched the wheel from me and began to twist it back and forth. 'We're stuck, grounded, and in high tide, too. Well done, Miles.'

We just stood there for a moment or two, none of us quite knowing how to gather our novice nautical wits. Peter made some calls on one of his gadgets, I haven't a clue to whom. I must say they were all jolly good sports. I would have strangled me, so it was pretty lucky that it was me who'd done the fucking up. We were about half a mile from shore. I offered to swim it but Anthony, being the well-mannered Etonian that he was, dived straight in. I was impressed. Peter wasn't. 'I doubt whether we'll see him again.' After an eternity of wet clothes and aching bones, Anthony reappeared in a white boat with a fisherman, to tow us off – my knight on a white horse.

Fidelity. Quite a subject is that. So many finer, more enduring virtues lie beneath the surface of lust. And to break up a marriage or a family over something as trivial and frail as lust seems to me to be foolish (as I, to my cost, found out ten years later). It would be as if Battersea Power Station were to pack in its relationship with the Thames just because one day a piddling little puddle comes between them, a puddle that'll soon dry out again, leaving no signs of ever having been there in the first place. That doesn't mean I condone infidelity, I don't. I just try to lift my heart to embrace the jealous one, sometimes me. It would be excellent if we could teach children to differentiate lust from love. What a step that would be! (And possible.)

I got to know a lot about lust when I was young, because I spent most of my time studying it. When I first moved to London from the country, I couldn't bicycle home to Ingatestone at weekends, so had to use the tube. I'd get on at Marble Arch, stay on it till Stratford East, pop across the platform to meet the Chelmsford train, leap on and get out at Ingatestone without – shoosh! Getting caught in a dark tunnel mid-station for too long always reminded me of getting stuck in the loo on that train. Fearful memories would engulf me. I'd start thinking about not breathing, and then I'd promptly lose my breath. I believe that fear and lust are tightly interwined. I'd often think about lusty things to take my mind off the fear of getting stuck in one of those foul tunnels. My task was made easy by the winks, come-ons and follow-mes coming from the men around me. As I sat there, all demure with my eyes to the floor, I'd often wonder what would happen if once – just once – I took up the challenge, got up and followed. This thought obsessed me for months, until I found myelf unable to contain my curiosity a moment longer.

I was returning to London from Barn Mead when the tube got stuck in a tunnel approaching Bethnal Green. I looked up from my paper and saw this guy giving me the eye, a nice, clean-looking guy for the kind of teddy-boy type that he obviously was. I returned to my paper, wondering if he was worth a second look. He was. As we crept slowly, inch by inch, through the dark tunnel towards Bethnal Green, there was plenty of time for the courting game. There he was, swinging himself from the silver bar at the exit doors, his eyes glinting with such a heat of urgency, I had no choice but to turn away. As I did so I felt that same urgent heat skewering me through my shoulder blades. I could almost see his eyes, so precisely was his horny body mirrored through the window, thanks to the darkness of the tunnel behind. Could he tell, I wondered.

The train pulled in, he beckoned me to follow. But my mind was already made up. At Bethnal Green he swung off the tube with confident ease. He was certainly easy when he twigged that I was going to follow, that I was about to call his bluff. Very cool indeed, I thought. He clambered King Kong-like up the steps of Bethnal Green station. I saw him framed in the entrance with the sunlight behind him, waiting for me, giving me time for second thoughts, for his body stance meant business. Like with the vodka, I'd set myself up with a dare, so I had to go through with it.

As I followed him down the street, he kept swinging his head back, hands swaggering on his hips, checking that I was still there, and smiling, more to himself, I thought, than to give me reassurance. We reached an entrance to a deserted alley-way. He beckoned me, I followed, my silly high heels kept buckling on the cobbles. My long wooden beads were bashing against my wobbly knees as I kept my distance down the empty alleyway. My heart, I noticed, was playing its usual jazz.

He stopped, leaned against a dirty grey wall, pulled a packet of Craven A from his pocket and lit a fag. I walked a little closer then stood very still.

'Wanna puff?'

'No thanks.'

'Come here, I won't bite.' He said it knowing I'd go to him. It was then that it dawned on me how often he must have performed this same trick with hundreds of other girls.

I didn't like the thought of that. In fact I was repelled by the idea of that being his spot, there against the wall. *That's* the difference between the sexes. That bloke was going to stuff me, probably with no finesse, then go off and forget everything about it. Not because he was cruel or heartless, but because that's just how it is. Man = Hunter. Had I been a bloke, the power of lust at that moment would have blinded me too. All thoughts regarding 'good', 'wrong', 'bad', 'how many', 'how often', would have been eclipsed by the overpowering need to get his end away.

'Come 'ere,' he said, needing it bad now. I stayed quite still, frozen. He came to me, led me to the wall, and put me against it, gently but with no nonsense. 'Needn't be frightened, just . . .' He didn't lean in for a kiss or anything like it, he merely went to the hem of my skirt with his cigarette hand.

I pushed him away, took off my shoes and ran. At the corner I turned back. He wasn't following and his stance showed no surprise whatsoever. He was slouching against his spot at the wall, drinking up the sun and taking another drag on his fag.

It reminds me of an upper-class actor I hardly knew who once asked me, 'Take your knickers off, my beauty.' I told him I didn't feel like it. 'Never mind,' he said, smiling. 'Seven out of ten do, you know.'

I'm sure my piece of rough trade was the same. As I ran off, I'm sure he thought, So she ran. I'll just go and pluck another. Better luck next time.

'Hold very tight, please.' Ting-ting!

CHAPTER FORTY-THREE

Y HAIR WAS certainly not conducive to infidelity. Ironing it or sticking thousands of flat steel clips down it protected me from any stray nights of passion – or indeed rape. Only Blacks know the aggravation attached to straightening our misplaced pubic frizz. So I decided to pop into the Afro shop I'd been told about in Kilburn and get it straightened once and for all. A friendly fat mama of a hairdresser took me to the basin. 'It's the opposite to a perm, you know that, do you, honey?'

I didn't know, and what's more I didn't care. All I wanted was for my hair to be permanently straight. Straight in the daytime, straight at night, straight when I made love and when I woke up again. And straight in the midst of fog, wind and rain. She threw a pink gown over me. 'OK,' said Mama. 'Let's git goin'.'

As I sat under the dryer, relieved to be almost through with the excruciating boredom of hair problems, I found myself next to a very dishy ebony creature, with legs like Mummy's.

'Don't see many white girls in here. What have you had done?' she asked really interested.

'I've just had my hair straightened.'

'So have I.' There was a moment's pause before she went on. 'I came here once before with dyed hair, and I lost most of it when they took me out of the dryer. I sure learnt my lesson.'

'What lesson was that?' None of it sinking in quite yet.

'Never straighten dyed hair.'

The penny dropped with an almighty plop. 'What?' I asked, hardly able to contain my rising panic.

'Is your hair dyed, then?'

I was out from under that dryer as quick as a flash.

As fat Mama undid the fat rollers, a great deal of my hair came rolling out too. I sat there, staring at great clumps of it all over the quite dirty floor. I began to cry. The ebony lady came over and put her arms around me. 'I know the feelin', I know the feelin', but believe me, it'll grow back in no time.'

There was quite a commotion in the Afro hair shop, as I saw, through my tears, clumps of my hair being swept up into a pan. Another black lady came up to me. 'Can I give you a tip, child?' I wasn't really in the mood, it was all too late for tips, so I turned my streaked face away. 'Watch me, watch what I'm doin'.'

I watched. This kind woman, using her own fizzy hair, showed me step by step how to straighten hair without using any chemicals. She just wrapped it around her head one way, and then went under the dryer, and then wrapped it the other way. And abracadabra! From pure frizz to straight as an arrow in merely half an hour. 'Never straighten your kinda hair, child. Dye or no dye, it ruins it for ever.'

I thanked her. 'I only wish you'd been here before it was too late.'

She began looking into my bald bits of scalp as if she was about to find Tutankhamen's tomb. 'It isn't too late, but whatever you do, don't go dyeing it again.'

'Why not?'

'Because if you dye it now on top of what it's already been

through, you'll be bald as a baby's bottom – just keep wrapping it.'

I decided not to mourn for what had gone, but to move onward, onward, with my black hair looking uncommonly stiff, stubborn, balding and prickly. So on my witch's broomstick, I flew over my two belly-flops: my West end début, and my Kilburn Afro aggro, licked my wounds and landed with a SPLASH at Worthing Rep. It had a reputation for almost guaranteed full houses, thanks to the abundance of elderly theatre enthusiasts, who tend to retire by the sea.

I commuted from Brighton, and lived with an old First World War friend of Daddy's, Norman Hoyte. They'd met again a few times after the war, when Norman was also part of the Bloomsbury Set in the twenties and early thirties. But if Daddy had re-established his friendship, he would have been quite taken aback at Norman's, by now, wildly eccentric nature.

Fortunately Norman lived at the other end of Brighton, as far away from Roedean memories as possible, in a very charming cottage near the station. He was an avid Ban-the-Bomber. Not until I met Norman did I know we were all going to get blown up within the sixties' decade. Mind you, this didn't overly concern me, since I was going to be dead at twenty-one anyway. I have doubts about all so-called eccentrics, for I'm never sure whether their outrageous behaviour stems from innocence or guile. After many a late night at the theatre I'd get a rude awakening from Norman, who'd draw my curtains, open the window, and place a plate of two lonely burnt bananas under my nose. I came to the conclusion that Norman was just a wicked calculating old bugger.

After three months of Worthing Rep I realized it was comedy that I was best at. I'd always secretly known this but had never been given the parts with which to prove it. At last I'd found my niche in life, and how satisfying it was! Bit by bit, inch by inch, I was turning weekly into a better comedienne. Although I had a long way to go to perfect the craft of comedy, at least I could make them laugh again like I used to do at school. It's the best sound in the world, laughter rippling through the stalls, the best way to blanket the fear.

Ma's Bit 'o' Brass was a strange northern comedy, almost a farce. It ended up a complete farce because at the beginning of the first act my character had to prepare and then cook a Lancashire Hotpot on stage. My poor leading man, Arthur Barrett, dreaded making his entrance at the end of the first act, because he had to sit down and eat my concoctions. 'I'd rather go back on the dole than eat another of Sarah's hotpots,' he said.

But he managed to get his revenge, all right, when he played my fiancé in, *The Reluctant Débutante*. Arthur Barrett was an actor who'd been at it for years – he knew the ropes intimately. During the scene in question I'd just returned from a ball without him. I chose a beautiful strapless apple green dress which shimmered under the lights. It fitted me like a glove, giving me great confidence for the necessary showy entrance. On the third night, entering to play the scene as usual, I heard the audience gasp at the shimmer of my green ball dress. As I did my nightly twirl I received another awesome gasp from the stalls. I knew I was looking particularly ravishing that night and was tickled pink with all the reaction I was getting. Full to the brim with feminine power and confidence I came and sat on the sofa beside my fiancé, Arthur Barrett, to play the intimate love scene.

He was looking rather strained and strangely stiff that night, I thought. However hard I tried, I wasn't able to pick the scene off the floor. Why would he not look me in the eye? Why were the audience tittering, and some of them whispering among themselves?

Perhaps there was a large bogey in my nose – no, all seemed safe in there. It was quite a passionate scene, but that night it seemed interminably cold and false. Arthur never once caught my eye, not once, and the audience were really beginning to shift now.

As I said my final goodnight to my fiancé on the sofa, my relief was enormous. I didn't forget, however, to give Arthur rather a dirty look as I exited back to the safety of my dressing room.

My dressing room didn't welcome me as usual. I gave my beautiful green shimmering ball gown one last little gloating glance in the long mirror, and there – staring me right in the face – was one completely naked breast with its nipple winking merrily away at me. When had it escaped? I stood there absolutely appalled, as indeed, the whole audience and Arthur Barrett must have been for the past ten minutes, all staring at its intimate whiteness, so alien somehow against my made-up neck and face. I truly wanted to die. Why hadn't Arthur done something – anything – to rescue my vulnerability? My hotpots weren't that bad, surely? A nudge, whisper, glance, even a passing glint in his eye might have saved my reputation.

I fairly skittled (having popped it back by now, of course) round to the prompt corner to ask the stage manager if she had seen it while I was on stage.

'It plopped out as you did your first little twirl at your entrance.'

'Entrance?' I asked, cringing with embarrassment. 'Why didn't you *do* something?'

Keeping her eyes glued to the prompt copy she replied, 'What could I do? You never looked in my direction.'

'But—'

'What did you expect me to do? Come on stage and pop it back?'

'But—'

'I couldn't very well bring the curtain down, just because your tit had popped out, could I?'

Arthur never brought it up, never mentioned it, and I was too embarrassed to bring it up myself. For many nights after that incident I kept waking up in a hot sweat of raw vulnerability and humiliation – I still do, occasionally.

During the week of an American comedy, *The Moon is Blue*, in which I gave my best performance so far, Robin rang to say that he was sending down a rather important film producer to see me. He wouldn't tell me which night he was coming. 'Make sure your breasts don't go flying all over the place this time, please.'

There must have been a mole or a tell-tale-tit lurking around the wings, for my tit-tale flew up to London Town, swelling, as only rumours do, into not one tit but a pair of Jayne Mansfields, swinging about for hours.

CHAPTER FORTY-FOUR

O N WEDNESDAY, I got a call from Robin telling me to drive up to London on the Friday, to audition for the leading part in a new film called *Term of Trial*. This news hit me very strangely. Was my childhood vision that day while the family stood posing in the rose garden about to become a reality? Was I about to become a movie star? 'And, Sarah, there will be a great many girls auditioning, so don't be put off, because everyone's after it. It's a great part, the lead opposite Laurence Olivier.'

There was a long silence. 'Hello, Sarah? Hello – have we been cut off?'

Naturally I made Robin repeat this news.

'Surely I stand no chance whatsoever of getting the part, do I?'

'As much chance as anyone else. Look sexy and don't be late. Romulus Films, Upper Grosvenor Street, three o'clock sharp.' The phone went dead.

I still had my clapped-out third-hand Mini Minor so getting to London and back in time for the evening performance was going to be a performance in itself. As I drove up the A24 on the dual carriageway, all kinds of thoughts were thumping against my skull. Would Laurence Olivier be there today? Would I be asked to read? Did I look sexy enough? I'd hitched my skirt up shorter than anyone's I'd ever seen. I wore white socks, since I was to play a school girl.

My hair was still my *bete noire*, not necessarily because I was so terribly vain – at least, I'd never been accused of being so – but because we were now living in 1960, and while no one went around with wild fuzzy hair it was unthinkable for movie stars. The new look was straight, crooked was *out* – not even out since it hadn't yet come *in*. Here was I still dyed black, crinkly, stiff and still slightly balding. I hadn't a hope in hell.

But welling up beneath all this was something instantly recognizable, yet I couldn't put my finger on it. Laurence Olivier was still my hero, I still kept his picture with me, though admittedly not under my pillow. It was hard to concentrate on the road, because maybe any minute now I was going to meet this hero of mine, my Heathcliff, who was calling to me from across the misty boggy moors of show-biz, my love, my life – my destiny!

My destiny suddenly crashed towards me. Not in the shape of Heathcliff, alas, just a stupid old cow adamant that we stop to exchange numbers – surely she could've seen me coming? Apart from which it was my right of way round Hyde Park Corner! Luckily her car turned out much less dented than mine, so I told her to stuff it, and drove off – couldn't be late, after all.

I just managed it, on the stroke of three. I took a quick gander in the mirror of the ladies' room in case of a straying tit or two. All seemed to be in order, except I noticed I couldn't touch up my eye-liner because my hand was shaking. When I got shown upstairs, there were at least three score girls and ten, all lined up, good as gold, waiting. I simply couldn't believe my eyes. What a cattle market. I reluctantly joined the end of the queue. I suppose up to this

343

point I had been terribly spoilt with Robin always seeing that everything was taken care of. Here I was in a longer queue than at the RADA auditions, which was hardly moving at all. I looked at the clock on the wall. It was already half past three, which meant I only had another hour before I had to head back to Worthing, otherwise I'd be missing curtain up.

Then something much more sinister began to dawn on my thick and frozen brain cells – something I'd tried to deny at first. As I was looking carefully around a second time, the truth came at me – vivid, harsh and numbing. Not only were they all dishy as can be, but they were *all* blondes. Each and every bird in the whole fucking queue was a bleedin' blonde Lolita. Why in God's name didn't Robin tell me they wanted a blonde? I could've saved myself the long journey up. I was becoming inwardly hysterical. The queue was still dead in its tracks. The time was coming up for a quarter to four, and I was late, black and bald. All the girls coming out of the audition room seemed so relaxed, teeth gleaming, blonde hair sleek and bouncy, that I was sure not only had they all been offered the part, but had been given the extra bonus of sitting on Olivier's knee.

The time was now a quarter to five. It'd take me two hours, probably more in the rush hour, to drive back to Worthing. This meant I'd have to leave now if I was to get to Worthing by seven o'clock, in theatrical language, that's the 'half'. All actors must be present in their dressing rooms half an hour before curtain up. And this actor wasn't going to make it. Neither was she going to make it into the audition room, by the looks of it.

I couldn't take any more. Having come all this way, I was damned if I was going all the way back to Worthing without even getting my toe in the door for this chance of a lifetime. So I moved up the queue, pushing past all the blonde little beauties to a chorus of, 'Get back in the queue! Who do you think you are?'

So great was the deserved animosity that I thought it best if I gave a little speech. 'I'm so sorry, everyone, but you'll have to let me in because I have to get back down to Worthing Rep, curtain goes up at seven thirty. Sorry! So sorry – excuse me – excuse me.' None of them liked it I could tell, but as soon as the next girl came out, I nipped in, so there was nothing they could do about it.

Once in the room a great wave of disappointment came over me. No Olivier. I needn't have bothered. All I wanted to do now was to get the hell out, because there seemed no point in wasting all of our time. There was one lady in the room, and two men. One was the director, a dark handsome chap in his fifties, same type as Vivien's beau Jack Merrivale, called Pete Glenville, and a fat man with a cigar, who looked like Uncle John and was apparently the boss, called Jimmy Wolf.

There was a moment of silence, so I took advantage of it. I couldn't stop myself, I was too far down the dark tunnel of panic. It all blurted out, spilling forth over them. What I actually said I can't remember, I think I was bleating about having to get back to Worthing in time for curtain up, but then couldn't resist adding, 'Besides, I'm not blind! It's perfectly obvious you're after a blonde. I'm a black head, so if it's OK with you I'll be on my way—'

'Hold on, hold on,' said Jimmy Wolf, 'you can wait five minutes, surely?'

But I was off again, and not a team of shire horses could

have held me back. 'Why is it imperative that all young girls have to be blonde to be sexy? It's such a cliché, sexy blonde, brunettes can be just as sexy you know, even black heads!'

'Calm down, calm down, and sit down a minute,' said Peter Glenville. 'Here's the page I want you to read. Take a moment to get your breath. Can you do a Northern accent?'

Thank God for my northern gang: Tom Courtenay, Mike Blackham and John Thaw!

'Yes, sir, I can,' I said trying to get myself into a better frame of mind. I had to admit to myself they all looked quite sweet, I was the only one who wasn't. I took the page he handed me.

'Mary will read it with you.'

I cleared my throat. 'I'm obviously Shirley, who is this Mr Weir?'

'That's the teacher you're in love with, your school master.'

'Laurence Olivier you mean?'

'Yes, that's right.'

'I'm not very good at reading – if you give me the script and let me learn it off by heart . . .?'

'Just read, please.'

I read as best I could, then I looked at my watch. 'I'll have to go now – sorry, so sorry!'

'Off you go,' said Pete Glenville. I flew out of there faster than an arrow from Cupid's bow.

CHAPTER FORTY-FIVE

ROBIN SAID they'd let me know. I heard nothing back. Luckily I hadn't told anyone I'd gone up to audition in the first place. I put the whole episode behind me. Every now and then I'd glimpse back and see just another belly-flop at the Chase pool.

Another rude awakening when Norman Hoyte called me one morning but not with burnt bananas this time. 'Robin Fox on the phone, Sarah.'

'It's down to twelve of you now so don't be late, and calm down this time, please, it might help.'

'It might have helped knowing they wanted a blonde.'

'You wouldn't have shown up if I'd told you that.'

'But, Robin, they still want a blonde.'

'Shut up and go up.'

Two days later there I was, at the end of a much shorter queue, all blondes nevertheless. I counted all of us and I was the eleventh. Did that mean there was someone yet to turn up. No, out came the first of the twelve. She didn't look too pleased with herself. I didn't think she looked young enough for the part.

One by one they all went in, and one by one they all came out again. None of them was looking too thrilled, and none of them stayed in very long either.

'Is Laurence Olivier in there?' I asked as one came out.

347

'You'll find out soon enough,' she snapped, cutting me to the quick.

I came to the conclusion that I lacked sufficient guts, grit for this acting game. I stood there wondering why I wore such short skirts. Perhaps because I got some kick from displaying a pair of ludicrously jittering naked knees.

What was it someone had told me about the essential ingredients for an actress to possess over the long haul? Ah yes . . . 'The heart of a lion, the skin of a rhinoceros and a loving spouse to go home to.' My heart, hardly that of a lion, was none the less a monster, the way it beat me to a pulp of fear. My skin was fine, not thick – and a spouse? I thought of my mother and father and how neither of them knew I was trying for this film. Hmm, *Term of Trial*, bad title, I kept forgetting it. I thought of Anthony Blond, I thought of Hatty, I thought of Norman Hoyte, who would doubtless be planning a march somewhere, I thought of Willy going bang bang! (You know, men's work.) Help! He'll be coming home pretty soon. This gave me a quiver of guilty excitement. But absence hadn't made my heart grow stronger, sadly it had made my heart go yonder.

As I stood there shame-faced, I realized that I was a fickle bitch who knew nothing about love. No, I had no heart, no spouse, nor a home, come to that – but then neither was I any kind of an actress either.

'Hurry up, we're waiting,' said Jimmy Wolf, puffing at his cigar in the doorway. How I love cigar smoke.

'You like the smell of cigars, then?'

'Yes, especially Cuban cigars.'

He looked at me very impressed, I hadn't a clue whether

he was smoking Cuban cigars until that moment. It seemed I'd won a point. Let's see if I could win another. He beckoned me to enter, and then went and sat down in the same place as last time, an enormous green leather chair.

Beside him sat Peter Glenville, who greeted me quite warmly I thought. 'Sarah Miles, isn't it?'

'Yes, sir, that's me.' He then turned to the chair on the other side of the room in front of the window. 'Sarah, I don't think you've met Laurence Olivier?'

There he was! I got a shock because he looked so like Daddy, bringing back that day at Brighton cinema, when Mummy commented on their likeness. He smiled at me. It wasn't a false smile at all, like Daddy had found it to be, far from it, I found it wonderfully warm.

'Hello,' he said.

'Hello,' I said.

Silence. I just stood there homing into his eyes with a love that I suddenly sensed had been with me since . . . who knows when? A timeless experience. I might have been fantasizing, but I got the impression that we were both craning our necks to take a peek at each other from around the bends of time.

Whenever I smell a rose, I feel a sweet intimacy, familiar, all consuming, as if I've been breathing in roses through eternity. Every whiff is part of every rose I've ever smelt through every lifetime, and here he was, aeons and aeons of sweet intimacy gathered together into that one moment when my foot passed through the door.

My monumentally important silence was finally interrupted by a trivial sound, the clearing of embarrassed throats. Not mine, though. I felt no embarrassment. Why should I? I was safely inside the door now. I became vaguely aware of Peter Glenville's presence above me, I could feel him flapping a script, though I couldn't be sure, so mesmerized was I.

'Could you kindly read this scene with Larry, Sarah?'

I never took my eyes off Olivier's, I couldn't. The spell was in mid-potency.

'Right. Off you go.' We didn't.

'Please start, Larry.' I can't remember playing the scene at all. I can't remember anything except being lost in Larry's eyes. I couldn't see their colour, though. He was facing away from the light.

'Thank you, that'll do nicely,' said Peter Glenville. There was another silence. On it went. Jimmy Wolf puffed out gentle coils of Monte Cristo (Romeo and Juliet, perhaps?) in our faces, but it had no effect whatsoever.

Finally they dropped the bomb shell.

'You read that very well, Sarah, but as you know, we want a blonde for the part.'

'Yes, I'm aware of that, I told Robin Fox not to waste your time, but he told me to come up anyway.' I felt no nerves. It's funny, I suppose it was Olivier's power that was feeding a particular kind of strength to me.

They spoke among themselves. What they said I can't remember, because it didn't matter.

Peter Glenville then addressed me. 'Sarah, would you be prepared to dye your hair blonde?'

I stayed as calm as I could. 'No, I couldn't do that, I'm afraid.'

'Oh?' said Jimmy Wolf, slightly aggressively I thought. 'And why is that?'

I turned away from Larry for the first time to explain why dyeing my hair would send me completely bald. But I could see I was making no headway whatsoever. To them I was just a silly spoilt brat, who for some vain reason didn't want to dye her hair. Fuck them all, I thought, and fuck Larry too if he was stupid enough not to believe me. Mind you, I thought Larry would go bald for a part, I'm sure he'd do anything for his art – I would too, but a sexy bald school girl isn't an artful answer.

(Miles Malleson, a wonderful old goat of an actor, was completely bald under his toupée. He once accepted the part of a bald barrister. Never liking to admit that he wore a toupée he trotted off to the studios to have a bald skull cap put over his toupée. Thus secured, he trotted off to give them his bald barrister. We actors! Larry would have tattooed his bum for Hamlet, if Shakespeare'd written it in, that is.)

One last try. 'I wouldn't have any hair left to play Shirley with – don't you see?'

They obviously didn't. There was another deafening silence.

'So,' said Peter Glenville finally, 'are you telling us that you *won't* dye your hair?'

'No, sir, not "won't", "can't"!'

After another quick chorus of incredulity, Larry piped up, 'I'd cut off my right hand for a part like this!'

That did it for me. How could he be so blind? 'Hmph!' I snorted. 'What a pair we'd make! Captain Hook and the new Bald Look!'

Feeling hellishly threatened by the lot of them, I turned to Peter Glenville, really on the defensive. 'Of course I'd dye my hair, but for what? To go bald and be replaced by one of those blondes?' How could Larry, my Larry, be so insensitive as to disbelieve my hair conundrum?

Although what I said and the way that I said it was somewhat cheeky, it was truthful. More silence – stony. I'd really gone and done it, pissed in my own strawberries. There was no more to be said. From a great deal of experience I've learnt, once I've put my foot in it, to pull it out quick and be off. I looked at my watch. 'Well, I have to go now—'

'Yes, we know. Worthing Rep and curtain up,' said Jimmy Wolf wolfishly.

I did a little curtsey to Larry but said nothing – nor did he, alas. I scarpered.

Driving back to Worthing was really bad. The skies were in relentless competition with my eyes. Everything was streaming with pain, rain and never again. Think of it, I'd never again set eyes on those of my Heathcliff!

With visibility disintegrating swiftly, I suddenly found myself being flashed at by a maniac who was heading directly towards me up the wrong side of the dual carriageway. I tooted my horn, I flashed my lights. Finally I had to swerve into the slow inside lane, a lane I was most unfamiliar with. What an idiot! I nearly got myself killed. He must have been as drunk as a lord. Just a glare of headlights as he shot merrily by – up *my* side of the dual carriageway.

Just as I was thinking what a twat he was, and how the world's full of them, another car came on the attack with headlights blaring. Now I was pissed off. What the hell was going on? Bloody idiots! I checked to make sure my tit hadn't plopped out again. It turned out they weren't twats at all. 'Twas I who was the twit. For it was I who'd been driving up the dual carriageway the wrong side. So what else is new? I shouldn't have been driving at all. I'd been on the brink of great things just a few moments ago. I'd read well, how could I not. It was like falling off a log, if the truth be known. All I had to do was be in love with the man I'd always been in love with.

I pulled up on the verge to collect my aching scattered wits and all I could think of was HAIR, and decided that to be a movie star you had to have great hair, silky, smooth, blonde sackfuls of the stuff. Bloody hard, trying to reverse up a dual carriageway to be going up it the right way, but until I found an exit, it had to be done, in case I met a copper.

There's no doubt that I fell right through those familiar plummeting depths into a far deeper despair that night. Such loss. Although a very different feeling from my Half Moon Street loss, this brand new chasm of loss had somehow to heal too. What's worse, the experience felt completely final somehow, no mere belly-flop in the Chase pool, no, this time it was like diving into the pool and finding no water in it.

CHAPTER FORTY-SIX

I STAYED IN BED for a whole decade, or so it seemed, until the phone rang, maybe two days later.

'Hello, Robin.' I was grumpy, I could hear it reverberating back at me through the mouthpiece.

'Sarah, they seem to be very keen on you for the part, and want to know whether you would deign to wear a wig?'

I was dumbfounded. 'Try me once more with that one, Robin.'

'They want to know whether you'd be prepared to wear a wig.'

That next week I was sitting with Stanley Hall who owned Wig Creations. He was a delightful man, the sort of professional who's gone now, the kind that went to the wall. 'So you want to be ash blonde rather than red blonde, do you?'

I wanted to look as much like Mummy as I possibly could, and Mummy was ash blonde. As our skin was the same colour, I knew it would suit me. 'Yes, please, I think ash blonde would be the best.'

As I sat there very nearly bald with my hair scraped back, ready for the wig, I looked at my face long and hard. And at that moment I saw my face go backwards through time. My eyes looked hot staring back at me from the mirror as if they were trying to tell me something extremely important, something that took place a very long time ago.

Although they were commanding me to listen, I couldn't

understand their message. Whatever it was, it came to me from the very depths of my sub-conscious. There was nothing I could do to recapture the message, through time long enough to comprehend its urgency. To have succeeded in trapping it from such a distance I would have needed some kind of cosmic butterfly net, and I'd forgotten to bring one with me to Wig Creations that day. . .

'There now, here we have three different shades.' Stanley Hall was back, piled high with blonde wigs of different shades. He started to place the first one on my head. It looked fairly good, I thought. 'It's a shame no one from the film company could come in today, but at least we can get a sense of where we're going.'

After he had tried them on, he decided that I was right and that the ash blonde was the best. 'Come on, let's go in to Larry and see what he thinks, shall we?'

I tried for an easy nonchalance. 'Is he here, then?' I noted my voice had gone up most of an octave.

'Yes, he asked me to bring you in.' I forgot how to walk quite suddenly. 'Come on, then, quick, quick!'

As I entered the next room and saw him sitting there, I realized I had been staring into his eyes through the wall. Maybe that was the message I was trying to pull out of my sub-conscious. I went all peculiar inside. I wanted to sit down because my knees were wobbling, but there was no chair, and the floor would have looked rather forward. 'Stanley, bring up another chair for the poor girl.'

I just stood there sort of swooning. Why was I so hot? I suppose because I hadn't been prepared for him being there. After a long silence Stanley brought a chair.

'Sit down, sit down, child,' said Olivier, pointing to the chair.

'Larry, what do you think of her with that colour hair? Does it complement her skin?'

'It's hard to tell, Stanley,' said Olivier, looking at me slyly sideways through the mirror. 'You're puce in the face, child. We'll have to wait till you've calmed down a bit.'

As I sat there watching him through the mirror, the fear slowly began to melt away. I think what triggered it was a moment of familiarity. He made a gesture with his hairbrush after Stanley Hall had finally finished, a gesture that took me back to childhood. He got hold of the little brush and dragged it back through his hair. Although it was thinning, I could tell it was once crinkly, because he repeatedly tried brushing it straight, to no avail, because it bounced back crinkly as ever. Exactly like Daddy's! Implacably stubborn and determined to do its own thing – rather like its owner, as I was to find out later . . .

'Looking forward to our stint in Ireland, are you, Dame Sarah?' he said with an Owly mock. That was the first time he called me 'Dame Sarah', and it stuck for over twenty years. It was always said as a tease, of course. As he sat there eyeing me through the mirror, although I was not frightened any more, I still felt hot and dizzy. Rather like the fainting spells I'd tried to feign in chapel at Roedean, always failing to make them sufficiently believable to get myself carried out. Now I could act it, however, because now I knew what it felt like for real. But I didn't want to be carried out this time, no, just up and away into happily ever after. (And to think, I had three whole years left before my twenty-first birthday!)

*

Yesterday, as I was finishing this last chapter, we had a fire here in our home. It took place in the conservatory, faster than lightning. This was the most special room in the house, designed and overseen by my brother Chuzzer. It was hand-made, lovingly, in oak, one of the most beautiful rooms I'd ever had the privilege of being in, let alone owning.

It certainly was a room for all seasons. Pardon the pun, but, then, it was my husband who coined the phrase in the first place. And since it's his conservatory, too, I think I can, on this occasion, plagiarize. This 'room for all seasons' was my whole world. Always used for meals, entertaining, medi-tating, reading, yoga-ing, praying, reading, sleeping, singing, chanting, and also where I did all my writing. Better the house had been taken than my world, the conservatory.

The bad news is: Owly went up in flames too. Old Owly, my oldest friend, my partner in crime, confidant, and best Pal. I started this book with Owly, and I end this book with Owly's end. I'm so very sorry to have lost Owly to the flames.

But the good news is: I'd written the whole of this book in the conservatory, but I'd taken my Apple Mac upstairs three days earlier. The conservatory was in dire need of a good spring cleaning.

The good news and the bad news: the fire took all the inside, all the interior away, all my treasures, everything I hold most dear PLUS – all my floppy discs.

So, if the fire had taken place three days earlier. I would have had no book at all. With my Apple Mac turned into thick gungy liquid, just like my floppy discs, there'd be no means whatsoever of recapturing any of the months it took to write.

It all depends from where you're looking.

'Look at that sunbeam, Ma, like gold and silver rainbows swirling through the window.'

'Aggravating the way they highlight every speck of dusk,' said Mummy, as she went off to get the duster.

Why did the fire happen, and what can I learn from it? All I have to do, is to keep learning the lessons laid out for me in the signs and symbols of everything around me, every new day of my life.

Life . . . it's a real bugger . . . isn't it?

An extract from

SERVES ME RIGHT

the second volume of Sarah Miles'
acclaimed autobiography

CHAPTER ONE

Never have *all* your dreams come true, ticking them off as
I did one by one. My dreaming was profoundly stimu-
lating, for potent, seductive feelings were present in the
anticipation, yet hardly at all in the fulfilment. Only you
serious lovers out there will know what the hell I'm on
about – as well, of course, as those who have had all their
dreams come true. But was I lucky to be loved by those I
dreamt of loving? Was I lucky to be a movie star? Was I
lucky to live in Shangri-la? Ha! Ha! Ha! SERVES ME
RIGHT.

Twenty-five years ago, when I was twenty-five, I made
a film called *Ryan's Daughter*, on the west coast of Ireland.
My character, Rosy Ryan, had recently married the
middle-aged local schoolmaster, Mr Shaunnessy, played
by Robert Mitchum. The local priest (a superb performance
by Trevor Howard which slid by unnoticed) has plenty of

reasons for concern when he sees Rosy mooning over the handsome young English major just arrived in the area. One day the priest bumps into Rosy hurrying guiltily along the beach alone, so he decides to confront her and to point out the damage ahead if she forsakes her marriage vows. They have an argument, and because Rosy remains defiant, the priest warns her.

'Don't go nursin' your wishes, Rosy, or by God you'll get what you're wishin' for.' Rosy Ryan retaliates, the conflict spirals until the priest loses patience with Rosy's arrogance and slaps her across the face in the hope of bringing her to her senses.

How devastating those words were for me at that time, for on the day we shot the scene, standing there on Inch beach, County Kerry, I realized that it was not only Rosy Ryan who was heading for tragedy by having her dreams come true, but Sarah Miles as well. My long list of dreams had been ticked off until it was finally complete. A cold shiver shot down my spine. A gang of goose-bumps poked up, warrior-like, through my thin pullover. I tried rubbing them away – they were most unglamorous for a movie star, I thought.

'Let's shoot the damn scene, for Christ's sake!' shouted Trevor Howard to David Lean, the director. 'The poor child is freezing to death.'

It might have been freezing, standing there with the Atlantic scuffing the grey waves, a Roedean-type howl to the wind and me dressed like an eternal spring day, but I hadn't noticed. My frozen limbs were merely surface stuff. A deeper freeze had set in.

'Right,' said David Lean. 'Rehearse the slap once more.'

Trevor gave me not so much a slap as a tickle. What I wanted was a slap. I wanted to be jolted out of the growing realization that I had no more dreams to come true. Maybe if Trevor really hit me – and meant it – he could shake me free of the fast-approaching despair. I decided to speak up.

'Trevor, would you mind not slapping me gently, it feels silly. Really slap me, as if you mean business.'

'You mean, make contact?' asked an incredulous Trevor.

'Yes, send me reeling.'

He tossed me a disbelieving look, and shrugged.

'OK,' said David through his silver and black cigarette holder, pretending that his pointed devil's ears hadn't heard a word we were saying. If he had colluded in the slap plan, if he'd admitted to hearing me say, 'Yes, send me reeling' then he'd have to tell Trevor not to listen to me, and that would have been inconvenient for David. He wanted Trevor to hit me, the harder the better, because it would be a hundred times better for the movie. And if anything happened to me – why, it was an accident. David's look escaped skyward.

'The seagulls look good – let's shoot.' (That's why there are so many seagull shots in *Ryan's Daughter* – it's David changing the subject.)

'Action!' shouts David, his hawk-eye glistening next to the camera lens. Playing the scene that cold afternoon on Inch beach, I caught a first glimpse of the chasm of nothingness that lay ahead of me. Yet there I was, still the same mass of yearning, still the same insatiable creature in need of shallow dreams to fill the vacuum within. 'Don't go nursin' yer wishes, Rosy, or by God, you'll get what you're wishin' for.' Rosy failed to heed the priest's warnings, and so had Sarah. Where in God's name was I to go from here? Was it too late to destroy my dream list and start all over again? Why hadn't I been more aware of the quality of my dreams? Why couldn't I have made sure that they were worthy dreams linked to a vocation or qualities that endure, rather than materialistic ones, linked to money, vanity, lust, fame and ego?

These thoughts were streaming through my mind as Trevor and I played the scene. When it came to the slap, I saw his grey woolly mitten come up and shoot in towards the side of my face. Christ! It was headed straight for my ear. I tried to turn away and stop the future, but it was all too late. Sweet, gentle Trevor had observed my wishes to the letter. He'd sent me reeling. He had decided to box my ears, just as any priest would do whose lamb had strayed from the flock. It was entirely in character and entirely my fault that I had neglected to warn him about the pain attached to my plastic-surgery, man-made ears. (They used to stick out like radar scanners.) Fortunately, so powerful was the impact that I went straight through the pain barrier – I was out for the count.

I returned to the land of the living in David Lean's caravan, with his mouth in close-up blowing cigarette smoke from his elegant silver and black holder into my face. I loathe the smell of Marlboro cigarettes, but David had me trapped. 'Take it gently for five minutes, Sarah.'

'I'm fine now.'

He looked at me, blue eyes sparkling with challenge. 'Are you game enough to have another go?'

'Yes,' I said. 'As long as Trevor really hits me again.'

He looked at me, his fiery eyes challenging mine, as if

checking that I meant it. He played cruel games with us actors. Not respecting us too much, finding our breaking point gave him a kick; so I was damned if he was going to find mine.

'Don't go nursin' yer wishes, or by God, you'll get what you're wishin' for!'

We completed the scene without Trevor knocking me out a second time.

How I wish I'd had the wisdom in those days to see the quiet path, the more subtle way of true worth forking up ahead of me. But I didn't. In need of swift, easy progress, I blundered onward down the wider path, so blinded by the desire for earthly things with which to stroke my vanity and ego that I failed to notice my path shrinking. It was slowly closing in on me, until I became hooked and pricked on those harsh jagged edges of dreams come true.

Years later when I'd still be down the same pathway tethered to those shallow dreams come true, 'Something' would intervene, thank God it would shake my blocked consciousness so violently that I'd have no choice but to go back up the path again. That damned 'Something' would have me retreating. I'd never done that before in my life.